Religion, Law and the Politics of Ethical Diversity

This book provides a multidisciplinary and comparative look at the contemporary phenomenon of conscientious objection or contestation in the name of religion and examines the key issues that emerge in terms of citizenship and democracy. These are analysed by looking at the different ways of challenging or contesting a legal obligation on the grounds of religious beliefs and convictions.

The authors focus on the meaning of conscientious objection which asserts the legitimacy of convictions – in particular religious convictions – in determining the personal or collective relevance of the law and of public action. The book begins by examining the main theoretical issues underlying conscientious objection, exploring the implications of the protection of freedom of conscience, the place of religion in the secular public sphere and the recognition and respect of ethical pluralism in society. It then focuses on the question of exemptions and contestations of civil norms, using a multidisciplinary approach to highlight the multiple and diverse issues surrounding them, as well as the motives behind them.

This book will be of great interest to scholars, specialists and graduate and advanced undergraduate students who are interested in issues of religious diversity. Researchers and policymakers in think-tanks, NGOs and government units will find the volume useful in identifying key issues in understanding the phenomenon of conscientious objection and its implications in managing ethical diversity in contemporary societies.

Claude Proeschel is Lecturer at the Université de Lorraine, France. She has been a member of the GSRL (Groupe Sociétés, Religions, Laïcités – EPHE-PSL-CNRS) since 2002.

David Koussens is Associate Professor in the Faculty of Law at the Université de Sherbrooke, Canada, where he holds the Research Chair in Law, Religion and Secularism.

Francesco Piraino is Postdoctoral Scholar at Ca' Foscari University – Venice, Italy. He is the Director for the Centre of Comparative Studies on Spiritualties and Civilizations at the Giorgio Cini Foundation in Venice.

Routledge Studies in Religion and Politics

Edited by Jeffrey Haynes, London Metropolitan University, UK

This series aims to publish high quality works on the topic of the resurgence of political forms of religion in both national and international contexts. This trend has been especially noticeable in the post-cold war era (that is, since the late 1980s). It has affected all the 'world religions' (including, Buddhism, Christianity, Hinduism, Islam, and Judaism) in various parts of the world (such as, the Americas, Europe, the Middle East and North Africa, South and Southeast Asia, and sub-Saharan Africa).

The series welcomes books that use a variety of approaches to the subject, drawing on scholarship from political science, international relations, security studies, and contemporary history.

Books in the series explore these religions, regions and topics both within and beyond the conventional domain of 'church-state' relations to include the impact of religion on politics, conflict and development, including the late Samuel Huntington's controversial – yet influential – thesis about 'clashing civilisations'.

In sum, the overall purpose of the book series is to provide a comprehensive survey of what is currently happening in relation to the interaction of religion and politics, both domestically and internationally, in relation to a variety of issues.

Religion, Conflict and Post-Secular Politics
Jeffrey Haynes

Democratization in Christian Orthodox Europe
Comparing Greece, Serbia and Russia
Marko Veković

Islam, Liberalism and Ontology
A Critical Re-evaluation
Joseph J. Kaminski

Religion, Law and the Politics of Ethical Diversity
Conscientious Objection and Contestation of Civil Norms
Edited by Claude Proeschel, David Koussens and Francesco Piraino

For more information about this series, please visit: https://www.routledge.com/Routledge-Studies-in-Religion-and-Politics/book-series/RSRP

Religion, Law and the Politics of Ethical Diversity

Conscientious Objection and Contestation of Civil Norms

Edited by
Claude Proeschel, David Koussens and Francesco Piraino

Routledge
Taylor & Francis Group
LONDON AND NEW YORK

First published 2021
by Routledge
2 Park Square, Milton Park, Abingdon, Oxon OX14 4RN

and by Routledge
52 Vanderbilt Avenue, New York, NY 10017

Routledge is an imprint of the Taylor & Francis Group, an informa business

British Library Cataloguing-in-Publication Data
A catalogue record for this book is available from the British Library

Library of Congress Cataloging-in-Publication Data
A catalog record has been requested for this book

ISBN: 978-0-367-67377-2 (hbk)
ISBN: 978-0-367-67379-6 (pbk)
ISBN: 978-1-003-13108-3 (ebk)

Typeset in Times New Roman
by Deanta Global Publishing Services, Chennai, India

Contents

Illustrations

Figures

Table

Acknowledgements

The editors would like to thank the Fondazione Giorgio Cini for co-organising the conference held in 2019 at Isola di San Giorgio Maggiore (Venice), at which contributors to this book presented and discussed drafts of many of its chapters.

The editors also express their gratitude to the Université de Sherbrooke (Chaire de recherche Droit, religion et laïcité; Centre de recherche Société, Droit et religion – SoDRUS), the Université de Montréal (Project PLURADICAL/FRQSC), CRIDAQ (Centre de recherche interdisciplinaire sur la diversité et la démocratie) and GSRL (Groupe Sociétés, Religions, Laïcités, CNRS-EPHE-PSL), which enabled the publication of this book.

Particular thanks are due to Ann Pattison and Thomas Windisch, who devoted considerable time and effort to the linguistic review and editorial work.

Contributors

Ravza Altuntas-Çakır is Lecturer in the Political Science and International Relations Department at Istanbul Sabahattin Zaim University, Turkey. Her intellectual and research interests lie at the intersection of modern Islamic thought and political theory, particularly the debates on religion and democracy, secularism and its discontents, diversity and pluralism and democratic and human rights struggles in Middle Eastern societies.

Samuel Blouin is 2016 Pierre Elliott Trudeau Foundation Scholar and Co-Investigator in a project funded by the Canadian Institutes of Health Research on the assessment of suffering of people requesting assistance in dying. He has been researching the topic of medically assisted death for the last five years in Canada and abroad.

Pierluigi Chiassoni is Professor of Jurisprudence at the Istituto Tarello per la Filosofia del Diritto (TiLPh) at the University of Genoa, Italy. He is founder of the Master's programme "Global Rule of Law and Constitutional Democracy".

Xavier Delgrange is Judge at the Belgian *Conseil d'État*. He teaches law and human rights at the Université Saint-Louis-Bruxelles, Université libre de Bruxelles and Université Catholique de Louvain, Belgium. A Member of the Interdisciplinary Centre for Constitutional Research of the Université Saint-Louis-Bruxelles (CIRC) and Associate Researcher of the Centre de recherche Sociétés, Droit et Religions de l'Université de Sherbrooke (SoDRUS), Canada, his main fields of research include institutional constitutional law, the role of the judge and human rights.

Samuel Dolbeau is a PhD candidate at the Université catholique de Louvain, Belgium, and the École des Hautes Études en Sciences Sociales, France. His research focuses on the development of the Emmanuel Community in French-speaking Europe (Wallonia, Romandy and France) from 1972 to the present day.

Isabelle Dumont is Assistant Professor in Social Work at the Université du Québec à Montréal, Canada. She has conducted research on therapeutic interventions designed for families having to cope with cancer.

Valentina Gaddi is a doctoral student in sociology at the Université de Montréal, Canada. Her research interests are related to religious pluralism, migration and the representation of the "other". She is an active member of several research groups, including Pluradical – on pluralism and radicalisation (FRQSC) and Religion and Diversity (CRSH). She recently co-founded the group Collectif Judeité(s) at the Université de Montréal.

Alexandre Grandjean is a PhD candidate at the Institute of Social Sciences of Religion (ISSR) at the University of Lausanne, Switzerland. Trained as a socio-anthropologist, he documents how and why esoterically driven agronomies are being *translated* and *adapted* into secular references as to become somehow "mainstream" in the Swiss public domain.

David Koussens is Associate Professor in the Faculty of Law at the Université de Sherbrooke, Canada, where he holds the Research Chair in Law, Religion and Secularism.

Hélène Lerouxel is Chief Secretary at the Belgian *Conseil d'État* and Assistant in Constitutional Law at the University of Saint-Louis-Bruxelles, Belgium, where she is a member of the Interdisciplinary Research Centre for Constitutional and Administrative Law (CIRC). Her research focuses on fundamental rights, and more specifically on their criminal or religious aspects.

Jocelyn Maclure is Full Professor in Philosophy at the Université Laval, Canada. He researches in the areas of political philosophy, ethics, analytical philosophy, philosophy of mind and philosophy of law.

Christophe Monnot is Lecturer of Sociology of Religion at the Université de Strasbourg, France, and Senior Researcher at the Université de Lausanne, Switzerland. His work focuses on religious institutions, establishment of the diaspora in a European Context and diversity. He is also a board member of the Research Network 34 (Sociology of Religion) of the European Sociological Association (ESA) since its founding in 2011.

Claude Proeschel is Lecturer at the Université de Lorraine, France. She has been a member of the GSRL (Groupe Sociétés, Religions, Laïcités – EPHE-PSL-CNRS) since 2002.

Vincent Valentin is Professor of Public Law at Sciences Po Rennes, France. He researches in the areas of neoliberalism, liberalism and contemporary libertarianism, particularly regarding philosophy of law and the history of ideas.

Daniel Weinstock is Full Professor at the Law Faculty of McGill University, Canada, where he was appointed Director of the McGill Institute for Health and Social Policy in 2013, and named a James McGill Professorship in 2014. He is Prize Fellow of the Pierre Elliott Trudeau Foundation (2004), and a recipient of the André-Laurendeau Prize given by the Association canadienne-française pour l'avancement des sciences. He was also awarded the 2017 Charles Taylor Prize for Excellence in Policy Research by the Broadbent Institute.

Introduction: contesting in the name of religion?

Claude Proeschel and David Koussens

On 29 March 1990, Belgium narrowly escaped a serious constitutional crisis when King Baudouin refused to sign the act that partially decriminalised abortion, due to a "serious issue of conscience" (Mabille, 1990).

In Quebec, when the process of making schools non-religious was completed in the mid-2000s with the introduction of a course in ethics and religious culture for all primary and secondary pupils, a number of Catholic groups challenged the new school curriculum in the courts in the name of their freedom of conscience (Lampron, 1998). In the same period, similar disputes were taken to the Spanish courts by Catholic movements who objected to the fact that their children were being compelled to take the new course in education and citizenship instigated by royal decree on 29 December 2006 (Proeschel, 2013).

On 4 October 2018, the European Court of Human Rights refused to hear the application put forward by 146 French mayors who spoke out against the infringement of their freedom of conscience that was inherent in the requirement to marry same-sex couples under the French Act of 17 May 2013 authorising equal marriage.

These are just a few examples of questions that have occupied sociologists since Max Weber, but they also more widely cut across debates in human and social sciences: It is not always sufficient to legislate for a legal norm to be acknowledged to be socially legitimate. Moreover, if the new legal provisions (decriminalisation of abortion, secularisation of education, opening up civil marriage to same-sex couples, allowing medical assistance with dying and so on) indeed fall within social and political environments that favour their emergence – in this case, the secularisation of society and the laicisation of institutions in the liberal democracies – they may also be perceived, by those for whom religion still matters and is a determining factor, as an external mechanism, removed from the social sphere, and whose legitimacy may, or even must, therefore be contested (Ewick and Silbey, 1998).

It is very much from this perspective that the Assembly of Catholic bishops in the United States adopted a strong stance, in a document that it published in 2012, in order to reaffirm that freedom of religion is "Our First, More Cherished Liberty", calling for disobedience when this freedom was threatened by civil laws, in areas as varied as contraception, abortion or state immigration laws

(United States Conference of Catholic Bishops, 2012). The reference made in that document to the famous "Letter from Birmingham Jail" sent by the Reverend and civil rights campaigner Martin Luther King Jr. in 1963 is not insignificant here: civil rights – in this context freedom of religion – are invoked as a defence against other civil norms too, even though these norms would be illegitimate from a strictly religious point of view.

> A just law is a man-made code that squares with the moral law or the law of God. An unjust law is a code that is out of harmony with the moral law … an unjust law is a human law that is not rooted in eternal law and natural law.
>
> (Luther King Jr., 1963)

Contestation in the name of religion as a secular trend

The idea of contesting the civil norm in the name of religion, which represents a clash between legitimate frameworks (civil and religious), is intrinsically modern and intimately linked with the very processes of secularisation that liberal democracies are experiencing.

If a norm is contested in the name of religion, it is indeed because religion exists within a secular framework that allows it the opportunity to express its views. Indeed, in a liberal democracy, secularisation leads to a progressive separation of the churches and the state in the desire for everyone to have an equal share of freedom (of conscience and of religion) (Maclure and Taylor, 2011; Laborde, 2017). And it is the exercising of freedom of religion that paves the way, in return, for objections to other civil norms on religious grounds.

Contestation in the name of religion, therefore, very clearly falls within a secular framework of guaranteeing civil rights. In this context, without contesting the legitimacy of the general norm, however, the individual can request to be exempted as an individual from the general norm because this would restrict their freedom of conscience and religion. But there are also cases where contestation then turns the secular guarantee of civil rights against itself. From this second perspective, it is indeed by invoking freedom of conscience and religion that contestation expresses itself in order to then better oppose another principle of secularism, that of the separation of the churches and the state. It has been noted that countless objections to the civil norm oppose laws that partly decriminalise abortion, laws that open up civil marriage to same-sex couples or laws that allow access to assisted suicide, all of which are measures that distance themselves from the religious norm in the legal and political regulation of life in society (Delgrange and Koussens, 2019; Leckey, 2007), that is, measures for the (informal) separation of the churches and the state.[1]

This is indeed a paradox inherent in secularism and, in broader terms, in a democracy. Whilst promoting the recognition of individual rights quite specifically for the members of minority religious groups, the secular framework also offers some individuals or religious groups the means for contesting them. In this case, campaigns by religious groups against the civil norm are to that extent the expression of a commitment to reinvest in a political sphere from which these groups had partly been excluded, precisely because of the principle of the separation of the churches and the state that is intrinsic to secularism. How, in such a context, can we envisage religion within the social order? How can we unravel what Olivier Roy (2010) describes as a "religious challenge" that liberal democracies face all the more intensely when they are pursuing their participation in a process of secularisation of their state institutions, and of their law?

In a secular context, the state is not considered to have a direct knowledge of religion. However, it is also because it is secular and must for this reason guarantee freedom of conscience and religion that it regularly needs to interfere in the religious sphere. This is how the state finds itself having to determine the scope of religion prospectively so that, retrospectively, it can guarantee freedom of conscience and religion for those who lay claim to it (Koussens, 2011: 813).

In most European states, the principle of freedom of conscience and religion was guaranteed when some denominations were either officially recognised by the state or given considerable preferential status by collaborative agreements with the public institutions. In Europe, national laws clearly take into account freedom of conscience in the individual dimension, but they also emphasise this freedom in the collective dimension in order to allow the churches to organise themselves by their own rules, but also so that it is easier to "identify" interlocutors whom they consider legitimate. In this context, recognising conformity with what, traditionally, is socially expected of a religion does indeed act as a "certification of legitimacy" (Roy, 2010: 252). It allows greater social and political readability of religious communities, and most often favours their recognition by the law.

In North America, on the other hand, the courts essentially determine the parameters of religion on an individual believer basis, that is, on the basis of what believers themselves subjectively define as the truth as they see it. In this way, their decisions embrace the views that sociologists of religion have been expressing in studies over the past 25 years or more regarding the processes that individuals adopt to validate those elements of beliefs to which they decide to adhere, based on the authenticity of their search for truth (Campiche, 1993; Davie, 1994; Hervieu-Léger, 1999). From this perspective, it cannot therefore be sufficient to understand religion within its objective dimension alone because "no external authority – neither an institution, nor a community – can dictate to an individual the truths they must believe in" (Hervieu-Léger, 1999: 187). All it can do is offer certain truths where a choice will then be made on an individual basis because "there is no 'true way of believing' other than the one that is personally adopted" (*idem*).

The difficulty of taking the religious factor into account in the law is therefore a direct consequence of the law's secularisation, as are the social issues that are external to the law but are contingent thereon (that is, the secularisation of society and hence the individualisation of relationships with beliefs and the privatisation of religion).

Theoretical issues

In democratic societies, claims of conscientious objection are without doubt one form of contestation in the name of religion that most challenges the law's ability to take religion into account. This is because such claims express a request for a legal system or a judge to endorse the right to be exempted from doing a duty (military service), or from providing a service (carrying out an abortion) which there is a legal obligation to perform. On the other hand, they can also express a request to carry out an act that is prohibited by the law (wearing a symbol indicating a religious affiliation) in the name of one's convictions. Looking at this analytically, two forms of claiming a conscientious objection can be identified.

The first route for expressing a conscientious objection in a democratic society is via the legal system. This means asking for a conscience clause to be included in the law, to allow exemptions from the act or the duty that this law addresses. Such a conscience clause goes some way towards recognition by the legal system, and therefore by the political community, of the ethically controversial nature of the subject or of the act that is potentially enabled by the new legislation (Proeschel, 2019). Moreover, it reflects a form of social recognition of the importance of dissent, and hence reflects the possibility of exempting from due process a person who believes that a law infringes their rights and their personal integrity.

The presence of a conscience clause in a legal instrument could be interpreted as an incursion of religious arguments into the public space, in other words, as the intrusion of ethics or of specific ethical issues in the law. However, if we analyse this from a Rawlsian perspective, the existence of such legislative clauses does not preclude, in principle,[2] the implementation of a democratic public space, which rules out arguments based on comprehensive doctrine that relate to public space (Rawls, 1993). Nor does it prohibit the creation of a common norm that is universally accepted, in the context of plurality. On the one hand, it is indeed the legislative system, with its sovereignty and legitimacy, that is adopting the exemption clause, guided in the course it steers by a political objective, namely respect for fundamental rights and for the diversity of ethics and values that coexist within society. Yet, such clauses rather reflect the manner in which the political debate in the public space acknowledges the existence of reasonable dissent, which can be resolved by enshrining this accommodation in the law. On the other hand, the fact that the legislative system takes this moral dimension into consideration does not result, in principle, in an effective measure that restricts the autonomy of others, which is often increased by the new legislation. These clauses, therefore, are a clear demonstration of one of the ways in which the law is morally bound to take the religious factor into consideration.

The second route for expressing a conscientious objection in a democratic society is via an application, in this case addressed in general terms to a judge, asking for acknowledgement of the legitimacy and legality, in a specific individual scenario, of an accommodation that is allowed in the name of religion. The areas in which applications of this type are deployed are very varied (reproductive rights, end of life, marriage and parenthood, education, the wearing of religious symbols and so on). In their consequences, these applications call into question the neutrality of laws. This is because, even if it is meant to be neutral in the justifications it gives or in the objectives it sets, any public policy will invariably engender instances of inequality among the various sectors of the population by virtue of their religious or moral views (Merrill, 2007).

Should we then implement, as Stephen Macedo recommends, "with a second stage: a stage where, having constructed a reasonable public view, we consider pleas for accommodations and exemptions from marginal groups" (Macedo, 1995: 483). The acceptance (or the rejection) of the objection, in this sense, can be considered to be a tool for managing and even integrating ethical differences (Guichard, 2014; Lépinard, 2016) and reflects the diversity of values within society and their protection by the political sphere. These are the political theory issues discussed in Part I of this book.

The opening chapter is by the philosopher of law Pierluigi Chiassoni, who describes the complex philosophical and legal issues surrounding the protection of conscience and convictions in a pluralist democracy, based on a two-pronged examination of the nature and the modalities of this protection. Starting with the premise that freedom of conscience is the essential counterpart of individual autonomy, he presents a strong defence of the right to conscientious objection, which makes it possible to guarantee what he calls the "four-legged religious freedom": the right to freedom *of religion*, the right to freedom *of non-religion*, the right to freedom *from religion* and the right to freedom *from non-religion.*

The discussion continues, in Chapter 2 written by Ravza Altuntas-Çakır, who keenly insists on the legitimate place of religion in the public democratic space. After setting out a number of contemporary philosophical positions, the author advocates a pluralist secularism model, which she considers best able to reconcile the presence of the religious element in the social public sphere with the democratic demands of secularism.

In Chapter 3, which deals with applications for exemptions in the medical field, the philosopher Daniel Weinstock analyses the extent of the principle of freedom of conscience or religion, and consequently of the exemptions that can be requested on this basis, not from the viewpoint of the person who cites such grounds, but from the patient's viewpoint. He argues in effect that patients have an interest in such exemptions being granted, provided they do not give rise to problematic consequences with respect to the supply of the legal medical services with respect to which exemptions are sought.

The spaces in which contestation occurs

Although they are very diverse, the applications made to judges share some common ground. The three main issues are as follows.

First, the question arises of whether granting such an objection to some is compatible with the rights of others. A judge is obliged to determine the balance between a number of individual autonomies, or between individual autonomies and the public interest. It is also the judge's remit to assess what might be an acceptable exemption that does not challenge the rights of the common good (for instance, in the case of exemption from vaccination, the public health requirements) (Navin, 2018) or the rights that have been opened up by the law (in the case of access to abortion for all women, for example).

Where individual autonomies are intertwined like this, contestation also raises the question of "burden-shifting", since exemption from a duty can engender a burden or an additional cost for other individuals. So, for example, this might involve assessing the additional cost that allowing dispensation from a day's work for religious reasons might entail for the employer, or even for those employees who do not benefit from this dispensation.

Second, and extending beyond an interpersonal relationship of this kind, applications for conscientious objection may conflict with the conditions necessary for living in a democratic society and for protecting individual autonomy. They then raise the question of the legitimacy of a state that cannot exert deliberate coercion with regard to specific ethical issues and therefore limits the practical consequences in order to ensure common values. It is a matter of knowing whether there is a "right to be exempted from measures reasonably designed to help secure the freedom of all" (Macedo, 1995: 486), or whether it is necessary to "pay a price for living in a free pluralistic society" (Macedo, 1995: 496).

This was the case with the refusal of the American judge to allow an application from Fundamentalist Christian parents for their children be exempted from a literacy course which used a textbook that presented the various religions in a neutral and impartial light. They had claimed that this was in contravention of their right to bring up their children to be convinced of the truth of their faith. Admittedly, the parents' request did not imply a challenge to the validity of public education as a whole, nor an attempt to apply a comprehensive doctrine interpretation of the education system. Yet, the aim of their application was to deprive children who were expected to grow up within the community of citizens of any confrontation with diversity, which is a key component of a basic education in citizenship. Conversely, in the case of the Amish, a group that lives largely outside society, the Supreme Court ruled that, whilst ensuring religious freedom, exemption from compulsory education after the 8th grade did not jeopardise the ability of individuals who wished to leave the group to be integrated into society, since the principles of common citizenship were considered to have been acquired by this stage in students' education, and the means for their emancipation was considered to have been provided.[3]

Third, as we indicated above, contestation before a judge in the name of religion raises the question of what precisely is religious and must be protected as such. How does a judge define religious convictions? How can they determine the sincerity of such convictions? And how then can they take religious arguments into account and what legitimacy do they accord to these arguments, either in the public space or in the present case, in the courts?

These questions become even more urgent when the spaces in which they are contested are vastly increased in number and are more inflammatory. This is because national and international legal instruments relating to the protection of basic rights have enlarged the window of opportunity for contesting a norm in the name of religion, which henceforth extends beyond areas to which it was traditionally confined.

The aim in Part II of this book is to document the emergence of new areas of contestation, both in the locations where contestation is expressed and in the causes that it champions. In Chapter 4, Vincent Valentin identifies the emergence of increasingly frequent "wars of conscience" within the private sector, contrasting the conscientious beliefs of individuals who regularly visit and work in an enterprise with the values advocated and defended by that enterprise. He starts by analysing the decisions of the European Courts and goes on to set out the challenges and new modes of regulation that might make it possible to resolve the tensions and conflicts between freedoms.

These new "conscience wars" diagnosed by Vincent Valentin give rise to new questions, specifically the question of knowing to what extent the potential beneficiary of an objection may no longer be an individual, subject to laws, but an institution or legal entity. Problems of this kind are followed up in Chapter 5 contributed by the law experts Xavier Delgrange and Hélène Lerouxel, who question the opportunity to extend conscience clauses for medical staff to health institutions in Belgium. On the basis of an analysis of the Belgian Catholic church's application for a conscience clause to be acknowledged in the law with regard to abortion, euthanasia and medically assisted reproduction for the sake of faith-based medical institutions, the authors believe that such a clause would result in new problems in terms of reconciling the rights and freedoms of individuals with those of institutions. This is a legal issue, but it is also strictly political in nature. Contestation in the name of religion is giving rise to involvement in a variety of campaigns by the churches or by interest groups that are guided by spiritual or religious issues in areas that are less so.

Chapter 6, contributed by Christophe Monnot and Alexandre Grandjean, which examines the eco-spirituality environment in Switzerland, further illustrates this argument. Starting with an analysis of the activities that revolve around the Laboratory for Inner Transition, a platform set up in 2016 in the Protestant NGO Bread for All, the authors proceed to unravel the range of campaigns and arguments that these eco-spiritual groups are mobilising in the public debate, based on a two-pronged spiritual and environmental approach. This chapter provides a very clear illustration of how religious or spiritual groups are attempting to win over wider audiences for their cause, a subject that is also of concern to the sociologist Valentina Gaddi in a research project she conducted among Hasidic Jews in the district of Outremont in Montreal in Quebec.

In a highly engrossing essay (Chapter 7), she describes how Hasidic Jewish communities are opposing the civil norm for reasons that affect the religious organisation of their everyday life. Is free parking of a vehicle permissible during the Sabbath? What temporary decorations can be put up on balconies during the period of Sukkot? Which buildings may be used for ritual purposes? The author goes on to show that, to be effective, contestation in the name of religion avoids expressing itself with reference to religion or in a religious argument, instead favouring secular arguments in order to be better heard in a secularised society such as Quebec.

The rhetoric of contestation

If considering the religious factor in order to guarantee basic rights in general, and freedom of conscience and religion in particular, is indeed a democratic right, in secularised societies that view religion mainly as a matter for the individual, contestation in the name of religion is also limited, as much in its foundations as in its rhetoric. First, the question may arise of the legitimacy of religious institutions in contesting, for religious reasons, choices made in the political sphere even when these institutions are attached to public service functions (hospitals, education, etc.) and benefit from public finance. Second, it is interesting to note how the terminology that religious groups mobilise to construct their arguments is evolving. Although religion is indeed at the root of contestation, religious views feature less and less frequently in the arguments that are deployed, since the social response to them in a secularised society is now minimal. The need to be heard that is highlighted by Hirschman (1991) seems to imply "constructing a rhetoric that is publicly audible (from the perspective of shared beliefs) and acceptable (from the perspective of norms for public discourse)" (Rennes, 2011). If the act of legislating and the law are resources for mobilisation and contestation on the grounds of religious convictions, they then imply a line of argument that is audible within the society in which the spaces for contestation are located. Discourse is then constrained by the requirements of reasoning. What is said cannot be subjected to an analysis that is independent of the place and time where it is said, and this is how "we see at work transformations in the argumentative resources that are and can be used, and the way they constrain or frame deliberative tests" (Chateauraynaud, 2004: 194).

How can the religious factor be made audible for the groups and individuals that contest norms in its name? What rhetoric is used nowadays to express such contestation? Such questions recur throughout the book; a perfect example of this can be found in the ethnographic surveys carried out by Isabelle Dumont and Jocelyn Maclure, Samuel Blouin and also Samuel Dolbeau.

On the strength of a series of semi-structured interviews with 20 doctors in Quebec, opposed to both secular and religious reasons to medically assisted dying, Chapter 8 by Isabelle Dumont and Jocelyn Maclure situates the thinking within contemporary philosophical debates about objecting. This leads them to take a stance in favour of a liberal interpretation of the right to object that has been established by the law, since in liberal democratic societies, the moral weight of actions does not necessarily have to be justified by citing a coherently structured set of tenets and convictions.

In the same vein, the comparative research conducted by Samuel Blouin (Chapter 9) in the canton of Vaud in Switzerland and in Quebec questions the possibility of contesting assisted dying in the name of religion in secularised contexts where religion is a private affair. How can such an objection express itself publicly nowadays in the face of social and political perceptions that relegate it to the level of private choice?

The book closes with Chapter 10 by Samuel Dolbeau, who analyses the politicisation of French Catholics from 1970–1980 onwards over issues concerning intimate relationships. He starts with a detailed analysis and review of one of the most dynamic ecclesiastical movements, the Emmanuel Community, and goes on to demonstrate the role played by the inclusion of lay medical experts in this politicisation, and its contribution to the legitimisation of lay people within the religious sphere.

As a whole, the various contributions presented in this book are in the nature of a reflection on the status, the role and the functions of the common norm in liberal democracies and in diverse societies where the various conceptions of what is good increasingly tend to clash in the legal arena. If contestation in the name of religion is a result of democracy (with its guarantee of rights), it also threatens it. Its legitimacy continues to be derived from delicately balanced situations, and constantly has to be renegotiated and find a balance between the rights of some and those of others.

Notes

1 Indeed, countless publications by lawyers and sociologists have clearly shown that this separation was not restricted merely to its enshrinement in a legal instrument as is the case in the United States, Turkey or France, for example, but extends beyond this, finding a wider expression by dissociating the religious and civil standards in the governance of the state (Hasquin, 1981; Blancarte, 2001; Ferrari, 2008; Baubérot and Milot, 2011).

2 This is, in effect, a theoretical principle. This is because the pragmatic aspect of how the objection has evolved in contemporary society is at times more or less explicitly translated into a strategy of globally challenging common norms in the name of a higher natural law or of civil or moral values. A claim for legal endorsement may then indicate a political use of conscience (Proeschel, 2017) and of religious convictions against a social and legal trend, and may give momentum in a moral crusade to "campaigns that aim not only to defend and promote certain values and norms, but also for them to spread beyond their followers alone and for compliance with them to be imposed on society in general" (Mathieu, 2005).

3 *Wisconsin v. Jonas Yoder*, 406 U.S. 205 (1972).

Bibliography

Baubérot, J. and Milot, M. 2011. *Laïcités sans frontières*. Paris: Éditions du Seuil.

Blancarte, R. 2001. "Laïcidad y secularización en México." *Estudios Sociólogicos* XIX (57): 843–855.

Campiche, R.J. 1993. "Individualisation du croire et recomposition de la religion." *Archives de sciences sociales des religions* 81: 117–131.

Chateauraynaud, F. 2004. "Invention argumentative et débat public: regard sociologique sur l'origine des bons arguments." *Papers in Political Economy* 47 (2): 191–213.

Davie, G. 1994. *Religion in Britain since 1945. Believing without Belonging*. Oxford: Blackwell.

Delgrange, X. and Koussens, D. 2019. "Les nouveaux arcs-boutants de la laïcité belge pilarisée." Pp. 93–99 in Bruyère, L., Crosetti, A.-S., Faniel, J. and Sägesser, C. (eds.)

Piliers, dépilarisation et clivage philosophique en Belgique. Bruxelles: Les Éditions du CRISP.

Ewick, P. and Silbey, S. 1998. *The Common Place of Law. Stories from Everyday Life*. Chicago: University of Chicago Press.

Ferrari, A. 2008. "Laïcité et multiculturalisme à l'italienne." *Archives de sciences sociales des religions* 141: 133–154.

Guichard, S. 2014. "De la liberté de croyance à l'obligation de s'intégrer: les arrêts du tribunal fédéral sur les dispenses de cours de natation pour des élèves musulmans." *AJP/PJA* 7: 983–992.

Hasquin, H. 1981. *Histoire de la laïcité, principalement en Belgique et en France*. Bruxelles: Éditions de l'Université de Bruxelles.

Hervieu-Léger, D. 1999. *Le pèlerin et le converti. La religion en mouvement*. Paris: Flammarion.

Hirschman, A.O. 1991. *Deux siècles de rhétorique réactionnaire*. Paris: Fayard.

Koussens, D. 2011. "La religion 'saisie' par le droit. Comment l'État laïque définit-il la religion au Québec et en France?" *Recherches sociographiques* 52 (3): 811–832.

Laborde, C. 2017. *Liberalism's Religion*. Cambridge, MA: Harvard University Press.

Lampron, L.-P. 1998. "Les arrêts *C.S. des Chênes* et *Loyola* : quand la valeur du pluralisme culturel perce le principe de l'autonomie confessionnelle." Pp. 229–245 in Koussens, D. and Foisy, C. (eds.) *Les catholiques québécois et la laïcité*. Ste-Foy: Presses de l'Université Laval.

Leckey, R. 2007. "Following Same-Sex Marriage : Redefining Marriage and the Impact for Polygamy." *Les Ateliers de l'Ethique* 2 (1): 30–35.

Lépinard, E. 2016. "Juger/inclure/imaginer les minorités religieuses. La prise en compte de la subjectivité minoritaire dans l'exercice du jugement au Canada et en France." Pp. 63–84 in Barras, A., Dermange, F. and Nicolet, S. (eds.) *Réguler le religieux dans les sociétés libérales. Les nouveaux défis*. Genève: Labor et Fides.

Luther King Jr., M. 1963. "Letter from Birmingham Jail." *Online King Records Access*. Retrieved on September 1st, 2020. (http://okra.stanford.edu/transcription/document_images/undecided/630416-019.pdf).

Mabille, X. 1990. "Le débat politique d'avril 1990 sur la sanction et la promulgation de la loi." *Courrier hebdomadaire du CRISP* 10 (1274): 1–33.

Macedo, S. 1995. "Liberal Civic Education and Religious Fundamentalism: The Case of God v. John Rawls?" *Ethics* 105 (3): 468–496.

Maclure, J. and Taylor, C. 2011. *Secularism and Freedom of Conscience*. Cambridge, MA: Harvard University Press.

Mathieu, L. 2005. "Repères pour une sociologie des croisades morales." *Déviance et Société* 29 (1): 3–12.

Merrill, R. 2007. "Neutralité politique." in Boudreau, V. and Merrill, R. (eds.) *DicoPo-Dictionnaire de théorie politique*. Retrieved on September 1st, 2020. (http://www.dicopo.org/spip.php?article).

Navin, M. 2018. "Prioritizing Religion in Vaccine Exemption Policies." Pp. 160–191 in Vallier, K. and Weber M. (eds.) *Religious Exemptions*. Oxford: Oxford University Press.

Proeschel, C. 2013. "La bataille judiciaire autour de l'éducation à la citoyenneté en Espagne." *Annuaire Droit et Religions* 7 (1): 241–257.

Proeschel, C. 2017. "Démocratie et militantisme moral: la conscience en politique." Pp. 287–298 in Dieckhoff, A. and Portier, P. (eds.) *L'enjeu mondial. Religion et politique*. Paris, Presses de Sciences-Po.

Proeschel, C. 2019. “Les politiques de la mort, lieu du réenchantement argumentatif ? L’instauration par la loi du 2 février 2016 d’un droit à la sédation pour les malades en fin de vie.” *Raison Publique* 23: 103–127.

Rawls, J. 1993. *Political Liberalism*. New York: Columbia University Press.

Rennes, J. 2011. “Les formes de la contestation. Sociologie des mobilisations et théories de l'argumentation.” *A Contrario* 16: 151–173.

Roy, O. 2010. *Holy Ignorance. When Religion and Culture Part Ways*. New York: Columbia University Press.

United States Conference of Catholic Bishops. 2012. *Our First, Most Cherished Liberty: A Statement on Religious Liberty*. Ad Hoc Committee for Religious Liberty, Washington, DC. Retrieved on September 1st, 2020. (http://www.usccb.org/issues-and-action/religi ous liberty/upload/Our_First_Most_Cherished_Liberty.pdf).

Part I

Theoretical issues

1 Protecting freedom of conscience in a constitutional state

Pierluigi Chiassoni

In this chapter, I aim to address a problem of constitutional engineering. This problem relates to providing adequate protection of freedom of conscience and religious freedom in a constitutional state, paying particular attention to the situation of people who happen to live in a religious society, that is, in a society where the cultural and political influence of religious groups, organisations and institutions is a pervasive phenomenon.

This problem of how to protect cannot be dealt with properly unless the object of protection has been sufficiently specified beforehand and the problem of what to protect has already been addressed, and, in some way solved. To be sure, the problem of what to protect could be avoided if there were a widespread consensus among scholars on what constitutes logically adequate conceptions of freedom of conscience and religious freedom. Unfortunately, that does not seem to be the case.

This chapter falls into two parts. The first part is conceptual. It defines the concept of freedom of conscience and the concept of religious freedom for a constitutional state in line with the principles of liberalism.[1] The second part is engineering. It outlines an integrated set of principles for the protection of freedom of conscience and religious freedom, by a constitutional state, in a religious society, combining a theory of the sphere of individual inviolability with a general right to conscientious objection, both in a negative and in a positive form.

The conceptual, protecting-what, problem

"Conscience" and "Freedom of Conscience"

In everyday discourse, by the term "conscience", we usually understand two different, though related, things.

First, "conscience" stands for the *moral code* of each individual human being, that is, the set of (fundamental) moral standards and convictions that govern the practical aspects of an individual's life.

Second, "conscience" is also used to refer to the *mental faculty* by means of which each individual identifies (establishes, specifies, revises, updates and so on) the moral code that governs the practical aspects of their life.

At any time in the life of an individual, conscience as a moral code (*conscience-code*) is, therefore, the product of conscience as a moral faculty (*conscience-faculty*).[2]

In everyday speech, the two senses of "conscience" are intertwined.[3] We are all familiar with expressions such as "My conscience forbade me to do that", "I will act according to the dictates of my conscience", "The voice of my conscience tells me not to do that", "If you do that, your conscience will persecute you for the rest of your life", "We will decide the issue by listening to our conscience" and so on.

Terms such as "dictates", "voice" and "persecution" reveal the persistence of an archaic way of thinking, one that is characterised by a primordial animism that inclines towards personification, turning the faculty of conscience into an "agent" that lives inside each individual as a demanding guest. This way of thinking goes along with a few well-known images about how the faculty of conscience works. To any individual, conscience is, firstly, a "never sleeping" *observer* who scrutinises each of their thoughts and actions; secondly, an inflexible *drill-sergeant* who issues commands for any situation in everyday life; thirdly, a *wise shepherd* leading them to do the right thing and abstain from doing the wrong (through "the pricks of conscience"); fourthly, and lastly, an *authority* that, acting at the same time as an *incorruptible judge* and as a *punctual executioner*, pronounces upon their transgressions and inflicts the corresponding inescapable torments.

Our everyday archaic way of thinking about conscience is based on metaethical objectivism. Conscience speaks *the truth* on moral matters. Far from being random or arbitrary, the dictates of conscience are assumed to voice moral precepts that are *objective* (non-subjective), *absolute* (not relating to only one moral point of view among others) and *intrinsically binding* (not optional for their addressees). Accordingly, conscience acts as an organ that "*hetero-organises*" individual actions: It is a kind of ethical *microchip* that conveys to each agent the heteronomous – external, objective, absolute and intrinsically binding – directives of true morality.[4]

One final piece of the puzzle is needed to complete this very swift account of conscience in our antiquated everyday thinking. The ministers of "institutionalised moralities" – for example, the ministers of certain institutionalised religions – hold the dictates of each individual's conscience to be truly objective, absolute and intrinsically binding, if, and only if, they comply with the opinion of institutional *moral experts*. These experts are, for instance, the official moral theologians who tell people, authoritatively, *how* the dictates of conscience are to be properly understood and acted upon. From this standpoint, therefore, the faculty of conscience of each individual, in order to work correctly, must ultimately become the organ of an *authoritarian "hetero-organisation"* of their conduct.

The authoritarian-heteronomous conception of conscience is characteristic of mainstream Christian medieval thought.[5] Modernity comes with the transition from the authority-controlled, heteronomous conscience to an authority-free, individualistic and autonomous conscience. The process involves two stages.

In the first stage, the faculty of conscience is seen as combining the heteronomy of moral standards with an anti-authoritarian and individualistic epistemological attitude. Conscience is still the vehicle of heteronomous objective standards of behaviour. But now each individual is entrusted with the delicate task of being the sole authorised interpreter of true moral requirements: They are the only agent competent to establish what those standards require, insofar as their conduct is in order, without any interference from intrusive and unwanted moral experts provided by authoritarian institutions.[6] Although not yet endowed with "full rights", each individual develops into a genuine *moral subject*, who is personally responsible for the correct cognition and application of the fundamental moral standards that should regulate their life (Sapir and Statman, 2005: 475–476).[7]

In the second stage, conscience is seen as having to do, not only with the identification of each individual's fundamental moral standards, but also, and primarily, with *establishing* the relevance and binding force thereof upon that individual. Conscience becomes the "place" where each individual's *moral autonomy* is located – the seat of the *moral power* to establish which standards are to be binding in their practical life. Individuals do not necessarily create the basic standards governing the practical aspects of their lives. However, those standards are relevant and binding for individuals, *if, and only if*, by exercising their moral autonomy, they have *accepted* these standards as their moral compass by making an ultimate (but usually revisable) free choice, that is, as the Polar star in their navigation through the high seas of practical issues.

The authoritarian-heteronomous conception and the non-authoritarian-autonomous conception of conscience make quite different demands on positive law.

The former requires the endorsement of an authoritarian view of freedom of conscience as the right of each and every individual to act according to the true dictates of the correct authority-controlled heteronomous conscience.

Conversely, the latter requires the endorsement of a liberal conception of freedom of conscience, one that encompasses for each and every individual: (1) the freedom to exercise their moral autonomy in creating, selecting, adopting and revising the standards that govern their practical life, without suffering any undue external influence (the *internal dimension* of freedom of conscience); (2) the freedom to live according to the moral standards they have created, selected, adopted and revised as fundamental to the practical aspects of their life, without suffering any undue external restraint (the *external dimension* of freedom of conscience).[8]

The authoritarian conception of freedom of conscience is at odds with deontological individualism and ethical pluralism. It favours moral imperialism, moral paternalism and the establishment of authoritarian states, usually of a religious-theocratic character. It justifies intolerance, political violence, subversion, civil war and internal and international terrorism.

By contrast, the liberal conception of freedom of conscience is at home with deontological individualism and moral pluralism, opposes moral imperialism and moral paternalism and requires the establishment of a democratic constitutional state, which is as neutral as possible in matters of conscience and religion.[9] Liberal freedom of conscience also protects each individual's freedom to put themselves under the direction of some external moral authority, be it of a religious or of a secular nature. This freedom to abide by the standards of some heteronomous morality, even by those standards that are the most authoritarian, strict and mortifying, cannot in any case involve the right to coerce others into being subject to the same bonds.

From the standpoint of liberalism, when constitutional states endorse the protection of freedom of conscience, they are committing to the liberal variety of freedom of conscience. This may seem to be a trivial point, but it is nonetheless worth making. People in religious societies are constantly exposed to religious people's claims about the *proper* way of understanding conscience and freedom of conscience, to the point that they may lose sight of the only concept that should inspire the institutions of a genuine constitutional state, that is, being in tune with its founding values of equal individual autonomy, dignity and inviolability (Nino, 1989: IV, V, VI).

Freedom of conscience and religious freedom

In the history of Western political thought and legal institutions, the right to freedom of conscience is closely connected to the right to religious freedom (Ruffini, 1901).

The uncertainties surrounding the concepts of "conscience" and "religion", however, make the relationships between the two rights (assuming, for the sake of argument, that they are two rights) far from established.[10] Any clarification, and resolution, of the uncertainty in question cannot but depend – if only by way of an uncommitted and detached analytical experiment – on some assumed normative ethical standpoint. There is indeed no true, absolute, freedom of conscience, no true, absolute, religious freedom, but only concepts and conceptions relative to, and dependent on, specific political philosophies and ethical outlooks. Hence, when we come to the law, the interpretation of recurrent phrases such as "freedom of conscience" and "religious freedom" cannot but depend on commitments to some political and moral philosophical outlook.

In very broad, tentative and pre-partisan tautological terms, religious freedom may be defined as *freedom in relation to religious matters*.

In common sense terms and in everyday language, the term "religious matters" refers to the following issues at least:

1. The existence of supernatural beings (gods, demons, nymphs, the souls of ancestors and so on) and their essential properties (goodness, omnipotence, wisdom and so on).
2. The relationships, if any, between supernatural beings (their will, desire, design, reason, understanding, whim, humour and so on) and the human condition on earth and in the afterlife.
3. The relationships, if any, between supernatural beings (their will, desire, design and so on) and the conduct of individual human beings, be they believers or non-believers, towards themselves, other humans, non-human animals, the environment and, last but not least, supernatural beings.

4. The rules, rituals, teachings and ways of life that emanate directly or indirectly from supernatural beings and the adoption, interpretation, development and application thereof by believers.
5. The ways of life, as defined by rules, rituals, teachings and so on, established by spiritual masters such as Buddha, Confucius, Jesus Christ and so on, and the adoption, interpretation, development and application thereof by the masters themselves or by their followers.[11]

Religious matters encompass a vast array of ontological, epistemological, cosmological, eschatological, anthropological and moral issues. If we consider such an array of issues from the standpoint of liberalism, the concept of religious freedom can be defined more precisely as being conceptually dependent on freedom of thought and freedom of conscience. It can be characterised as a *specific form of liberal freedom of thought and liberal freedom of conscience in relation to religious matters* (Atienza, 2014; Post, 2007).[12] To put this in very general terms, the ontology, epistemology, cosmology and eschatology of theistic and non-theistic religions are protected by religious freedom as a specific form of freedom of thought; the moral dress, food, rituals and codes of worship of theistic and non-theistic religions are protected, instead, by religious freedom as a specific form of freedom of conscience.

The liberal reduction of religious freedom to a *specific variety* of the liberal rights to freedom of thought and freedom of conscience *as they relate to religious matters* is at odds with a stance that believers in theistic religions often adopt; in other words, the stance that *their own* right to religious freedom is a fundamental right in itself, not just a specific form of some other more general fundamental right, and entitles *them* to special privileged forms of protection over the claims of conscience made by non-religious people or by those who follow different religions. In so claiming an exclusive right to ecclesiastical liberty (Ruffini, 1901: 5–10), believers in theistic religions raise what, in scholars' jargon, has come to be known as the "special status problem".[13]

A well-designed liberal theory of religious freedom must openly face, and determine, the special status problem.

To support their vindication of a privileged position, theistic believers use three arguments: the deity's blessing, tradition and the feelings of the majority, and the benefit to society.[14]

First, theistic believers argue *their* right to religious freedom should be accorded a special status and privileged protection since it relates to the true design of the true deity for mankind and has that deity's sacred blessing.

Second, theistic believers argue *their* right to religious freedom should be accorded a special status and privileged protection since *their* religious creed and religious institutions played, and still play, a paramount role in the history, culture and tradition of the country, and the feelings of the (moral, if not statistical) majority of the people would be hurt were such a right not to be granted the status it deserves.

Third, theistic believers argue *their* right to religious freedom should be accorded a special status and privileged protection since *their* religious creed and religious institution, by their very existence, contribute directly or indirectly to the well-being of society as a whole and of its many individual members.

From the standpoint of liberalism, the three arguments above, far from being conclusive, can easily be refuted.

The first argument calls for an outright rejection. Were the laws of a constitutional state to accept this view, they would be abandoning their political secularism and moral neutrality, and violating what, in American constitutional law, amounts to the Establishment Clause.

The second argument is a subtle appeal to the negative side of the equality principle ("Unlike cases should be treated differently").[15] It is presumably for this reason that the majority of the country would feel hurt, were the right to religious freedom denied the special legal status that it cherishes. From a liberal standpoint, however, matters of conscience, and claims based on religious grounds as a variety thereof, are not suitable candidates for applying the principle of antiquity (*prior in tempore potior in iure*), since they belong to the timeless dimension of ethical principles, where argumentation requires *substantive* reasons. By the same token, no special status can be accorded to a religious creed on the basis of its (alleged) correspondence to the feelings of the majority. Matters of conscience (and religion) are not suitable candidates for being decided according to the majority principle, belonging as they do to the "sphere of inviolability" that the constitutional state must guarantee to each and every individual *against* undue interference by other people, even though they are in an overwhelming majority. Finally, the fact that the feelings of many people may be hurt by denying a special legal status to their right to religious freedom, even though they happen to be the majoritarian feelings, must be considered devoid of any legal relevance whatsoever, since such a "wound" does not pass muster in Mill's harm principle.

The third argument appeals to the ostensible benefits that society at large, and each and every one of its members, derives from the very existence of the religious creed and religious institutions connected with a certain right to religious freedom. Whether, and to what extent, particular religions are beneficial to a society is a matter of asking for careful empirical inquiry, once the relevant conceptual issues have been established (Which benefits? To whom? How are they measured?). Religions may indeed be beneficial, but can also be obnoxious.[16] Be it as it may, from a liberal standpoint, the entire issue must be considered irrelevant with regard to the problem of special status. Even supposing a certain religion *does* in fact bestow benefits on a society, why should the right to religious freedom (and the related claims of conscience) of its believers be entitled to privileged legal protection? They ask for special status as a matter of *right*. Such a right, however, looks like the right to a "virtual contract" or "trade-off", that is, the special protection looks like the *price* that theistic believers ask *in exchange for* the benefits that their religion bestows on a society. That being the case, three remarks are in order. First, religions do something supposedly beneficial to society *on their own initiative*. As a consequence, they cannot claim to have any *legal right* to that society's recognition in the form of a special status for their right to religious freedom. Second, religions in a constitutional state do enjoy the precious inestimable benefit of public protection of religious freedom: They are, in this sense, compensated in advance for whatever benefit they may bestow on society. Third, the net balance of the beneficial effects of a religion on a society is, to say the least, uncertain and arguable. Conversely, the beneficial effects any religion derives from the public protection of (liberal) religious freedom are solid and certain.

Religious freedom: a cluster of rights

From a liberal standpoint, the right to religious freedom amounts, broadly speaking, to the *specific definition of the liberal rights to freedom of thought and freedom of conscience in relation to religious matters.* Some analysis suggests that the liberal right to religious freedom could be conceived as being endowed with a *double dimension* and a *four-legged structure.*

To begin with, it is worth distinguishing between the *internal* and the *external* dimensions of the right to religious freedom.

In its *internal dimension,* this right amounts to the freedom, for each and every individual, to adopt, revise, change and reject beliefs and attitudes concerning religious matters and, in particular, religious ways of life. This freedom covers a broad spectrum, including believing in a theistic or in a non-theistic religion, embracing agnosticism or atheism, believing a certain religious way of life to be the one that is truly conducive to clear material benefits such as a meaningful worldly existence, eternal life, universal salvation, perfection on earth and beyond, endorsing or rejecting a religious moral code and so on. Protecting the internal dimension of the right to religious freedom against undue forms of invasion of, and influence upon, the human mind by public or private powers is necessary to be sure, and becomes more so as mind-control techniques evolve. It is not sufficient, however. An adequate protection of the right to religious freedom also requires the protection of its *external dimension,* that is, public manifestations, alone or together with other people, of one's beliefs and attitudes concerning religious matters, public practice of religious rituals, public adherence to religious rules, practices and teachings (with regard to, for example, food, clothes, holidays, education, sex, violence and so on).

The liberal right to religious freedom in a broad sense, however, has not only an internal and an external dimension, along the same lines as the right to freedom of conscience, as we have seen. It also has a *four-legged structure* that cuts through the two dimensions. The right to religious freedom in a broad sense is a *complex right* amounting, at a lower level of abstraction, to the combination of two pairs of fundamental things – the right to freedom *of religion,* the right to freedom *from non-religion,* the right to freedom *of non-religion* and the right to freedom *from religion.*

The right to freedom *of* religion is the freedom to adopt some theistic or non-theistic religion and carry out the public manifestation and exercise of its rituals, practices, worship, teachings, observances and so on.[17] The complement to this right is the right to freedom *from non-religion,* that is, the right of people who adhere to a religious creed to be *free from undue interference* from people of secular or different religious beliefs.

Likewise, the right to freedom *of non-religion* is the freedom to reject any theistic or non-theistic religion, to adopt an atheistic, agnostic, secular way of life and carry out public manifestations and exercise of its principles, rules and teachings. Concomitant to this right is the right to freedom *from religion*, that is, the right of secular people to be free from undue interference from people with religious beliefs.[18]

Sapir and Statman argue for a narrow construction of the right to freedom from religion, seeing it as providing protection to "secular people" from being "forced to perform an act, or to participate in a ceremony, of a clearly religious nature", whenever this makes them "feel ... alienated from themselves", being "forced to behave in a manner that is inauthentic and against their integrity" (Sapir and Statman, 2005: 502), such as being obliged to participate in a religious form of marriage (*Idem*, 2005: 502, 506–508).

Sapir and Statman's view has the merit of aiming at determinacy and precision. Nonetheless, it is unfit when it comes to providing "secular people" with a level of protection adequate to the requirements of a liberal constitutional state.

According to Sapir and Statman, the act or ceremony which secular people are forced to perform must be "of a clearly religious nature". On a narrow reading, an act or ceremony is "of a clearly religious nature" if, and only if, it is prescribed by the ritual code of some religion. Being forced into performing a rabbinic marriage or attending a Catholic mass would be clear examples of this. On a broader reading, on the other hand, an act or ceremony is also "of a clearly religious nature" if it is required by religiously inspired positive laws, that is, by laws the content of which tacitly endorses the moral or ritual dictates of a religion or set of religions. Sapir and Statman seem to be opting for the narrow reading of the "clearly religious nature" condition. So understood, however, their concept of freedom from religion leaves secular people defenceless from the imposition of acts or ceremonies required by positive laws that tacitly endorse the moral or ritual dictates of a given religion or set of religions.[19] Accordingly, only a broader reading is in tune with liberal religious freedom.

Sapir and Statman's concept of freedom from religion takes into account only *one kind* of religiously dependent norms, that is, the *positive imperative norms* requiring people "to perform an act, or to participate in a ceremony, of a clearly religious nature". However, religiously inspired laws can also harm secular people by means of *negative norms*, such as *negative imperative norms*, which impose duties to abstain from performing certain acts, or *inability norms*, which make people unable to validly perform certain acts. Positive legal orders are still replete with religiously inspired laws that, for example, prevent women from dressing as they like, prevent women from travelling abroad without their father's, brother's or husband's consent, make abortion and sodomy among consenting adults a crime, prevent any form of valid same-sex marriage and so on. Accordingly, the adoption of Sapir and Statman's narrow conception of freedom from religion makes secular people defenceless too in the face of these very alienating and very harmful laws.

Taking stock

Let me review the argument so far.

1. In order to provide a solution to the conceptual, protecting-what, problem, I have identified in turn (i) a non-authoritarian, individual autonomy-centred, conception of conscience; (ii) a corresponding liberal conception of the right to freedom of conscience; (iii) a broad concept of the right to religious freedom, as a specific definition of the liberal rights to freedom of thought and freedom of conscience, endowed with a double dimension (the internal and external dimension) and a four-legged structure, including the more specific rights to (iv) freedom of religion (the one usually expressly conveyed by constitutional and international covenants clauses), (v) freedom of non-religion, (vi) freedom from non-religion and (vii) freedom from religion, the latter to be understood as establishing a broad protection, targeting not only openly religious laws, but also religion-inspired laws.
2. I have argued, through a comparison with rival concepts and rights, that the concepts and rights reiterated above are those most in tune with the liberal spirit of a contemporary constitutional state. In so doing, I have rejected in turn (i) the authority-controlled, heteronomous conscience of Christian medieval thinking, (ii) the authority-free but still heteronomous conscience of some stances in modern thought, (iii) the authoritarian conception of the right to freedom of conscience, (iv) the claim of theistic believers to a right of religious liberty (ecclesiastical liberty) of their own, having a special status and entitling them to privileged protection, (v) a narrow concept of the right to freedom from religion (as advocated, for example, by Sapir and Statman).

It is time to move on to the second part of the chapter, that is, the part that addresses the constitutional engineering, protecting-how problem.

The engineering, protecting-how, problem

The problem of effective protection of the right to freedom of conscience in a religious society: strengthening the democratic process

The protection problem I will deal with has a limited scope. It consists in looking for the most effective and viable ways of protecting the liberal right to freedom of conscience, and, in particular, the right to freedom from religion. In what follows, for brevity's sake, I will refer to this protection problem as being about "the right to freedom of conscience".

Political majorities can, and often do, interfere with the right to freedom of conscience through the democratic process, by enacting religiously inspired laws of universal mandatory application.

One way of protecting freedom of conscience consists in strengthening the democratic procedures, so as to ensure that religiously inspired laws be enacted after a society-wide process involving true and deep debates between the different opinions at stake. Some years ago, Carlo Augusto Viano, a staunch defender of political secularism living in a (clear instance of a) religious society, outlined a set of rules purporting to establish the conditions for legitimate access by religious groups, organisations and institutions to the democratic process and its benefits. Let us examine them briefly.

1. Religious groups, organisations and institutions enjoy a full right to participate in the process of legislation by campaigns (including propaganda and public advertisement) addressed at public opinion.
2. The exercise of this right should, however, be subject to *limits* concerning the *places* and the *forms* of religious campaigns.
3. Religious campaigns in favour of a piece of legislation:
   a. Should be regarded as totally free, whenever performed inside buildings devoted to worship, such as churches and oratories.
   b. Should be regarded as totally prohibited, whenever claiming to take place inside public buildings, such as public hospitals, public schools, barracks, police districts and so on.
   c. Should be regarded as permitted, whenever performed inside public spaces likely to be "visited" by all citizens (such as national television or radio programmes), *on condition* that the religious points of view be exposed and argued for in the presence of people of different beliefs and allegiances, so as to ensure an effective "fair trial" (Viano, 2007).

The strengthening of the democratic process is likely to provide a limit to religiously inspired legislation, and, accordingly, is a measure worth adopting. By itself, however, it cannot provide an adequate protection for individuals' freedom of conscience. It does not rule out the possibility that a religiously inspired statute will nonetheless come to be enacted, which may interfere with the freedom of conscience, and the freedom from religion, of some individuals. In a constitutional state that is informed about the principles of liberalism, however, individuals have rights, and there are things the state cannot do without violating their rights, even though violations may come from a democratically enacted law. Such premises suggest a well-known conclusion, namely that the democratic protection of the right to freedom of conscience must be supplemented by further guarantees offered by the institutions of the constitutional state.

The problem of effective protection of the right to freedom of conscience in a religious society: an integrated doctrine of constitutional protection

In a constitutional state, the axiological basis for protecting the right to freedom of conscience is provided by the following hypotheses:

1. The law contains a set of supreme constitutional principles, expressly stated in specific constitutional provisions, or implicit in constitutional discourse (the "implicit" or "unwritten constitution"), and immune from change, even in the form of due constitutional amendment.

2. The liberal right to freedom of conscience (and freedom from religion) figure among the supreme principles of a constitutional state.
3. The liberal right to freedom of conscience implies a general right to conscientious objection, the exercise of which is subject only to the limits that can be derived from a fair, liberal reading of the harm principle (Mill, 1859: 16–17, 83–103; Feinberg, 1984: 1–27; Dworkin, 2006: ch. 3).
4. The general right to conscientious objection comes in the two varieties of the negative and the positive right to conscientious objection (Chiassoni, 2009, 2011; Saporiti, 2013a, 2013b).
5. Constitutional provisions establishing a general right to conscientious objection are to be considered as normatively redundant. Nonetheless, they may perform a very important declarative and symbolic function.
6. Statutory provisions establishing a right to conscientious objection for specific classes of cases (such as military service, medical care of abortion or animal experimentation) cannot be read to imply, under the *expressio unius est exclusio alterius* directive, the denial of a similar right for different situations. Such provisions should rather be read as expressing non-exclusive specific definitions and implementations of the general constitutional right to conscientious objection.
7. Apart from the limits imposed by a liberal reading of the harm principle, whenever a legal provision, be it in internal or international law, declares the right of conscientious objection to be subject to the "laws that regulate the exercise thereof" (or similar forms of words),[20] these limits should be read as authorising the enactment of laws that introduce *facilitating restrictions*, that is, the limits necessary to coordinate and facilitate the exercise of the right to conscientious objection by people, while any law introducing *obliterating restrictions*, that is, intended to unduly restrict or virtually suppress such a right, is to be deemed invalid.

In the light of the axiological basis above, an adequate constitutional protection of the right to freedom of conscience can be provided by reconciling the practice of legislatures and tribunals with the twin doctrines of the *sphere of individual inviolability* ("protected area" [Galeotti, 2008]; "*coto vedado*" [Garzón Valdés, 2004]) and *constitutional conscientious objection.*

The two doctrines offer *complementary forms* of protection that combine to form an *integrated doctrine of protection* that is characterised by the following tenets:

1. The legal space of constitutional states contains a set of matters upon which political majorities, even very broad and extensive majorities, cannot validly produce either *imperative norms* or *inability norms*.
2. Those matters concern individual morality and individual ways of life ("ethical matters" and "ethically sensitive issues") and form the sphere of individual inviolability, which is reserved for each individual's moral autonomy (the moral power of self-determination in practical issues).

3. The inviolability limits to the competence of the democratic legislature, if not expressly stated by any constitutional provision, must be considered to apply by way of an implicit constitutional principle, that is, the right to freedom of conscience, which is a supreme constitutional principle.
4. Whenever a democratic legislature decides, these principles notwithstanding, to enact a law containing imperative or inability norms on matters that pertain to the sphere of individual inviolability, it must provide the law with a set of provisions that regulate the right to conscientious objection.
5. Whenever a democratic legislature has enacted a law containing imperative or inability norms on matters that fall within the sphere of individual inviolability, without providing it with provisions concerning the exercise of the right to conscientious objection, the people who assume that their right to freedom of conscience has been violated are entitled to file a judicial complaint asking for the complete invalidation of the law, or, subordinately, for the recognition of their constitutional right to conscientious objection.
6. Where a judicial review is submitted to a constitutional court, the judge ordinary before whom the lawsuit has been brought should adopt temporary measures protecting the complainant's right to freedom of conscience while the constitutional process is underway.[21]
7. In their decision-making, legislatures and judges should take into account the negative and positive versions of the right to conscientious objection according to their respective functions and competences.

The right to freedom of conscience does not "imply" a general right to conscientious objection as a matter of logical implication, but, rather, by way of *pragmatic implication*, that is, as a means that is necessary, and likely to contribute, to its effective protection against abusive practices, and as an instrumental right the existence of which prevents the right to freedom of conscience from being just a "paper right".

Drawing a distinction between a negative and a positive right to conscientious objection is by no means usual. The remaining part of my chapter will be devoted to casting some light on this and suggesting that it is viable with regard to providing adequate protection for the right to freedom of conscience in a religious society. Before doing so, however, two preliminary issues must be briefly considered. The first issue, calling for a very short digression, is conceptual; it concerns the difference between conscientious objection and the right to conscientious objection. The second issue, which demands a more extensive treatment, is substantive. It concerns the sceptical stance that some scholars entertain about the very possibility of a constitutional state granting a general right to conscientious objection.

"Conscientious objection": entitlement, not resistance

Conscientious objection is often understood as a peaceful, but unlawful, form of resistance, akin to civil disobedience, consisting in violating an existing law for reasons of conscience. Isolated individuals, wishing to publicly bear witness to their opposition in conscience towards a certain piece of legislation, violate that very piece of legislation even though they may not consider the legal regime, as a whole, to be immoral or unjust.

That is an altogether different concept from the one under discussion here, that is, the *right* to conscientious objection as a fundamental individual right, explicitly or implicitly granted by a constitutional state to each and every of its subjects, with a view to protecting their right to freedom of conscience (and freedom from religion) against constitutionally illegitimate laws.[22]

A general right to conscientious objection? Overcoming sharp criticism from sceptics

The idea of a general right to conscientious objection was, and apparently still is, anathema to Western contemporary constitutional culture. The rights to conscientious objection actually granted to people so far – in relation to military service, medical assistance with abortion, medical experimentation on animals – were, and commonly are, regarded as *exceptions* to a general regime where conscientious objection is considered as a form of unlawful, punishable, protest (Dworkin, 1968, 1983). Furthermore, international legal instruments appear to treat the right to conscientious objection, if any, as something to be granted specifically by national governments.[23]

Nonetheless, the present age allows for – and indeed requires – the adoption of a different view. As a matter of political and moral philosophy, any government seriously committed to the protection of individuals' right to freedom of conscience should recognise a general right to conscientious objection as part and parcel of the constitutional system, as a default guarantee along the tenets of the integrated doctrine outlined above.

Some scholars, however, have assumed a sceptical stance. Among the arguments they have compiled against the idea of a general right to conscientious objection, five deserve consideration since they seem to deliver a fatal blow to this idea. These are the international law argument; the ineffectiveness argument; the consequentialist argument from instability and anarchy; the consequentialist argument from general welfare and common good; and the procedural drawbacks argument (Galeotti, 2008; Leiter, 2013: 94 ff.; Raz, 1979: 287–288; Mastromartino, 2018: 159–181).

The international law argument

The first argument to be considered, the international law argument, turns upon international legal instruments, such as, in particular, the International Covenant on Civil and Political Rights (art. 8, 3 *c* (*ii*)), the European Convention on Human Rights (art. 4, al. 3), and, more recently, art. 10 of the Charter of Fundamental Rights of the European Union, according to which:

> The right of conscientious objection is recognised in accordance with the national laws governing the exercise of this right.

The instruments are taken to support two mutually conspiring conclusions. First, there is no way of entertaining the idea of a *general* right to conscientious objection. Indeed, as the international legal instruments suggest, only limited, *situation-specific*, rights to conscientious objection are available to individuals. Second, there is no way of entertaining the idea of an *implicit* general right to conscientious objection, waiting to be made explicit in relevant sets of cases. Indeed, as the international legal instruments suggest, only *explicit* rights to conscientious objection are available to individuals, the existence of which depends on *ad hoc* national laws regulating the exercise thereof.

Three replies are in order.

First, international legal instruments do not provide any clear, knockdown evidence for the twin suggestions I have just recalled. The ICCPR and the ECHR only mention conscientious objection in relation to military service. Such a mention, however, is not sufficient, in itself, to draw the conclusion that only specific rights to conscientious objection exist and, what is more, *can* exist, in the realm of law.

Second, if my account of the axiological basis of a constitutional state is correct (as I think it is), even though international legal instruments had the content that the critique to a general right to conscientious objection claims them to have, any reference to what they say becomes totally irrelevant from the viewpoint of people's *domestic* constitutional rights.

Third, the international legal instruments at stake (the ICCPR, the ECHR, the European Charter of Fundamental Rights) can only be used to *enhance* the set of fundamental rights that people enjoy within their national states. They cannot be used, however, either to *deprive* people of the fundamental constitutional rights that they already have according to their own national legal system, or to *downsize* these rights. Constitutional states recognise a fundamental right to freedom of conscience. This right involves a general right to conscientious objection. Hence, the citizens of constitutional states do have a general right to conscientious objection, irrespective of the international law situation.

The ineffectiveness argument

The ineffectiveness argument runs as follows. Once people's fundamental right to freedom of conscience is being protected by a constitutional system that allows religiously inspired norms to be declared invalid whenever they violate the sphere of individual inviolability, there is no use in *also* granting people a general right to conscientious objection. Such a right would be utterly pointless.

The ineffectiveness argument makes an appeal to constitutional parsimony. It is too easy to be (totally) good, however. When religious societies are at stake, the invalidity guarantee may not work by itself. The symbolic force of a given religiously inspired law may be so strong that it weakens, postpones or altogether prevents the proper exercise of a judicial review. The constitutional court may balance its duty to nullify an illegitimate piece of religiously inspired legislation with the need to maintain its own "legitimacy" as a "neutral law-applying body" and find the second obligation overwhelming. Accordingly, individuals must be granted a *default protection device* for their right to freedom of conscience. Such a default device is, precisely, a general right to conscientious objection, in line with the tenets I am outlining there, for instance.

The consequentialist arguments from anarchy and general welfare

Perhaps the strongest argument against a general right to conscientious objection is the consequentialist argument from anarchy (the "Hobbesian argument"). It runs as follows: Granting a general right to conscientious objection is likely to have disastrous, overwhelmingly negative effects, for it would open the door to political and legal instability and would compromise the very existence of a peaceful government under the law, ultimately leading to anarchy.

Two replies are in order.

First, in point of fact, the prediction that the argument from anarchy turns upon is by no means reliable. Indeed, it is more likely that the effect of granting a general right to conscientious objection would be the strengthening of social bonds, and social harmony, under a general law of individual freedom (Walzer, 1970: 120 ff.). Each and every individual, under that regime, would appreciate an effort to treat everyone with equal concern and respect – always, of course, within the limits allowed by a liberal reading of the harm principle.

Second, from the viewpoint of rational argumentation, the consequentialist argument from anarchy is, on the whole, ill-conceived. It assumes that *either* we grant an *absolute* right to conscientious objection, but in such a case we are doomed to anarchy and the dissolution of society, *or* we cannot grant any such right *at all*. The argument is too swift to be good. First, no constitutional right – apart from, of course, the rights that relate to the protection of life and the ban on torture and inhuman or degrading treatments – is, as a matter of principle, an absolute. Second, a *relative* right to conscientious objection, subject to limitations inspired by a liberal interpretation of the harm principle, is viable, all things considered (I will return to this issue, shortly).

The same line of reasoning, based on the *prima facie* relative nature of the general right to conscientious objection can also be applied to counter the general welfare or public good version of the consequentialist argument. The general right to conscientious objection, it is submitted, would endanger the general welfare, by allowing people to opt out of social solidarity and of contributing to general well-being. Now, this is likely to be the case if, and only if, the right to conscientious objection were, by its very nature, incapable of being applied by balancing conflicting rights and interests. But such a characteristic can be safely ruled out.

The procedural drawbacks argument

In one of the finest essays on the subject, Joseph Raz identifies two *procedural drawbacks*, as I shall call them, which are concomitant to granting a general right to conscientious objection.

The first drawback is cheating. People are likely to cheat about the reasons of conscience that compel them to object to a certain piece of legislation, but, Raz claims, it is very difficult, if not altogether impossible, to discover their cheating.

The second drawback is favouring "public intrusion into the private affairs of individuals", due to the need to investigate the sincerity of people's claims of conscience.[24] To be sure, when discussing this drawback, Raz makes clear that it is irrelevant "unless the right is applied on the basis of a simple declaration by the objector (a method that makes abuse all the more easy)".

To sum up, Raz suggests that granting a general right to conscientious objection opens the door *either* to undetectable cheating and abuses or to unwelcome intrusions in the private sphere of individuals.

The procedural costs – in terms of cheating or intrusions – that Raz brings to the fore need to be taken into account. Nonetheless, they do not seem capable of supporting a conclusive, knockdown argument against a general right to conscientious objection.

First, judicial decisions have only to establish the *potential harmfulness* of a piece of legislation to individuals' right to freedom of conscience. This only calls for hypothetical judgements. Suppose somebody (really) entertains such and such a secular or religious conviction of conscience. Would law *X* violate right to freedom of conscience?

Second, it seems necessary to distinguish between cases of the exercise of the right to conscientious objection where a simple declaration by the objector should be regarded as sufficient (that is, when paternalistic or perfectionist laws are at stake, for example, those preventing early abortion, same-sex intercourse and same-sex marriage) and cases where, on the contrary, a sincerity test must be applied, since allowing the conscientious objection would impose (relevant) costs on society and individual people (that is, when non-paternalistic and non-perfectionist laws are at stake).

Third, the level of scrutiny can change according to the costs that society and individual people are likely to derive from allowing a conscientious objection claim.

Fourth, investigation, when it is deemed necessary, can be arranged in such a way as to respect people's private lives.

Two varieties of the right to conscientious objection: preliminary remarks

It is worth distinguishing two varieties of the right to conscientious objection. I will now explain these in further detail, and demonstrate their viability in a constitutional state, contrary to the view that regards specific cases of a negative right to conscientious objection as the only ones that are viable.

The *negative right* to conscientious objection (the right to negative conscientious objection) can be characterised as the *faculty* (permission, liberty or privilege), ascribed to an individual who is the object of a *positive legal duty* (the duty to do something, provide a certain service, perform a certain act), *not to comply* with that duty, and *omit* to perform the action required, for reasons of conscience.

By contrast, the *positive right* to conscientious objection (the right to positive conscientious objection) may consist in the following:

(a) The *faculty* (permission, liberty or privilege), ascribed to an individual who is the object of a *negative legal duty* (the duty of not doing something, abstaining from performing a certain action), *not to* comply with that duty, and *perform* the otherwise forbidden action, for reasons of conscience.
(b) The *power* (permission, capacity, authorisation or ability), ascribed to an individual who is the addressee of an *inability norm* concerning a certain legal act (a norm making people incapable of validly performing that act), *validly to perform* that act, for reasons of conscience.

Many constitutional orders recognise the right to negative conscientious objection, yet not as a general right, but in relation to specific situations (military service, medical treatment of abortion and so on) (Walzer, 1970: 125 ff.; Viano, 2008).

The right to positive conscientious objection, by contrast, has never been expressly considered. Perhaps, this is due to the idea, most of the time tacitly entertained by scholars, that there exists a *radical asymmetry* between the negative and the positive right to conscientious objection, making the claim to read a positive right into the very texture of the law of constitutional states utterly weird, unreasonable and in any case non-viable.

The idea of a radical asymmetry between the negative and the positive right to conscientious objection is wrong.[25] This conclusion appears to be supported even by a superficial comparative analysis of a few case studies.

The right to negative conscientious objection: two typical cases

According to the law of several countries, a gynaecologist working for a public hospital where gynaecologists are required to perform abortions has the right not to perform such interventions for reasons of conscience (for instance, if his religious creed considers abortion a crime). Likewise, in many countries where military service is compulsory, a physically and mentally fit youngster may avoid conscription for reasons of conscience (for instance, if he is a sincere secular pacifist).

Why do most people (now) consider these exemptions from a positive duty to be justified? Apparently, the question dictates an easy answer. Most people (now) think that, in both cases, if the laws did not grant such an exemption, the laws would be constitutionally illegitimate: They would violate the religious gynaecologist's and the young secular pacifist's freedom of conscience.

Let us assume, for argument's sake, that both cases are obvious, typical instances of situations where granting a negative right to conscientious objection is (morally and) legally justified, and indeed required, in order to protect the constitutional right to freedom of conscience of the people involved.

Once we so assume, it is worth bringing to the fore the structural aspects they share, so as to have some grounds for comparing these seemingly obvious cases of a justified *negative* right to conscientious objection with some cases which, it may be claimed, are clear cases of a justified *positive* right to conscientious objection.

First, in both cases, people have a *perfect legal duty* (a duty backed up by coercive legal sanctions) to perform certain activities, derived from an employment relationship or from citizenship.

Second, in both cases, people find themselves in a predicament, represented by a *conflict of duties*, that is, their *positive legal duty* to perform certain activities is at odds with their *negative moral duty* not to perform them.

Third, in both cases, it is assumed that the prevalence of the legal duty over the corresponding, opposite, moral duty would amount to the *violation of a fundamental constitutional right* of the people involved, namely, their right to freedom of conscience – and, in the gynaecologist's case, religious freedom, as freedom of religion and from non-religion.

Fourth, in both cases, it is clear that the prevalence of the negative moral duty (via the constitutional right to freedom of conscience) over the positive legal duty results in *negative consequences*, both to society at large and to other people individually considered.

On the one hand, exemptions from a positive duty have *costs* – to public hospitals (they have to pay somebody else to do the job the objectors fail to perform), to the women deciding to have an abortion (in terms of delay, stress, being obliged to go searching for a different medical centre and so on), to the military defence of the country (if pacifism becomes a widespread phenomenon, the state will have to invest more in professional soldiers) and to "ordinary" conscripts (those who are neither pacifist nor war-freaks), who may incur a higher risk of being killed or maimed in war.

On the other hand, the exemptions from a positive duty fly in the face of *legal principles*, even momentous ones, namely, the principle of social solidarity, which is the grounds for the duty to participate in the defence of the country; the principle of good administration; the right of women to health, which may be compromised by a widespread phenomenon of conscientious objection to abortion.[26]

Fifth, and last, these exemptions reflect a *balancing* against each other of the several legal rights and interests that are at stake, giving priority to freedom of conscience over different, competing, rights.

Bearing in mind the above structural features of the two clear cases of a justified negative right to conscientious objection, let us move on to consider two cases where apparently, for coherence's sake, granting a *positive* right to conscientious objection, far from being weird or unviable, should likewise be considered to be justified.

The right to positive conscientious objection: two typical cases

I will consider, in turn, two cases where a positive right to conscientious objection is at stake. The first is based on an actual case, and involves a negative imperative legal norm. It is the "kirpan case" decided by the Canadian Supreme Court (*Multani v. Commission Scolaire Marguerite-Bourgeois*), and was commented on, negatively, by Brian Leiter.[27] The second case is fictitious and involves a legal inability norm; it concerns the discipline of living wills (or biological wills) in the imaginary constitutional state of Freedonia, a merry, jolly, island in the middle of an ancient sea.

Bringing a kirpan to school

A school commission enacts a rule that prohibits students from carrying weapons into the school building. A boy of the Sikh religious faith claims to have the duty to carry a ritual sword (*kirpan*) with him at any time. Does he have a good case to be permitted to carry the *kirpan* into school for reasons of conscience?

The Canadian Supreme Court, in the *Multani* case, said yes. Brian Leiter, in a book published some years ago, says no. Both sides argue in terms of granting or denying, "exemptions" or "exceptions".

A better way of coping with the issue would consist, however, in asking whether, in the case at hand and in like cases, the plaintiff is justified in claiming a positive right to conscientious objection. To argue for this suggestion of mine, I will consider the arguments Leiter provides for maintaining that, in cases such as that decided by the Canadian Court, every claim to exemption should be rejected, be it grounded on religious rules, as is the case with the Sikh boy, or on some social or family tradition, as it is the case with the "rural boy". Leiter imagines a boy who, according to the rules of his ancestors, should always carry his great-grandfather's knife with him as all his forerunners have always done during their lives. Leiter grounds his negative answer on two arguments.

First, in evaluating claims such as that made by the Sikh boy (to conscientious objection, I would say), courts should not defer to subjective interpretations of religious – or, at any rate, traditional – rules of behaviour. Rather, they should take into account, and give priority to, objective interpretive practice and understandings (Leiter, 2013: 66). This would prevent courts from becoming the dupes of individuals' whims, or, even worse, of individuals' cheating. In the *Multani* case, however, the Court relied on the boy's own strict interpretation of carrying a *kirpan*, overlooking the fact that such an interpretation was by no means the only or dominant one in the relevant religious community.

Second, in evaluating claims such as that made by the Sikh boy (to conscientious objection, I would say), courts ought to avoid conceding privileges that fly in the face of the equality side of the right to freedom of conscience. For instance, they should not grant an exemption in favour of the Sikh boy if they are not also willing to grant a like exemption to the rural boy. But, according to Leiter, that is precisely what was likely to happen, had the rural boy applied to the same (or any) court.

Leiter makes two thoughtful and provocative arguments, raising two key problems: the first concerns the proper way of coping with subjective claims of conscience; the second concerns how to avoid unlawful discrimination in like claims of conscience.

Nonetheless, the first of Leiter's arguments should be rejected, while the second should play a role in relation to, and within, a careful evaluation of conscientious objection claims from the standpoint of the harm principle.

As to the first argument, one may argue, contrary to what Leiter claims, that a moral case can be made in favour of a subjective conception of freedom of conscience, provided this is not, at least *prima facie*, preposterous. In their book *Secularism and Freedom of Conscience*, Maclure and Taylor argue for such a view, in the very name of individual autonomy, under the requirement of sincerity (Maclure and Taylor, 2011: 100–104). Their conclusion can be strengthened by the following remark. Freedom of conscience is not tantamount to the freedom to follow the moral or religious rules approved by the relevant community. If *that* were the case, freedom of conscience would amount, for any individual, to freedom for authority-controlled, heteronomous consciences. Hence, the only way of protecting freedom of conscience that is likely to be compatible with the genuine protection of each individual's moral autonomy consists in adopting a liberal conception of conscience. This in turn requires adopting a subjective conception of the rights and duties one has "according to one's conscience". In any case, the point is whether such a conception – be it sincere or not – deserves protection from the standpoint of liberal freedom of conscience and the harm principle.

As to the second of Leiter's arguments, it can be maintained that, from a liberal standpoint, the case of the Sikh boy and the case of the rural boy must be treated by assuming, in both cases, the existence of a *prima facie* right to positive conscientious objection, understanding it as a *relative* individual right, limited by a liberal reading of the harm principle. Accordingly, courts should consider, first of all, whether *their* – and *other like claimants' – bringing a weapon* into a public school does, or does not, constitute a danger to the life and limb of third parties, likely and relevant so as to justify a prohibition[28] based on the harm principle.

Living wills in Freedonia

The political majority in Freedonia approves a law that incapacitates individuals from making valid living wills: that is, wills containing *binding instructions* to doctors and medical personnel at large about the end-of-life treatments they are allowed to apply to the testator's body, once she has lost consciousness.

Taking into account the cases of the religious gynaecologist and the young secular pacifist, where a negative right to conscientious objection has been granted, would individuals, aware of the integrated doctrine of the sphere of individual inviolability and constitutional conscientious objection, *also* be justified in claiming a *positive right* to conscientious objection against the Freedonian law on living wills?

I think the answer must be a clear yes. To argue for this conclusion, I will consider, in turn, the structural features of the present situation from the standpoints, respectively, of a legislator who voted for the law (I will call him the ethical legislator), and of a jurist defending the prerogatives of a constitutional state.

Living wills in Freedonia: the case of the ethical legislator

From the vantage point of the ethical legislator, the main features of the case are as follows:

1. The enacted law on living wills contains an *inability provision*, establishing people's incapacity to make living wills binding on doctors and medical personnel at large.
2. The law gives rise to a *normative conflict* between the *legal norm of inability*, on the one hand, and the opposite, *moral norm of ability*, on the other, which happens to be part of many people's consciences (i.e. moral code).
3. The legal norm of inability finds its ultimate justification in the constitutional *right to life*, which is a fundamental individual right; it has been enacted, the ethical legislator claims, "to defend life" and to "build up a barrier against euthanasia".
4. The moral norm of competence, conversely, finds its ultimate justification, if any, in the constitutional *right to freedom of conscience* (and religious freedom as freedom from religion), which is also a fundamental individual right.
5. As a consequence, the enacted law about living wills, insofar as some people's consciences are concerned, leads to a *clash between two fundamental principles* (the principle of sanctity of life and the principle of freedom of conscience) and their corresponding *fundamental rights*.
6. The fact that the right to freedom of conscience trumps the right to life would entail *unbearable costs*, the right to life being much more valuable than the right to freedom of conscience; accordingly, the fact that the right to life trumps the right to freedom of conscience cannot but have less relevant, bearable, costs.
7. A proper *balancing* of the two rights at stake must, accordingly, give priority to the right to life over the right to freedom of conscience, and, by the same token, to the inability norm over the ability norm.

Living wills in Freedonia: the case of the constitutional jurist

From the vantage point of a jurist eager to defend the prerogatives of Freedonia as a genuine constitutional state, the structural features of the case need to be presented in a different way:

1. The enacted law on living wills, where it contains the *inability provision* that incapacitates people from making living wills binding on doctors and

medical personnel at large, gives rise to a *normative conflict* between the *legal norm of inability* and the *moral norm of ability* that happens to be part of many people's consciences (i.e. moral code).

2. Supporters of the inability norm claim it to be justified by the *right to life*: "to defend life" and "build up a barrier against euthanasia", as they like to say.
3. Unfortunately, they ground their argument upon an understanding of the right to life that is biased by deference to a peculiarly religious vision of such a right, that is, to an authoritarian, paternalistic and anti-individualistic vision according to which life is a fundamental good (being the gift of a supernatural being), and must be protected at all costs, even at the cost of overriding the will, and moral autonomy, of individuals.
4. The Freedonian law on living wills is, accordingly, a religiously inspired law that violates people's sphere of individual inviolability and their right to freedom of conscience in the name of a *peculiarly religious conception* of the right to life.
5. As a consequence, individuals have a good case of conscience for asking judges either to invalidate such a law altogether, since it is clearly unconstitutional, or to retain the law, but read into it a positive right to a conscientious objection clause, making them capable, for reasons of conscience, of modifying binding living wills.
6. People who think that granting such a positive right to conscientious objection would be absurd, unreasonable or even unlawful would do better to consider the following points.

First, in the past, Freedonian law has granted a negative right to conscientious objection to religious gynaecologists and young secular pacifists.

Second, such negative rights have been granted although it was clear that they had negative consequences, both for society and for individuals, in terms of actual costs and the actual impairment of rights.

Third, granting a right to positive conscientious objection against the inability norm on living wills would have no such negative consequences: neither in terms of social and individual costs, nor in terms of the impairment of rights. There is indeed no violation at all of the right to life in the only understanding compatible with a liberal, constitutional state, but only the violation of the right to life as understood by the ministers and believers of a specific religious faith.

Fourth, provided Freedonian legislators have granted people rights of negative conscientious objection in cases of abortion and military service, even though those rights had negative consequences in terms of costs and the infringement of individual rights, they should *a fortiori* grant people a right of positive conscientious objection in the living will case, since the granting of such a right does not have any negative consequences, except on the moral feelings of those religious people who uphold the law. The moral feelings of believers in a religion, however, are not entitled to protection under a liberal constitutional state.

Final remarks

1. The right to freedom of conscience and to religious freedom, in the liberal reading I have outlined here, are fundamental legal rights – among others, to be sure – of any morally decent society.
2. The protection of these rights requires constant effort when devising adequate institutional mechanisms.
3. The right to conscientious objection has been, so far, a Cinderella of constitutional engineering, as a consequence of the unjustified sceptical stance adopted by scholars.
4. It is time to discard such an unwarranted stance, in the name of a comprehensive, unprejudiced evaluation, for relevant classes of cases, of the forms and limits of a general right to conscientious objection, in both the negative and positive variants, subject to Harm Principle considerations.

Notes

1 Two principles are paramount to liberalism: the principle of equal (moral, political and legal) sovereignty of individuals and the harm principle. The first claims each individual to be sovereign before the social bodies and institutions inside which they happen to dwell in the different stations of their life. The second sets the proper boundaries of each individual's sovereignty by establishing the requirement that individual actions should never do harm to others. See Mill (1859: ch. I) and Feinberg (1984: "General Introduction").

2 On "conscience", see, for example, Viano (2011: 16 ss.); Dent (1998: 579); Sapir and Statman (2005: 472); MacKlem (2006: 68); Galeotti (2008: 2) and Nussbaum (2008: 19).

3 The *Concise Oxford Dictionary* defines "conscience" as the "moral sense of right and wrong", where "sense" suggests, at the same time, the faculty by which we get to know what is morally right and wrong as if by instinct, and the output of the exercise of such a faculty.

4 An example of such a view is provided by a few verses from John Milton's *Paradise Lost*: "And I [God] will place *within* them [men] *as a guide*/My Umpire Conscience" (quoted by Walzer, 1970: 121, italics added).

5 This is, for instance, as is well known, the position adopted by St. Augustine (see, for example, his *Letter to Boniface*, quoted by Saada-Gendron, 1999: 87–90), and by Thomas Aquinas, who emphasised the Church's "mercy" in warning heretics "twice" before excommunicating them and having them put to death by the secular power "in order that they be cut off from the world" (*Summa Theologiae*, III, II.2, q. 11, quoted by Saada-Gendron, 1999: 45–49). It did not disappear, of course, with the Modern Age, surviving inside the Catholic Church, the Orthodox Church, and Protestant Sects. See Ruffini (1901: 31–41) and Acton (1907).

6 A heteronomous, anti-authoritarian conception of conscience is found in the well-known words uttered by Martin Luther at the Diet of Worms, on 18 April 1521: "Nisi convictus fuero testimoniis Scripturarum aut ratione evidente (nam neque Papae neque Conciliis solis credo, cum constet eos errare saepius et sibi ipsis contradixisse), victus sum Scripturis a me adductis captaque est conscientia in verbis Dei: revocare neque possum neque volo quidquam, cum contra conscientiam agere neque tutum sit, neque integrum. Hier stehe ich. Ich kan nicht anders. Gott helff mir. Amen (Here I stand. I can do no other. God help me. Amen)" (quoted by Passerin D'Entrèves, 1969: 46, n. 9). In another seminal passage, Luther claims that: "In the consciences [of humans]

God wants to be alone and wants only his word to reign" (quoted by Ruffini, 1901: 37). Sapir and Statman (2005: 473–474) quote the following passage from Luther: "I lift my voice simply on behalf of liberty and conscience, and I confidently cry: No law, whether of men or of angels, may rightfully be imposed upon Christians without their consent, for we are free of all laws". From this, they assume that they have evidence for a Protestant conception of conscience, that is, one that is "essentially individual and subjective", representing "a profoundly subversive and antinomist understanding of the concept of conscience, one that presents a threat to the existing religious, social and political order", since it coincides with "the dictates" of people's "hearts". They also recognise, however, that according to "Luther and Protestant philosophers", "the Divine will is revealed to human beings through their conscience". Accordingly, I consider the account I have provided in the text, of a heteronomous and epistemologically individualistic conception of conscience, to be in line with Luther's thinking. This conception is individualistic but not "subjective"; that is, the "dictates of the heart" do not create moral norms, nor condition their binding force upon an individual's acceptance, but simply reproduce norms that emanate from the will of the deity, norms that men can also get to know by a direct reading of Scripture and by making use of their reason.

7 A knowledge of the correct principles of human conduct automatically "brings with it" the duty to act accordingly. This is a very old and still persistent way of thinking that is nowadays known as "internalism".

8 The dual dimension of liberal freedom of conscience is often overlooked.

9 The proper characterisation of the neutrality of the liberal constitutional state is still a major issue in political philosophy. See, for example, Maclure and Taylor (2011: 16–17) and Leiter (2013: 14–15). As Thomas Paine underscores in a celebrated passage of his *Rights of Man* (1791: 136–137): "The French constitution hath abolished or renounced *Toleration*, and *Intolerance* also, and hath established *universal right of conscience*. Toleration is not the *opposite* of Intolerance, but is the counterfeit thereof. Both are despotisms. The one assumes to itself the right to with-holding Liberty of Conscience, and the other of granting it. The one is the pope armed with fire and faggot, and the other is the pope selling or granting indulgencies. The former is church and state, the latter is church and traffic". See also Gianformaggio (1993) and Baroncelli (1993).

10 For instance, in the *Oxford Dictionaries*, "Freedom of conscience" is defined as "The right to follow one's own beliefs in matters of religion and morality". Retrieved on 15 September 2020.

11 In my definition of "religious matters", I have followed the approach adopted by Alston (1964). This is not a commonly shared view among scholars. For instance, Brian Leiter (2013: ch. 2) purports to define "religion" by means of a set of three necessary and jointly sufficient properties: (1) commands endowed with an experienced categorical character; (2) purposive insulation of beliefs from the evidence and reasons governing common sense and scientific knowledge; (3) function of existential consolation. For a careful conceptual criticism, showing such a definition to be unable to differentiate religion from morality (unless, perhaps, in quantitative terms), see Himma (2014). See also MacKlem (2006: 141). In *Religion without God*, Ronald Dworkin advocates the replacement of the "troublesome special right" to religious freedom with "the general right to ethical independence", suggesting that "we treat religious freedom as part of ethical independence", as a "central case of a more general right to ethical independence" (Dworkin, 2013: 144–145, 146).

12 Religious freedom can also be understood as encompassing freedom of *religious* expression, i.e., as freedom of expression regarding religious matters.

13 Sapir and Statman (2005: 486–487); Leiter (2013) and Himma (2014) come to the same conclusion.

14 These remarks of mine are grounded on the argumentative strategy employed in Italy by top Catholic Church dignitaries during the 1990s and 2000s, up to the election of Pope Francis.

15 The tradition argument may also work as an appeal to the "majoritarian" historical and cultural identity of a people, claiming a certain religion should be given a privileged legal status because of the prominent and unique role it is assumed to have played in the moulding of this identity. Again, it turns on the negative side of the equality principle.

16 Sapir and Statman (2005: 470 ff.) invite us to also consider the *costs* – in terms of social discrimination, prejudice and fanaticism – that the presence of religious creeds and institutions can impose on individuals and societies, and how the balance is by no means clear. See also Leiter (2013: 62–64, 83–85).

17 According to art. 18 of the Universal Declaration of Human Rights, for instance, the "right to freedom of religion" includes the "freedom, either alone or in community with others and in public or private, to manifest his religion … in teaching, practice, worship and observance". Retrieved on 15 September 2020. https://www.un.org/en/universal-declaration-human-rights/#:~:text=Article%2018.,%2C%20practice%2C%20worship%20and%20observance. See, for similar clauses, the International Covenant on Civil and Political Rights (art. 18, al. 1), retrieved on 15 September 2020, https://www.ohchr.org/en/professionalinterest/pages/ccpr.aspx, and the European Convention for the Protection of Human Rights and Fundamental Freedoms (art. 9, al. 1), retrieved on 15 September 2020, https://www.echr.coe.int/Documents/Convention_Eng.pdf.

18 The rights of freedom from non-religion and freedom from religion may be read, for instance, in art. 18, al. 2, of the ICCPR: "No one shall be subject to coercion that would impair his freedom to have or to adopt a religion or belief of his choice". See also the U.N. Declaration on the Elimination of all Forms of Intolerance and Discrimination Based on Religion or Belief (25 November 1981), the U.N. Resolution on Elimination of all Forms of Religious Intolerance (20 December 1993), and, more recently, the U.N. Resolution on Elimination of All Forms of Religious Intolerance (16 March 2009). In his account of "freedom from religion", Vitale (2004: 99 ff.) emphasises the state-duty side thereof, seeing it as the duty of the state to make sure that each and every individual be able to exercise a genuine freedom of choice as to religious matters.

19 Think, for instance, of a law imposing on workers the duty of going on holiday on the very days of religious holidays; or imposing on the women involved in a procedure of homologous artificial insemination the duty to have all the permissible number of fertilised eggs implanted into their uterus.

20 See, for example, art. 10 of the Charter of Fundamental Rights of the European Union: "The right of conscientious objection is recognised in accordance with the national laws governing the exercise of this right". Retrieved on 15 September 2020, https://www.europarl.europa.eu/charter/pdf/text_en.pdf.

21 The scope of temporary judicial protection can be quite broad if a class action has been filed.

22 On conscientious objection as an "act" or "practice" of disobedience, see, for example, Passerin d'Entrèves (1973); Raz (1979: 263, 276 ff); Bobbio (1983: 317, 318) and MacKlem (2006: 69 ff.).

23 Art. 8, al. 3, c (ii) ICCPR: "For the purpose of this paragraph, the term "forced or compulsory labour" shall not include: … (ii) Any service of a military character and, *in countries where conscientious objection is recognised*, any national service required by law of conscientious objectors" (italics added, ndr); likewise, art. 4, al. 3, ECHR: "For the purpose of this Article, the term "forced or compulsory labour" shall not include: … (b) any service of a military character or, *in case of conscientious objectors in countries where they are recognised*, service exacted instead of compulsory military service" (italics added, ndr). A quite different tone is employed in art. 10 of the Charter of Fundamental Rights of the European Union, as is well known and we shall see shortly.

24 Raz (1979: 287) also considers a third drawback, that is, the encouragement of "self-doubt", "self-deception" and "in general, undesirable forms of introspection". This is not, however, a procedural drawback, since it points rather to the psychological costs

that a general right to conscientious objection may impose on individuals. Those costs, of course, would depend on each individual's sensitivity and proneness to self-doubt etc. See also Galeotti (2008) and Leiter (2013).

25 For (rebuttable) arguments against positive conscientious objection, see Mastromartino (2015: 633–636).

26 This point casts a dubious light on the legitimacy of granting an unconditional right to conscientious objection to gynaecologists, from the standpoint of a liberal interpretation of the harm principle. I will not pursue it further.

27 Laws making sex between consenting, same-sex, adults a crime provide an even clearer case where a positive right to conscientious objection appears to be fully justified.

28 Courts may adopt, in balancing the arguments for and against, an Alexy-like formula of the following sort : $CIV^{P1/P2/C} = AIV^{P1} \times EIC^{P2>P1}/AIV^{P2} \times EIC^{P1>P2}$, where $CIV^{P1/P2/C}$ stands for the Comparative Institutional Value of Principle P1 (freedom of conscience) in relation to Principle P2 (right to life and safety of limbs) as to the individual and generic case at hand C (bringing weapons in a public school building for ethical reasons); AIV^{P1} and AIV^{P2} stand for the Abstract Institutional Value of Principle P1 and Principle P2; $EIC^{P2>P1}$ and $EIC^{P1>P2}$ stand for the Expected Institutional Cost to Principle P1 of the prevalence of Principle P2 and the Expected Institutional Cost to Principle P2 of the prevalence of Principle P1, respectively.

Bibliography

Abbagnano, N. 1964. *Dizionario di filosofia*. Torino: Utet.

Acton, J. E. E. D. (Lord). 1907. *The History of Freedom and Other Essays*. London: MacMillan.

Alston, W. 1964. *Philosophy of Language*. Englewood Cliffs, NJ: Prentice Hall.

Atienza, M. 2014. "Las caricaturas de Mahoma y la libertad de expression." Pp. 133–144 in García Jaramillo, L. (ed.) *Nuevas perspectivas sobre la relación/tensión entre la democracia y el constitucionalismo*. Lima: Grijley.

Baroncelli, F. 1993. "Tolleranza. Il fascino perverso di una definizione." Pp. 229–248 in Comanducci, P. and Guastini, R. (eds.) *Analisi e diritto 1993. Ricerche di giurisprudenza analitica*. Torino: Giappichelli.

Bobbio, N. 1983. "Disobbedienza Civile." Pp. 316–320 in Bobbio, N., Matteucci, N. and Pasquino, G. (eds.) *Dizionario di politica*. Milano: TEA.

Ceccanti, S. 2006. "Laicità e istituzioni democratiche." Pp. 27–47 in Boniolo, G. (ed.) *Laicità. Una geografia delle nostre radici*. Torino: Einaudi.

Chiassoni, P. 2009. "Libertà e obiezione di coscienza nello stato costituzionale." *Diritto & questioni pubbliche* 9: 65–89.

Chiassoni, P. 2011. "Obiezione di coscienza: negativa e positiva." *Notizie di Politeia* 101: 36–54.

Cohen, C. 1968. "Conscientious Objection". *Ethics* 78 (4): 269–279.

Dent, N. 1998. "Conscience." P. 579 in Craig, E. (ed.) *Routledge Encyclopedia of Philosophy*. London: Routledge.

Dworkin, R. 1968. *Civil Disobedience*, in Dworkin, R. (1977), 206–222.

Dworkin, R. 1970. *Taking Rights Seriously*, in Dworkin, R. (1977), 184–205.

Dworkin, R. 1977. *Taking Rights Seriously*. Cambridge, MA: Harvard University Press.

Dworkin, R. 2006. *Is Democracy Possible Here? Principles for a New Political Debate*. Princeton: Princeton University Press.

Dworkin, R. 2013. *Religion Without God*. Cambridge, MA: Harvard University Press.

Feinberg, J. 1984. *The Moral Limits of the Criminal Law. I. Harm to Others*. Oxford: Oxford University Press.

Galeotti, E. 2008. "The Place of Conscientious Objection in a Liberal Democracy." *Diversity in Europe: Dilemmas of Differential Treatment in Theory and Practice*, 17–31. SFIP. Retrieved on September 15th 2020. http://eprints.sifp.it/195/1/the-place-of-conscientious-objection-in-liberal-1.html.

Garzón Valdés, E. 2004. "Para ir terminando." in Atienza, M. (ed.) *El derecho como argumentación*. Cátedra Ernesto Garzón Valdés 2003, a cura di R. Vázquez e R. Zimmerling, México, Fontamara.

Gascón Abellán, M. 1996. "Lineamenti di un diritto generale alla disobbedienza." Pp. 77–89 in Comanducci, R. G. (eds.) *Analisi e diritto 1996. Ricerche di giurisprudenza analitica*. Torino: Giappichelli.

Gianformaggio, L. 1993. "Il male da tollerare, il bene del tollerare, l'intollerabile." Pp. 203–228 in Comanducci, P. and Guastini, R. (eds.) *Analisi e diritto 1993. Ricerche di giurisprudenza analitica*. Torino: Giappichelli.

Himma, K. E. 2014. *Compensating for a Legally Imposed Disability: Is there a Special Fundamental Right to Religious Freedom?* Paper presented at the International Conference 'Fundamental Rights – Justification and Interpretation', Faculty of Law, University of Belgrade, 24–25 October 2014.

Leiter, B. 2013. *Why Tolerate Religion?* Princeton, NJ: Princeton University Press.

MacKlem, T. 2006. *Independence of Mind*. Oxford: Oxford University Press.

Maclure, J. and Taylor, C. 2011. *Secularism and Freedom of Conscience*. Cambridge, MA: Harvard University Press.

Mastromartino, F. 2015. "Contro l'obiezione di coscienza positiva." *Ragion Pratica* 45: 629–237.

Mastromartino, F. 2018. "Esiste un diritto generale all'obiezione di coscienza?" *Diritto & Questioni Pubbliche* XVIII (1): 159–181.

Mill, J. S. 1859. *On Liberty*. in Id. *On Liberty and Other Essays*. Oxford: Oxford University Press, 1991.

Nino, C. S. 1989. *Ética y derechos humanos. Un ensayo de fundamentación*. Barcelona: Ariel.

Nozick, R. 1974. *Anarchy, State and Utopia*. New York: Basic Books.

Nussbaum, M. 2008. *Freedom to Conscience. In Defense of America's Tradition of Religious Equality*. New York: Basic Books.

Paine, T. 1791. "The Rights of Man: Being an Answer to Mr Burke's Attack on the French Revolution." in Id. *Rights of Man, Common Sense and Other Political Writings*. Oxford: Oxford University Press 1995.

Passerin D'Entrèves, A. 1969. *La notion d'État*. Paris: Sirey.

Passerin D'Entrèves, A. 1970. *Obbedienza e resistenza in una società democratica*. Milano: Comunità.

Passerin D'Entrèves, A. 1970–71. "Legittimità e resistenza". Studi Sassaresi, *Autonomia e diritto di resistenza* III: 33–45.

Passerin D'Entrèves, A. 1973. "Obbligo politico e libertà di coscienza." *Rivista internazionale di filosofia del diritto (IV)*: 50.

Post, R. 2007. "Religion and Freedom of Speech: Portraits of Muhammad." *Constellations* 14: 72–90.

Rawls, J. 1999. *A Theory of Justice. Revised Edition*. Oxford: Oxford University Press.

Raz, J. 1979. *The Authority of Law. Essays on Law and Morality*. Oxford: Clarendon Press.

Ruffini, F. 1901. *La libertà religiosa. Storia dell'idea*. Introduzione di A. C. Jemolo, Milano, Feltrinelli, 1967.
Rusconi, G. E. 2004. *Come se Dio non ci fosse. I laici, i cattolici e la democrazia*. Torino: Einaudi.
Rusconi, G. E. 2006. "Laicità ed etica pubblica." Pp. 47–70 in Boniolo, G. (ed.) *Laicità. Una geografia delle nostre radici*. Torino: Einaudi.
Saada-Gendron, J. 1999. *La tolerance*. Paris: Flammarion.
Sapir, G. and Statman, D. 2005. "Why Freedom of Religion does not Include Freedom from Religion." *Law and Philosophy* 24: 467–508.
Saporiti, M. 2013a. *La coscienza disubbidiente. Ragioni, tutele e limiti dell'obiezione di coscienza*. Milano: Giuffrè.
Saporiti, M. 2013b. "For a General Legal Theory of Conscientious Objection." *Ratio Juris*, 1–13.
Viano, C. A. 2007. *La libertà dalla religione*, manoscritto.
Viano, C. A. 2008. *L'obiezione di coscienza*, manoscritto.
Viano, C. A. 2011. "La coscienza : voci e mistificazioni." *Notizie di Politeia* XXVII (101): 11–28.
Vitale, E. 2004. "Libertà di religione. E dalla religione?" Pp. 91–106 in Bovero, M. (ed.) *Quale libertà. Dizionario minimo contro i falsi liberali*. Roma-Bari: Laterza.
Walzer, M. 1970. "Conscientious Objection." in Id., *Obligations. Essays on Disobedience*, War, *and Citizenship*. Cambridge, MA: Harvard University Press.
Walzer, M. 1997. *On Toleration*. New Haven: Yale University Press.

2 Contesting philosophical secularism

The case for pluralist secularism

Ravza Altuntas-Çakır

Recent critiques of secularism often refer to the authoritarian tendencies of laicism, which is also defined as "philosophical secularism" (Laborde, 2018a: 167), "ideological secularism" (Modood, 2010: 5), "ethical secularism" (Bhargava, 1999: 492), "nationalist secularism" (Asad, 2003: 199), "aggressive secularism" (Kuru, 2007: 576), "fundamentalist secularism" (Plesner, 2005: 1) or "militant secularism" (Soroush, 2007). The limitations created by philosophical secularism are considered a threat to established liberal democracies' pluralism record, as well as a barrier for genuine democratic consolidation in developing democracies such as those in Muslim majority countries.

In this chapter, I first identify the failures of philosophical secularism to undermine religiously sanctioned normative systems in motivating everyday life. I then propose a conception of pluralist secularism, which aims to achieve a normative reconciliation of the potentially conflicting concepts of secular statehood and public religious presence. Pluralist secularism, I argue, can bring out alternative political and social-legal responses in demonstrating how "religion can legitimately play a role" in contemporary democratic politics (Abou El Fadl, 2005: 202). I then make a case for institutional pluralism, largely derived from the Western multiculturalist discourse, as it shows how broader political platforms can be made available, enabling individuals and groups with religious demands to play public roles. As such, I will critique philosophical secularism to accommodate claims made in the name of religion by presenting a different normative framework for the relationship with the state and religion.

Critiquing philosophical secularism

Philosophical secularism has been the most prominent model of secularism experienced – often coercively imposed – in Muslim societies. This type of secularism in the Muslim world has promoted a strict separationist theoretical approach in dismissing religion from the public sphere and limiting it to the private realm. In practice, philosophical secularism has also endorsed a moralising attitude in controlling and managing the ability to define a national religion for the citizenry to follow, thus lending support to Talal Asad's assertion: "[r]eligion is seen by secularism [the secularist state] to take the form it should probably have" (2003:

199). The principle of state neutrality towards religion has also been used as "a technology of modern governance that ensures the state's sovereign right to regulate all domains of social life, a necessary part of which is religion" (Mahmood and Danchin, 2014: 5). Overall, philosophical secularism has manifested an innate "obsession with religion, and it leads to the desire to legislate about religion instead of accepting true separation" (Berlinerblau, 2017: 95 with quotes from Oliver Roy). This is due to philosophical secularism's perfectionist ideology that imposes "some eternal, comprehensive set of ultimate ideals" (Bhargava, 1999: 492).

As such, a nationalist secularist outlook and policies have emerged, seeking to control alternative visions of a religiously defined good life by *managing religion*. Bryan Turner emphasises that religion, as an important "carrier of identity" (with its latent capacity to generate social unity), has been too valuable a tool to leave to non-state forces (2007: 124). Accordingly, religion has become an essential tool for monolithic nationalism, where national political identity and group identities are assumed to be unproblematic. Therefore, *the management of religion* was a vital component for the nationalist secularist state's claim to absolute authority, which "seeks to regulate all aspects of individual life even the most intimate, such as birth and death – no one, whether religious or otherwise, can avoid encountering its ambitious powers" (Asad, 2003: 199).

Philosophical secularism has been a significant barrier in the social and political democratisation in Muslim contexts that continues to hinder the normative reconciliation between religion and the state and hence contributes to a highly contentious political sphere. With Talal Asad's observation, countries with a nationalist secular establishment, such as Turkey, Algeria and Tunisia, face a wide-ranging impasse in which both nationalist secularists and Islamists pursue state power because of the nation-state's monopoly over "the claim to constitute legitimate social identities and arenas" (2003: 200). Secularists have strictly viewed "religion as a private lifestyle option" and "resist the 'deprivatisation' of religion" (Turner, 2012: 166). Meanwhile, political scientists like Jocelyne Cesari and Hakan Yavuz observe that when the attitude of the secularist ideology was authoritarian, Islam re-emerged as a political ideology, which channelled the defensive and reactive political struggle "on the periphery" as political opposition aiming to recapture the platform of the state (Islamist "backlash") (Cesari, 2004: xv; Yavuz, 2003: 484). Similarly, Charles Kurzman and Ijlal Naqvi also identify that when the state has not provided channels for effective political participation or restricted Islamic visions of a good life, this has led to "driving Islamists underground", stiffening their political ideology or "helping to radicalize them" (2010: 35). In essence, those authoritarian secular solutions have increased the intensity of Islamist struggles for power and have not helped democratic learning and development in contexts where religion is an important marker of social identity. This is rather another manifestation of the fact that there is "a deep, quite irreconcilable conflict between ethical secularism and religion" (Bhargava, 1999: 495). With more pluralistic applications of secularism, I make a similar argument to that of the inclusion-moderation thesis: The Islamist backlash could have been substantially lessened, and the democratisation process could have been more fruitful had religion been able to have an independent role in the public sphere.

During recent decades, revising the meaning and objectives of secularism for the development of contemporary democratic societies has occupied the works of political theory. Theorists like Jürgen Habermas, Jocelyn Maclure, Alfred Stepan and Charles Taylor, who have criticised old-fashioned assertive secularism, have sought to develop, from within revised political secularism(s), a notion of modern democracies that supports the political inclusion of religious views into the public realm (Habermas, 2006; Maclure and Taylor, 2011; Taylor, 1998, 2008; Stepan, 2000). Despite these recent theorisations, however, critics like Jacques Berlinerblau have maintained that proponents of "political secularism have rarely conceptualised the state's relation to religions accurately" (2017: 94).

The concept of pluralist secularism developed here aims to address the relation between the state and religion and to offer normative reconciliation. I show how philosophical secularism and its provisions of an excessively centralised and absolute sovereign state can be replaced by more democratic forms. The theoretical argumentation in this chapter cannot decisively adjudicate on the question of redefining this relation between religion and politics without consideration of the issues regarding jurisprudence, public administration, sociology, demographics and even economics. This chapter situates itself within a normative discussion, which seeks to open up new debates about the relationship between the state and religion in modern democracies through its conceptualisation of pluralist secularism. More specifically, it opens new avenues for contesting nationalist secularism's obsession with singularity in light of arguments formulated in the name of religion in favour of institutionalised pluralist modes of being, thinking and acting. To do this, this chapter will first conceptualise the notions of the state and religion within the framework of pluralist secularism. And finally it will demonstrate how pluralist secularism would reconcile the secular state and public religious life within the context of institutional pluralism.

Pluralist secularism

Conceptualising the notion of the state within the idea of pluralist secularism

John Locke famously commented on the importance of the "just" relationship between the state and religion in liberalism:

> I esteem it above all things necessary, to distinguish exactly the business of civil government from that of religion, and to settle the just bounds that lie between the one and the other.
>
> (Locke, 1689: 6)

Sceptics such as Stanley Fish questioned the possibility of "just bonds" between the state and religion, however, given the fact that the state is the sovereign entity, which decides the boundary of accepted public religiosity. Fish asserts that, in theory, "the rejection of any absolutism [absolute authority]" is key to liberal thought. In reality, however, Fish insists the nation-state that draws the boundary between the public and private and ethics and politics makes the prospect for a "just" relationship in liberal democracies an "impossible mission" (1997: 2274, 2255). Similarly, Berlinerblau also identifies that regardless of its kind, secularism has the foundation of sovereignty designating the supreme right of the state "to make legally binding decisions about religion" that "*always* implies an asymmetric relation of power" (2017: 94).

Locke astutely discerned a just state-religion equilibrium to be central to democratic politics, and Fish is accurate in diagnosing the problems residing within the notion of a statist framework that impedes a "just" reconciliation. Under the notion of pluralist secularism, I shall endeavour to postulate a *fair* balance, amongst possible others, to bring perspective to the issue. The position proposed here, or elsewhere, cannot be rich enough in scope to settle all issues surrounding the relationship between religion and politics. It is sufficient here to make a case for a fairly earned equilibrium, which should introduce new and more nuanced vistas in political theory on this issue.

Pluralist secularism, an alternative form of political secularism, assesses the state's relation to religion in a new light. It asserts that "democracy can better be advanced by mixing, not separating religion from politics", while detaching religion or any comprehensive doctrine of good from the state realm (Bhargava, 1999: 495). This amounts to emancipating the state from religion and equally "emancipating religion" from the state for the religion's own sake, which elsewhere is broadly defined as "two-way protection" (Stepan, 2000: 35, Ghobadzadeh, 2014: 8; Gutmann, 2009: 190). I support the argument put forward by Abdullahi Ahmed An-Na'im that this double emancipation can promote an environment for voluntary reflection to observe religion and is a necessary condition for its public articulation (2008: 3–4).

To create a genuine two-way protection, pluralist secularism resorts to a limited idea of the state. It underpins a morally thin and non-philosophical state framework, as the institutional realm of compromise and consensus that endorses Veit Bader's idea of "priority for moral minimalism". The state is impartial in understanding citizens' normative systems to act and refrains from establishing, controlling or imposing a "contested truth-claim of any kind, whether religious, philosophical, or scientific" (Bader, 1999: 602). Therefore, a morally minimalist state does not "impose moralistic controls on family, sexuality and personal conduct" and ensures pluralism by preventing the imposition of a particular value system (Zubaida, 2011). Instead, it is "sensitive to the different expectations and needs of individuals and communities" by creating sufficient space for genuinely pluralistic politics (Barzilai, 2010: 6). Pluralist secularism is a condition of interrupting philosophical secularism's systematic ordering, organising and disciplining of human beings, their moral doctrines and their practices in favour of accommodating the diversity of and within these practices.

Key liberal thinkers also agree with some form of a limited state idea in theory. For instance, Ronald Dworkin and Jonathan Quong maintain that the state should be "independent of any particular conception of the good life", because the substantial good's intractable nature of disagreement will make its legal enforcement illiberal (Dworkin, 2015: 7; Quong, 2011: 192). Similarly, Maclure and Taylor assert that "since the state must be the state for all citizens, and since citizens adopt a plurality of conceptions of the good", the state must not officially endorse one particular worldview and "must avoid hierarchizing the conceptions of the good life" (2011: 20, 13). In liberal democracies, the state's neutrality to "all religious and secular movements of thought" safeguards the "equal moral value" of its citizens (Maclure and Taylor, 2011: 20).

I will blend the idea of the limited state advanced in some liberal theories with ramifications emerging from multiculturalism, as the latter has effectively helped understand the opportunities and constraints of liberalism in relation to religious claims and needs. Multiculturalism has provided more advanced and pluralistic conceptualisations of the link between religion and state through the more informed and pluralistic reconfiguring of law, rights and citizenship. One of the most essential ramifications it provides is the rethinking of the liberal principle of equality. Advocates of multiculturalism promote "liberal notions of equality rooted in the recognition of difference" as they attempt "to reconcile equality with difference" (Göle and Billaud, 2011: 127). Multiculturalist scholars have advocated the inclusion of religion in politics, moving away from religion being a private matter. Religion has become central to understanding public demands, an outcome of a multiculturalist understanding of the equality principle (Shachar, 2008; Bader 2009). Pluralist secularism seeks to respond to religion-based collective demands departing from individualistic and universalist liberal positions towards a pluralistic and egalitarian relationship between the state and religion. This leads to the construction of a greater decentralised and differentiated public institutional design. At the same time, pluralist secularism is as keen as individualistic theories of liberalism when it comes to safeguarding the constitutional separation of religion, moral equality and also domestic and civil liberties, such as freedom of conscience and the right to difference and dissent.

In their attempt to give public space to religion within the context of a limited and impartial state, scholars such as John Keane and Amyn B. Sajoo have argued democracy does not only need the institutional separation of the state from religious and other comprehensive moral views, it also "requires the institutional division between a certain form of state and civil society" (Keane, 1993: 28; Sajoo, 2004: 226). With its morally minimal outlook, pluralist secularism here posits functionally differentiated public spheres, namely, *the social public sphere* and *the state public sphere*. The analytical category of *the social public sphere* – a distinct form of political sphere where religious communal life is organised by civil society associations – is separate from *the state public sphere* – where the secular state controls the common institutional framework. This dual typology of the public sphere will be discussed later in the section on institutional pluralism.

What is needed here is a careful balance between the secular state and the principle of recognition of communal normative difference. However morally minimalist a state might be, by definition, "the liberal democratic state enjoys sovereignty over all other groups and associations on their territory" (Laborde, 2018b: 162). Although the debate is ongoing, when it comes to the domestic supremacy of sovereignty, liberal theory seems to favour the state as the final arbiter in deciding the boundary between right and good, public and private and legal and moral (Locke, 2016: 156). Yet, here, being the *final* arbiter does not mean being the sole arbiter and thus closing the process of negotiation with other groups and associations in their demands for redefining this boundary. There are surely different kinds of secularism within liberal democracies in addressing this relationship, yet it is philosophical secularism that views absolute sovereignty in an uncontested manner.

Regardless of theory, in reality, the boundaries are contested and blurred (Shachar, 2008: 420). Modern categories of private and public (as well as legal and moral) were invented in modernity and do not fully reflect social realities (Hallaq, 2010: 143). As critics have suggested, today, a secularist political structure "does not simply divide our lives, and from a certain angle at least, it really divides our lives in a superficial sense" (Macedo, 2000: 164). Challenging philosophical secularism, the former Archbishop of Canterbury, Prof. Rowan Williams of Cambridge, famously identifies that citizens may take their moral light from different sources, secular or divine, in deciding on these boundaries. Some communities in the UK, he cites, "while no less 'law-abiding' than the rest of the population, relate to something other than the British legal system alone" (Williams, 2008). And if the state insists on a strict notion of secular absolute sovereignty and

> [i]f the law of the land takes no account of what might be for certain agents a proper rationale for behaviour … it fails in a significant way to communicate with someone involved in the legal process.
>
> (Williams, 2008)

According to Williams, democracies should recognise that people do have multiple affiliations and various modes of belonging, whether political, religious or cultural. This would require a formal inclusion or circulation of different normative and legal systems when dealing with the actual lives of the citizenry. For Muslims, Williams explains, God is the ultimate source of justice, and *sharīʿa* sets certain moral obligations for human action in order to live an ethical life and gain God's blessing. Thus, inhibiting Muslims' connection with *sharīʿa* would delimit their autonomy for a good life (Williams, 2008). Williams refers to Ayelet Shachar's theory of Transformative Accommodation (2008) as a model of institutional pluralism, which can provide societal space for Muslims to adhere to their comprehensive religious views, as opposed to the statist models.

I join Williams and Shachar in making the argument that institutional pluralism or jurisdictional autonomy does not contradict the state sovereignty principle of liberalism but rather proposes a more informed notion of sovereignty, reflecting the practical relationship between the state and religion in a more sociologically intelligible way. In the institutional pluralism feature within pluralist secularism, the supremacy of the state is still implied. Yet sovereignty in this understanding cannot extend to include the shaping of religion or fitting differences into a certain value mould. State sovereignty under pluralist secularism respects religion's intellectual and political independence, albeit within limits that ensure the very state's sovereignty and its coercive forces in order to guarantee constitutional supremacy and democratic benchmarks. Within a pluralist secularism framework, democratic benchmarks are to be grounded in as thin a moral foundation as possible to maintain effective levels of neutrality. As such, normative thinness here is premised on a minimalist understanding of universal human rights rather than a specific normative system. The state can continue to have its domestic sovereignty on a morally thin foundation due to a political conception of minimalist human rights while these communities with competing truth-claims can be present and accommodated within *the social public sphere.*

This argument will be described in detail in the institutional pluralism section. The section will critique philosophical secularism and initiate an inquiry into how pluralist secularism can deal with claims in the name of religion.

Conceptualising the notion of religion within the idea of pluralist secularism

As Cecile Laborde identifies, religion can be classified in very broad terms, such as

> cognitive statements of truth, identificatory symbols, comprehensive ways of life, modes of voluntary association, moral and ethical obligations, vulnerable collective identities, and so forth.
>
> (2018b: 2)

In fact, "[e]ach facet of religion raises its own set of normative questions" that would imply different factions of the relationship patterns with the state (Laborde, 2018b: 2). I will take Charles Taylor and Jocelyn Maclure's categorisation of religion and its relation to the liberal state as one of the most informed postulations in liberal theory. I will engage with their theorisation in order to establish and articulate my idea of pluralist secularism concerning religion. Taylor and Maclure define religion within the broader notion of freedom of conscience and ethical independence, rather than dealing with religion as a special facet. According to Taylor and Maclure, "convictions of conscience" include "both deeply held religious and secular beliefs", preferences, values or lifestyles (2011: 13). If we adopt a firm understanding of state neutrality and impartiality, the liberal state seems to compel us to categorise religion on the basis of individual consciousness and to safeguard the equally protected status of the choices of belief and unbelief. Taylor and Maclure themselves state, however, that secularism consists of four principles – equality of respect, freedom of conscience, state neutrality towards religion and separation of church and state. They assert that not all these principles carry equal significance. The moral equality of persons and the protection of the liberty of conscience and religion are the two constitutive principles, which are the moral cores of secularism from which the ultimate aims are derived. State neutrality and separation of church and state, Taylor and Maclure maintain, are, on the other hand, the two "institutional" and operative modes that are intended to realise the constitutive principles (2011: 21–28).

If we consider this ranking of principles that takes equality as a supreme value and turn to multiculturalism, we come to see that "[e]quality is increasingly understood to require that we recognize social difference and allow some departures from uniform or 'universal' citizenship"[1] (Carens and Williams, 1996: 162). Monica Mookherjee also argues that we are to take moral equality in a more pluralist understanding, rather than a single, universal, "reasonable" pattern; in most cases, people's capacities, freedoms and needs are interpreted and practised in "culturally variable ways" (2009: 58, 149). Thus, a more concrete account of rights and freedoms would integrate people's multifaceted lives, not only as individuals but also as members of cultural associations (Mookherjee, 2005: 34).

I agree with Bryan Turner that it is difficult to separate concerns about multicultural equality from concerns about freedom of religion; "[t]herefore any policy relating to multiculturalism is automatically a policy about religion" (2011: 175). The question raised here is whether there is something particular to culture and religion that makes them distinct from other conscientious beliefs and gives them a particular status in their claim for public accommodation. I argue that this is the case. There are certain beliefs and practices peculiar to organised religions and cultures, which gives them unique functions to perform. Multiculturalist theorists such as Ayelet Shachar and Veit Bader have maintained that the followers of organised faiths provide a normative ordering, juridical theory and jurisdictional order, which would impact the societal lives and collective practices of their adherents. In addition, they relate particular societal needs to a distinct conception of a good life. Especially for religions like Islam and Judaism, which have their jurisdictional codes, multicultural accommodation is argued to require inclusive legal methods (Shachar, 2001: 147; Bader, 2009: 51). Therefore, I argue that organised religions are not any conscientious acts, but

> unique in the sense that they have offered to their believers a structured and sacred text that has embedded detailed normative guidelines of alternative order in all spheres of life.
>
> (Barzilai, 2004: 3)

For instance, Islamic law has a tradition of centuries of legal reasoning, sources, structures and functions, similar to Judaism (Hallaq, 1985: 79). This rich tradition of ethics, logic, law and jurisprudence has had lasting effects on the intellectual history and collective memory of Muslims.

Critical religion theorists such as Talal Asad and Saba Mahmood argue that the liberal conception of religion is individualistic, Protestant-centric and aesthetic/spiritual and marginalises other religions that do not go through the same formation of secular modernity (Mahmood, 1995: 9–12). Mark Juergensmeyer also suggests that the Enlightenment notion of religion is restricted to a particular set of doctrines limited to particular communal issues (2017: 82). Veit Bader criticises liberalism's approach to more legal-based religions, particularly with respect to Islam and Judaism, for its underestimation of their political and legal relevance and hence failing to give it special public consideration (2001: 10). Similarly, Ayelet Shachar argues that secular models, which emasculate organised religions' special nature, constitute the most severe constraint for their believers, who belong to multiple communal authorities and are subject to more than one set of laws (2001: 91).

My demonstration of religion as a unique kind of normative system is not singling out religion as a category to be accommodated. In making this argument, I am not taking sides on the issue of which categories of normative systems or deep commitments are to be protected. Neither is this a moral argument claiming that religious commitments should be favoured when it comes to public recognition because of their divine features. On the contrary, I concur with Taylor and Maclure that different normative systems, godly or godless beliefs, religious or non-religious conscientious commitments, should be respected and accommodated. I also strongly support their belief that it is not the role of the secular state to decide whether metaphysical foundations or non-spiritual foundations are more integral to individual identity, self-esteem and well-being, or which forms of "meaning-giving beliefs and commitments" are worthier than others (Taylor and Maclure, 2011: 75–76). The limited and morally minimalist democratic state would entail an even-handed accommodation of different normative systems.

On the other hand, I argue here that organised faiths should not be categorised merely as individual morality or as being individualistically conscientious, undermining their collective and communal aspects for an individual member's moral well-being in the context of rights and freedoms. Pluralist secularism approaches religion as a distinct category but not because the individual moral depth of religious commitments is seen as more respect-worthy than other conscientious commitments. Different substantive claims have different natures, however, and not all normative systems appeal as comprehensively to all spheres of life as organised religions. Individual rights and freedoms may be sufficient for the actualisation of a secular-based philosophical belief. When it comes to organised religions, due to their divinely inspired ethical and legal dimensions, their followers would have distinct societal needs and collective demands, which require different multicultural techniques of recognition and accommodation.

In this discussion, I am not engaged with the nature of religious law,[2] but I am interested rather in current arguments about its relation to the secular state. On this issue of the legal relationship between religion and the state, Hallaq's critique is important:

> [T]he modern state is systemically and systematically geared towards the transformation and homogenisation of both the social order and the national citizen, features that have a direct bearing on law.
>
> (2010: 142)

Yet, regardless of this affirmed political hegemony and its accompanying intrusions in differentiating the public (secularism) and the private (religion), in reality, the "political field", as described by Sami Zubaida, has not been under the monopoly of the state (1993: 118). There was an "absence of a monopoly on norms, identities, and practices [espoused by individuals and groups]" as non-state (religious, cultural, ideological) forces have been operating alongside the state whether as structural or micro-level practices (Moussa, 2020: 2). Similarly, Yüksel Sezgin argues that the real world does not follow a clear division or rigid boundaries, showing the interdependence of the public and the private as state law and non-state normative ordering, which cooperate "within the same social-legal space" (2013: 23). In recent years, as Sezgin emphasises, the universality of the Westphalian nation-state, which was based on the fully uniform legal system, normative unification, centralisation of state power and undivided domestic sovereignty, has been increasingly questioned by scholars.[3] Thus, "differing levels and forms of decentralization and fragmentation by maintaining plural institutions and practices in various issue areas such as personal status or family law" are sought with the assertion that some aspects of internal affairs should be outside the interventions of the state's monopoly[4] (Sezgin, 2013: 22–23).

Yet the modern secularist nation-state resists these calls for devolving power, to a considerable extent, due to its comprehensive and moral nature. Referring to Benedict Anderson and Ninian Smart, Mark Juergensmeyer defines religion and state nationalism as "species of the same genus", that is, as "ideologies of order" (1995: 380). Juergensmeyer views religion and secular nationalism not as political ideologies in a narrow sense but in a Geertizan sense as systems of order that invoke identity and loyalty, giving social meaning and order to individuals. As such, their competition for their claims to a social role, morality and law is intricate under the unitary nation-state structure (Juergensmeyer, 1995: 381). As in the democratisation processes in the Muslim societies, this potential rivalry over social identity has not been resolved, either institutionally or socially. The secularist state has enjoyed the monopoly to define, order and regulate the social, political and legal spheres. Counterclaims to redefine and reclaim the societal arenas in the form of de-privatisation of religions or "the potential entry of religion into space already occupied by the secular" faced a stern secularist backlash (Asad, 2003: 199).

I believe pluralist secularism can resolve this competition in favour of the free will of the people to decide on their social lives while maintaining the political secularisation of the state, as well as recognising the distinct societal role of religion. To better address the theoretical and practical inadequacies of ideological secularism in capturing the empirical relationship between religion and politics, pluralist secularism perceives religion as relevant within the sphere of public and political but not related to state power (Bader, 2001: 10). A process of differentiation in the public sphere between "state public sphere" and "social public state" can open up new ways for thinking about the place of religion in society. A novel agenda for thinking and speaking about institutional pluralism taking positions can be seriously formulated in the name of religion on the basis of this differentiation that critiques philosophical secularism.

Institutional pluralism

I will now conceptualise the idea of institutional pluralism within pluralist secularism. Institutional pluralism is a pluralistic alternative to the institutional hegemony of philosophical secularism, which facilitates a moralising, homogeneous public sphere. Multiculturalist thinkers have long debated that the orthodox liberal regime of equality may not bring justice to "deep and irresolvable normative conflicts" in normatively diverse societies (Macedo, 2000: 17 with quotes from Stephen Arons). Some form of diversification of public services and of expanding the actors in public policy is argued to be necessary (Hirst, 1997: 13). In turn, pluralist secularism calls for an institutional turn for democratic decentralisation of state power in addressing the political and public demands of religious groups. Here, religious freedoms are given a collective role, complementary to individual rights, in order for the followers of organised faiths to be able to pursue their definition of a good life. This entails going beyond the unitary nature of the state that strictly controls public life to an institutionalised cooperation and regulated interaction of state and non-state authorities in welfare and jurisdictional domains.

When it comes to the welfare sector, institutional pluralism proposes, "democratically negotiated freedom of religion from state interference" should also entail a degree of formalised influence for groups "in civil society and political society" (Stepan, 2000: 42). This approach amounts to granting "democratically controlled voluntary associations" "greater control of their affairs" in organising, funding and providing public services that might not adequately and impartially be provided by the unitary nation-state (Bader, 2003: 132; Hirst, 1997: 25). In an institutionally pluralist structure, national governments and civil society actors, such as faith-based or cultural associations, become "social partners" in specific policy areas, including the provision of social services, control over linguistic policy, management of schools, health care, seniors' care, social work and more (Modood, 2017: 357).

According to this understanding, religion has "an autonomous life in the hands of social actors". When it comes to religion's role in democratic public life in Muslim societies, Abdullahi Ahmad An-Na'im argues for divorcing Islam from the state authority. He also asserts that the "connectedness of Islam" and the public sphere should be available. For this, he suggests that "the distinction between the state and politics" has to be established: "the organs and institutions of the state" – or the "more settled and deliberate operational side of self-governance" – and politics – or the more "dynamic process of making choices" for "organized political and social actors" holding "competing visions of the public good" – are to be differentiated from one another (An-Na'im, 2002: 3–5). This degree of division becomes vital to guarantee the state's impartiality to "mediate and adjudicate among the competing visions and policy proposals" as well as allowing pluralistic societies to enjoy peace and stability by "regulating the relationship between religion and the state through secularism" (An-Na'im, 2002: 3, 2002b: 8). As such, I argue that the connectedness between Islam and politics does not indicate a shift – in Lockean terminology – the "immovable" boundary between the state and religion that stays in place (Locke, 1955: 27). Rather, this connectedness implies conceptually distinguishing the state and the public sphere to rethink the relationship between the political and the religious. In my conceptualisation, I have articulated this redefinition through the categories of *the social public sphere* and *the state public sphere*.

The social public sphere is a sphere of civil society politics, where the role of religion in politics is facilitated on the basis of "an extensive interpretation of associational freedoms" (Bader, 2007: 53). Religious groups are given resources and opportunities for certain public services through voluntary mechanisms to perform some of the functions of the state (Vallentyne and van der Vossen, 2014). Institutions in the social public sphere are designed to accommodate moral pluralism, in which religious liberty is not a tool to shape the religion in a paternalistic or moralising way (as critical religion theorists warn) but to give an autonomous sphere for its free articulation and development. Meanwhile, the pluralist secular framework simultaneously ensures voluntariness and the freedom of citizens to choose among governmental and societal organisations through democratic mechanisms and constitutional safeguards. In essence, institutional pluralism thus does not make civil society a competitor to the state but views it as a complementary force, in which the social public sphere focuses on the interaction and accommodation of religious difference in a resourceful and pluralist way.

While cherishing its merits, it is also critical to carefully recognise the long-standing problems regarding state sovereignty, social order and national community when it comes to institutional pluralism. It is particularly important to understand what institutional pluralism proposes on the theme of coexistence. The state public sphere addresses the concerns of reconciliation between religious freedoms and the state's authority. The state is responsible for maintaining social order and tranquillity to provide the basis for the enjoyment of all civil rights. In fact, "without some powerful framework of shared interests and shared institutions", a democratically functioning institutional pluralist framework would not be sustainable (Turner, 2011: 329). I argue that institutional pluralism can only work with a robust democratic secular superstructure as a political foundation, which maintains the state's moral and normative impartiality in balancing collective religious freedoms with citizenship rights. Therefore, the institutional pluralism model advocated here is acutely aware of the risk of excessive fragmentation in plural societies, which can create dangerous separateness of "communities antagonistic to one another" (Zubaida, 1993: 153). The state public sphere can ameliorate the latter development in which all citizens cooperate in governmental institutions, and which is designed to develop and maintain the shared political culture, civic unity and the common good, and democratic toleration is key to an institutional pluralism framework (Murphy, 2013: 115).

This analytical differentiation between politics and the state in the form of the social public sphere and state public sphere is derived from several important sociological observations regarding philosophical secularism. First, philosophical secularism imposes a superficial division of lives as public and private in which the public (or political) is inaccessible to religion. This enforced division compels individuals with comprehensive religious visions to live a contradictory life, which is divided into two hollow parts. Second is the acknowledgement of the difficulty of the state's delivery of adequate services to people with different accounts of a good life; hence the importance of a right to the collective good. Third, groups, if excluded from political influence, are likely to become reactionary by feeding extremism or revolutionary action to reclaim political authority. Institutional pluralism can help to generate transformativeness in the practices of these groups as well as the perceptions of their constituencies inclined towards a heightened sense of belonging to the state that normatively accepts them (Murphy, 2013: 117).

Overall, by making a conceptual differentiation of the state and political, I aim to rearticulate the boundary between religion and the state in a way to ensure two significant imperatives: (i) the state does not intervene in the moral character of religious communities and (ii) religion does not assert moral or political authority in government. As such, the institutional link between religion and state institutions is removed, while the connectedness of religion and public institutions can be performed in certain areas. As Fish has identified, a "just" solution may be impossible to reach in this intricate relationship. However, I think such an analytical differentiation would serve for a solution that seems more reasonable in rethinking the relation between secularism and religion in democratic politics. Consequently, I maintain that this framework, which compels an interaction between the state and religious groups, has the potential to create a more inclusive governing of a diverse citizenry as well as a more interactive model of peaceful coexistence between the state and comprehensive moral doctrines.

This section will now go on to conceptualise the second facet articulated under the broader umbrella of institutional pluralism – jurisdictional pluralism. Redefining the role of religion and the provisions of membership in the political community, as well as the reconfigurations of state-community relations, gave rise to the discussions on jurisdictional pluralism (Sezgin, 2013: 42). On this topic, Ayelet Shachar's (2001, 2009) "joint governance" and Veit Bader's (2003) "nonconstitutional pluralism" conceptualise "the idea of permitting a degree of regulated interaction between religious and secular sources of law" that confines religious arbitration to the disputes regarding private law (typically around the regulation of marriage, divorce and adoption) (Shachar, 2009: 133). In my categorisation, jurisdictional pluralism is a function of the social public sphere and state law reigns in the state public sphere where public and criminal law are carried out.

In defining jurisdictional pluralism, for this chapter, I shall use Ayelet Shachar's definition, which envisages an agreement-based voluntary accession mechanism to legal authority for the administration of semi-public law (2009: 143). Shachar takes religious law not as an opposing system to the secular establishment but as a complementary normative system with an ongoing interaction, negotiation, dialogue and mutual learning developing between the state and groups for a more responsive system (2008: 146–147). She develops a conceptual framework where the state and religious groups engage in a "non-exclusive competition" to provide better social and legal services and to be more accountable to their shared constituencies. This provides the individuals themselves with potential influence over both state and groups for reforms (Shachar, 2001: 122, 107). To ensure this outcome, she proposes a framework within which the recognition of collective jurisdictional identity and the introduction of constitutional scrutiny on the firm protection of individual citizenship rights (such as "credible threats of exit") can democratically work together (Shachar, 2008: 143, 149). Thus, it is important to emphasise that Shachar's model is not a form of legal pluralism (where a non-state law can function as an alternative to the state law), but a form of jurisdictional pluralism (where a non-state law can function as a form of third-party arbitration).

In summary, I argue that institutional pluralism (including jurisdictional pluralism) in the public domain can only take place provided that a number of conditions are satisfied – an established democratic secular superstructure, the actual enforcement of individual rights and freedoms, the defence of minority rights, the constitutional protection of the rights of vulnerable group members (i.e. the protected right to exit the group) and the instilment of democratic checks and balances to ensure the democratic character and social solidarity of the polity in practice (Turner, 2011: 321; Shachar, 2009: 133). In addressing the criticisms facing it, institutional pluralism in this form would not be an "obvious threat to state sovereignty" or an "erosion of citizenship" (Turner, 2011: 318).

It is important to note that there can be various models of institutional pluralism based on the already existing relationships and institutions between the state and religious communities, as well as the nature of the group and the already established political context. Due to the theoretical nature of this study, I do not engage with the legal, sociological, anthropological and economic dimensions of institutional pluralism and have not mapped out specific criteria by which to decide which groups should be merited recognition under which arenas (Carens and Williams, 1996: 163). My main concern in the arguments stated in the preceding sections was to develop a normative justification for pluralist secularism to overcome the authoritarian policies of philosophical secularism towards religion.

Conclusion

To conclude, pluralist secularism offers an alternative approach to secularism, with a particular focus on the relationship between the state and religion. The state is conceptualised as an enterprise that is impartial towards all normative systems in a society. It endorses moral minimalism by dissociating religious authority, absolutist truths and moral systems from the government while allowing religious reference and presence (the political roles and implications of citizens' different accounts of ontological morality and definitions of a good life) to be part of politics. Religion is conceptualised as a personal and a communal issue, which has the capacity to play a social and political role in democracies within the social public sphere where a degree of separation of the state from civil society politics is maintained (An-Na'im, 2008: 5). In this chapter, the configurations of the differentiation between politics and the state have enabled us to think about different ways in which the aspirations for religiously motivated societal lives and liberal commitments to individual rights could be reconciled.

Finally, pluralist secularism has been used as a concept to advocate moving away from a unitary nation-state to pluralist forms of the state. I have argued that in order to resolve the state's relation to religious affairs, some form of institutional pluralism (institutionalised state and religious interconnectivity devolving certain public credentials from the state to authentic civil society organisations) is necessary. Ultimately, the pluralist secularism framework has aimed to balance state political sovereignty with collective religious freedoms, social solidarity with accommodation of normative difference and hence the state public sphere with the social public sphere. I believe this model has certain virtues in addressing the disadvantages the current secularist systems place on religious individuals and groups. It also opens new avenues for debate on rethinking secularism based on normative stances on state-religion relations made in the name of religion.

Notes

1 Iris M. Young's "differentiated citizenship" (2011), Will Kymlicka's "multicultural citizenship" (1995) and Monica Mookherjee's "affective citizenship" (2005) are some of its prominent examples.
2 For a detailed discussion on the nature of Islamic law, see Wael B. Hallaq (2010).
3 See Barkey (1994), Jessop (1990), Estin (2011), Galanter (1981), and Merry (1988).
4 See Mégret (2012), and Melissaris (2009).

Bibliography

Abou El Fadl, K.A. 2005. *The Great Theft: Wrestling Islam from the Extremists*. New York: Harper San Francisco.

An-Na'im, A.A. 2002. "Muslims Must Realize That There is Nothing Magical about the Concept of Human Rights, Interview with Asghar Ali Engineer." Pp. 5–13 in Noor, F.A. (ed.) *New Voices of Islam*. Leiden: ISIM.

An-Na'im, A.A. 2008. *Islam and the Secular State: Negotiating the Future of Shari'a*. Cambridge, MA: Harvard University Press.

Asad, T. 2003. *Formations of the Secular: Christianity, Islam, Modernity*. Stanford: Stanford University Press.

Asad, T. 2012. "Thinking about Religion, Belief, and Politics." *The Cambridge Companion to Religious Studies*, March, 36–57.

Bader, V. 1999. "Religious Pluralism: Secularism or Priority for Democracy?" *Political Theory* 27: 597–633.

Bader, V. 2001. "Associative Democracy and the Incorporation of Ethnic and National Minorities." Pp. 187–202 in Hirst, P. and Bader, V.M. (eds.) *Associative Democracy: The Real Third Way*. London: Frank Cass.

Bader, V. 2003. "Democratic Institutional Pluralism and Cultural Diversity." Pp. 131–167 in Harzig, C. and Juteau, D. (eds.) *The Social Construction of Diversity: Recasting the Master Narrative of Industrial Nations*. New York: Berghahn Books.

Bader, V. 2007. *Secularism or Democracy? Associational Governance of Religious Diversity*. Netherlands: Amsterdam University Press.

Bader, V. 2009. "Legal Pluralism and Differentiated Morality: Shari'a in Ontario?" Pp. 49–72 in Grillo, R. et al. (eds.) *Legal Practice and Cultural Diversity*. Surrey: Ashgate.

Barkey, K. 1994. *Bandits and Bureaucrats: The Ottoman Route to State Centralization*. Ithaca, NY: Cornell University Press.

Barzilai, G. 2004. “Legal Categorizations and Religion: On Politics of Modernity, Practices, Faith, and Power.” Pp. 392–409 in Austin, S. (ed.) *The Blackwell Companion to Law and Society*. Malden: Blackwell Publishing.

Barzilai, G. 2010. *Communities and Law: Politics and Cultures of Legal Identities*. Ann Arbor, MI: University of Michigan Press.

Berlinerblau, J. 2017. “Political Secularisms.” Pp. 85–102 in Zuckerman, P. (ed.). *The Oxford Handbook of Secularism*. New York: Oxford University Press.

Bhargava, R. 1999. *Secularism and Its Critics*. Delhi, NY: Oxford University Press.

Carens, J.H. and Williams, M.S. 1996. “Muslim Minorities in Liberal Democracies: The Politics of Misrecognition.” *Public Policy and Social Welfare* 21: 157–186.

Cesari, J. 2004. *When Islam and Democracy Meet: Muslims in Europe and in the United States*. New York: Palgrave Macmillan.

Dworkin, G. 2015. “The Nature of Autonomy.” *Nordic Journal of Studies in Educational Policy* 2: 28479.

Estin, A.L. 2011. “Family Law, Pluralism, and Human Rights.” *Emory International Law Review* 25: 811–828.

Fish, S. 1997. “Mission Impossible: Settling the Just Bounds between Church and State.” *Columbia Law Review* 95: 2255–2333.

Galanter, M. 1981. “Justice in Many Rooms: Courts, Private Ordering and Indigenous Law.” *Journal of Legal Pluralism* 19: 1–47.

Ghobadzadeh, N. 2014. *Religious Secularity: A Theological Challenge to the Islamic State*. New York: Oxford University Press.

Göle, N. and Billaud, J. 2011. “Islamic Difference and the Return of Feminist Universalism.” Pp. 116–144 in Triandafyllidou, A., Modood, T. and Meer, N. (eds.) *European Multiculturalisms: Cultural, Religious and Ethnic Challenges*. Edinburg: Edinburgh University Press.

Gutmann, A. 2009. *Identity in Democracy*. Princeton, NJ: Princeton University Press.

Habermas, J. 2006. “Religion in the Public Sphere.” *European Journal of Philosophy* 14: 1–25.

Hallaq, W.B. 1985. “The Logic of Legal Reasoning in Religious and Non-Religious Cultures: The Case of Islamic Law and the Common Law.” *Cleveland State Law Review* 34: 79–97.

Hallaq, W.B. 2010. “Islamic Law: History and Transformation.” *The New Cambridge History of Islam* 4: 142–183.

Hirst, P. 1997. *From Statism to Pluralism: Democracy. Civil Society and Global Politics*. London: University College London Press.

Jessop, B. 1990. *State Theory: Putting Capitalist States in Their Place*. University Park: Penn State Press.

Juergensmeyer, M. 1995. “The New Religious State.” *Comparative Politics* 27 (4): 379–391.

Juergensmeyer, M. 2017. “The Imagined War between Secularism and Religion.” Pp. 71–85 in Zuckerman, P. (ed.). *The Oxford Handbook of Secularism*. New York: Oxford University Press.

Keane, J. 1993. “Power-Sharing Islam?” Pp. 15–31 in Tamimi, A. (ed.) *Power Sharing Islam?* London: Liberty for Muslim World Publications.

Kuru, A.T. 2007. “Passive and Assertive Secularism: Historical Conditions, Ideological Struggles, and State Policies Toward Religion.” *World Politics* 59 (4): 568–594.

Kurzman, C. and Naqvi, I. 2010. "The Islamists Are Not Coming." *Foreign Policy* 177: 34.

Kymlicka, W. 1995. *Multicultural Citizenship: A Liberal Theory of Minority Rights*. Oxford: Clarendon Press.

Laborde, C. 2018a. "Toleration and Laïcité." Pp. 162–177 in McKinnon, C. and Castiglione, D. (eds.) *The Culture of Toleration in Diverse Societies: Reasonable Tolerance*. Manchester: Manchester University Press.

Laborde, C. 2018b. *Liberalism's Religion*. Cambridge, MA: Harvard University Press.

Locke, J. 1689. *Treatise of Civil Government and A Letter Concerning Toleration*. Translated by Popple, W. Indianapolis: Bobbs-Merrill.

Locke, J. 1955. *A Letter Concerning Toleration*. New York: Bobbs-Merrill.

Locke, J. 2016. *Second Treatise of Government and a Letter Concerning Toleration*. New York: Oxford University Press.

Macedo, S. 2000. *Diversity and Distrust: Civic Education in a Multicultural Democracy*. Cambridge, MA: Harvard University Press.

Maclure, J. and Taylor, C. 2011. *Secularism and Freedom of Conscience*. Cambridge, MA: Harvard University Press.

Mahmood, S. 1995. "Talal Asad: Modern Power and the Reconfiguration of Religious Traditions. An Interview with Talal Asad." *Stanford Humanities Review* 5 (1): 1–16.

Mahmood, S. and Danchin, P. 2014. "Contested Genealogies of Religious Freedom." *South Atlantic Quarterly* 113 (1): 1–8.

Mégret, F. 2012. "Is There Ever a "Right to One's Own Law?" An Exploration of Possible Rights Foundations for Legal Pluralism." *Israel Law Review* 45 (1): 3–34.

Melissaris, E. 2009. *Ubiquitous Law: Legal Theory and the Space for Legal Pluralism*. Burlington: Ashgate Publishing Limited.

Merry, S.E. 1988. "Legal Pluralism." *Law & Society Review* 22: 869–896.

Modood, T. 2010. "Moderate Secularism, Religion as Identity and Respect for Religion." *Political Quarterly* 81 (1): 4–14.

Modood, T. 2017. "Multiculturalizing Religion." Pp. 354–368 in Zuckerman, P. (ed.) *The Oxford Handbook of Secularism*. New York: Oxford University Press.

Mookherjee, M. 2005. "Affective Citizenship: Feminism, Postcolonialism and the Politics of Recognition." *Critical Review of International Social and Political Philosophy* 8 (1): 31–50.

Mookherjee, M. 2009. *Women's Rights as Multicultural Claims: Reconfiguring Gender and Diversity in Political Philosophy*. Edinburgh: Edinburgh University Press.

Moussa, M. 2020. "Patronage in Reverse and the Secular State in Egypt." Pp. 284–296 in Sadiki, L. (ed.) *Routledge Handbook of Middle East Politics: Interdisciplinary Inscriptions*. London: Routledge.

Murphy, M. 2013. *Multiculturalism: A Critical Introduction*. London: Routledge.

Plesner, I.T. 2005. "The European Court on Human Rights between Fundamentalist and Liberal Secularism." In Seminar on The Islamic Headscarf Controversy and the Future of Freedom of Religion or Belief, Strasbourg, France, 1–16.

Quong, J. 2011. *Liberalism without Perfection*. New York: Oxford University Press.

Sajoo, A.B. 2004. *Civil Society in the Muslim World: Contemporary Perspectives*. London: I.B. Tauris.

Sezgin, Y.K. 2013. *Human Rights Under State-Enforced Religious Family Laws in Israel, Egypt and India*. Cambridge: Cambridge University Press.

Shachar, A. 2001. *Multicultural Jurisdictions*. Cambridge: Cambridge University Press.

Shachar, A. 2008. "Privatizing Diversity: A Cautionary Tale from Religious Arbitration in Family Law." *Theoretical Inquiries in Law* 9: 573–587.

Shachar, A. 2009. "Entangled: State, Religion, and the Family." *Harvard International Law Journal* 49: 135–142.

Shahar, I. 2008. "Legal Pluralism and the Study of Shari'a Courts." *Islamic Law and Society* 15: 112–141.

Soroush, A. 2007. "Militant Secularism." Retrieved on September 23rd, 2020. http://www.drsoroush.com/English/On_DrSoroush/E-CMO-2007-Militant%20Secularism.html.

Stepan, A.C. 2000. "Religion, Democracy, and the Twin Tolerations." *Journal of Democracy* 11 (4): 37–57.

Taylor, C. 1998. "Modes of Secularism." Pp. 31–53 in Rajeev Bhargava (ed.) *Secularism and its Critics*, New York: Oxford University Press.

Taylor, C. 2008. "Foreword." Pp. xi–xxii in Brahm, G. (ed.) *Secularism, Religion and Multicultural Citizenship*. Cambridge: Cambridge University Press.

Turner, B.S. 2007. "Managing Religions: State Responses to Religious Diversity." *Contemporary Islam* 1 (2): 123–137.

Turner, B.S. 2011. "Legal Pluralism, State Sovereignty, and Citizenship." *Democracy and Security* 7 (4): 317–337.

Turner, B.S. 2012. *Religion and Modern Society: Citizenship, Secularisation and the State*. Cambridge: Cambridge University Press.

Vallentyne, P. and van der Vossen, B. 2014. "Libertarianism." in E.N. Zalta (ed.) *Stanford Encyclopedia of Philosophy*. Retrieved on September 23rd, 2020. https://plato.stanford.edu/archives/fall2014/entries/libertarianism/.

Williams, R. 2008. "Civil and Religious Law in England: A Religious Perspective." Lecture by the Archbishop of Canterbury Dr Rowan Williams at the Royal Courts of Justice, February 7th, 2008. *The Guardian*. Retrieved on June 18th, 2020. http://www.guardian.co.uk/uk/2008/feb/07/religion.world3.

Yavuz, M.H. 2003. *Islamic Political Identity in Turkey*. New York: Oxford University Press.

Young, I.M. 2011. *Justice and the Politics of Difference*. Princeton, NJ: Princeton University Press.

Zubaida, S. 1993. *Islam, the People and the State: Political Ideas and Movements in the Middle East*. London: IB Tauris.

Zubaida, S. 2011. "Turkey as a Model of Democracy and Islam." *Open Democracy*. Retrieved on February 10th, 2019. https://www.opendemocracy.net/north-africa-west-asia/sami-zubaida/turkey-as-model-of-democracy-and-islam.

3 Are there consequentialist grounds for exempting religious health care professionals from medical assistance in dying?

Daniel Weinstock

Introduction

There has been in recent years a robust debate over the question of whether physicians and other health care professionals (HCPs) should be exempted from certain legally permitted medical practices if they find them morally unacceptable. Advocates of exemptions argue that there is nothing in the medical context that should prevent us from carving out reasonable accommodations for HCPs in the medical field just as we do in many other fields of endeavour, and that such exemptions follow from liberal-democratic premises (Maclure, 2016; Maclure and Dumont, 2017; Wicclair, 2011). Opponents of exemptions argue that the interests of patients should in the medical context be prioritised in all contexts, and that this priority is threatened by any regime of exemptions. They argue that in deciding to become HCPs, individual agents by that very fact agree that they will make themselves available to perform any legally prescribed medical procedure where the interest of their patient warrants it (Schuklenk, 2019; Savulescu and Schuklenk, 2017; Schuklenk and Smalling, 2016; Stahl and Emanuel, 2017).

A common assumption undergirds much of the literature of the past few years, despite the appearances of quite substantial disagreement. I will refer to this as the "self-regarding" assumption. According to this assumption, the main reason that there is to affirm the right of patients has to do with the interests of patients, and the main reason that there is to affirm the rights of HCPs has to do with the interests of the people who fulfil roles in the health care system. Absent from the discussion, as far as I can tell, is any discussion of the possibility that there may be other-regarding reasons to which we might have to attend in determining how to balance the claims of patients and those of HCPs. That is, nowhere is it considered that there may be patient-centred reasons that add weight to the claims of HCPs, or indeed HCP-centred reasons that weigh in favour of the claims of patients.

There can be no doubt that this is largely the way in which the philosophical debate about the foundations of rights has proceeded. Regardless of their other differences, rights theorists tend to look for the foundation of rights in the interests of rights holders, either their general interests or their agency-based interests (Kramer, Simmonds, and Steiner, 2000). And there can be no question that the debate over exemptions in the health care field has been largely carried out in terms of rights. I want in this short chapter to adopt a more consequentialist stance towards the problem of exemptions and ask the question of whether patients might not have an interest in accommodating the conscience-based claims of HCPs at least to some degree. That is, I want to consider whether, when we consider the range of institutional regimes that we might consider putting in place in order concretely to realise the respective rights of patients and of HCPs, where on the continuum from "conscience absolutism" to "patient-centred absolutism" do we want to calibrate this regime?[1] I take it that unlike deontologically minded rights theorists, consequentialists in answering this question ought to be sensitive to all manner of possible consequences to which the adoption of different regimes might give rise, and thus be open in particular to the kinds of "other-regarding' considerations that I have just briefly described. I want to consider three kinds of reasons of this sort that I shall refer to as "expectation-based", "diversity-based" and "capacity-based". I will define these terms in due course.

I will proceed as follows. I will first rehearse an argument that I developed some years ago in order to identify a range of cases that fall under the general rubric of "conscience-based exemptions" that seem *least* amenable to justified accommodation. These arguments I refer to as "irreducibly religious". The burden of this chapter will be to show that even in these kinds of cases, there are defeasible consequentialist grounds to consider a carefully crafted regime of exemptions with respect to practices such as medical assistance in dying (MAID). I will show that all three kinds of reasons I have briefly referred to above, and that I will develop at greater length below, apply even in this least auspicious of cases.

Irreducibly religious reasons

In an earlier article (Weinstock, 2014), I argued that the idea of conscience-based refusal is ambiguous between two quite different sets of phenomena, which differ in ways that are morally significant from the point of view of the question of whether or not exemptions should be granted. Some HCPs claim exemptions because they have moral objections to a practice that is legally prescribed in the jurisdiction in which they practice. Though they have not necessarily articulated the argument in detail, they have conscientiously thought about the question of whether or not the practice is morally permissible, and they have come to the conclusion that it is not.

Some exemptions are, on the other hand, made on religious grounds. Those who make them view certain professional obligations as incompatible with their religious obligations. Now, care must be taken in distinguishing these two categories. It is a mistake often made by those of us whose ethical convictions are grounded in secular moral theories that only such theories count as moral theories at all (Parfit, 1986). Religiously grounded moral theories are according to this view really grounded in barely concealed appeals to authority. I believe that this is a mistake. On the one hand, many contemporary moral theories have identifiably religious origins, origins that still have an impact on contemporary articulations of the theory. As Ian Shapiro has classically shown, this is true in particular of contemporary rights theory, and may also be true of contemporary virtue theory (Shapiro, 1986). On the other hand, moral theories explicitly grounded in religious traditions are very often distinguished from others not on the basis of claims about the ultimate authority of the moral arguments therein, but rather on the basis of conceptual repertoires and ways of prioritising certain values over others. Natural law arguments formulated by contemporary natural lawyers such as John Finnis or Robert George shock sensitivities that have been steeped in theories like utilitarianism not for metaethical but at the end of the day for first-order ethical reasons.

If this is plausible, many of the arguments, and accompanying claims to exemption, that some would categorise as religiously grounded turn out to be moral in nature. What I think of as irreducibly religious arguments are of several kinds. Among them are explicit appeals to authority – "I can't do that because Scripture/my Imam/Rabbi/Priest has told me that I cannot", but also appeals to tradition and identity. As Samuel Scheffler has recently shown, religions are, among other things, traditions, and traditions have import in the lives of many people because of the way that they anchor them temporally. They make sense of our individual lives in terms of broader narratives in ways that might be psychologically important for some. They are also, relatedly, at the basis of the identities of many people. For some, religion performs a role similar to that played for others by nationality – an answer to the question posed by others (but also sometimes posed by oneself): "Who are you?"

As important as identity and tradition might be for individual moral psychologies, we do not make the practice of medicine any better by carving out exemptions for HCPs whose objections to certain practices are grounded in such considerations (or even less, in considerations of authority). I have argued, however, that we *do* make the practice of medicine better by empowering HCPs to think critically about the practices that their profession encompasses, and within limits, to act on the conclusions of their critical reflections through the request for exemptions. This is not the place to rehearse that argument in detail. Suffice it to say, however, that the practice of medicine is morally complex, and that we all benefit if the institutions through which it is practised give some place to the privileged epistemic standpoint of those HCPs who are at the coalface of many of the decisions that we make about what is and what is not permissible within that practice.

There seems to be no reason, from the point of view of the practice of medicine, to accommodate those whose objections are irreducibly religious. Accommodating them would seem, at first blush, to serve them by allowing them to harmonise their professional practice with their identities or with the traditions to which they cleave. But given the priority which, as we have seen, should always be given within the medical system to the interests of patients, these self-regarding considerations seem not to have much normative weight at all.

In what follows, I want to suggest that things might not be so simple. First, even those whose reasons for requesting exemptions are irreducibly religious (or whose reasons are inchoate[2]) may have a claim to exemption, if they entered the profession at a time when the practice that they are now being asked to perform was illegal. At the moment of legal reform, moreover, even those who favour MAID (and who may at some point in their own lives be inclined to request it) have reason to grant exemptions on these grounds, lest those who claim them use their institutional and social power to block reform in a wholesale manner. Second, and independent of such considerations, there may be reasons that even patients who might see themselves as at some point making a request for MAID would recognise for granting exemptions to those whose reasons for exemption are irreducibly religious.

Expectation-based reasons for exemptions

Many of the theorists who have argued most strenuously against granting any conscience-based accommodations for HCPs have done so on the grounds that joining a profession implies, at least in the context of a tolerably just liberal democracy, accepting the norms through which the society they belong to has chosen to regulate the profession in question. In a liberal democracy, no one forces anyone to become a physician, a nurse or anything else, and so it can rightly be assumed that people who have chosen those professions, and the norms that accompany them, have done so freely. They can on this view be held responsible for their choices, and in particular, they can be held accountable by reference to the professional norms that they have freely undertaken to uphold.

I will assume that this argument is largely correct for the sake of the present argument, though I don't believe it to be bullet-proof. That one's society is governed in a tolerably liberal-democratic way is not a sufficient condition for considering that all of the medical practices are ethical within it. Indeed, medical change in recent decades has been driven in part by the recognition that certain permitted practices (for example, in the area of assisted reproduction) were morally problematic, and that citizens of a liberal democracy conversely ought to have a right to certain proscribed practices (abortion and MAID, to name but two examples). It follows that even in the context of liberal democracies, it can be supposed that at any given time, HCPs under a regime that did not tolerate any conscience-based exemptions would be proscribed from performing morally permissible procedures and required to perform morally problematic procedures.

I do not want to dwell on the weaknesses of this argument in the present context, however, but consider what would seem to be one of its implications, which appears to run against the thrust of the argument made by those who would deny HCPs any room for conscience-based exemptions. This argument has to do with the moral situation of those who practice a profession at the moment of fundamental norm change, and with the legitimate moral claims made by those in that situation, in a context of fundamental norm change. The argument I am considering is to the effect that if one joins a profession, one by that very fact accepts the professional norms that accompany it. But what if those norms change over the course of one's career? What if the expectations that one has reasonably formed on the basis of the norms that were in place when one joined the profession, and the existence of which may have formed part of the reason that one made the career choice one did, are violated by some significant change in those norms? On the face of it, it would seem that the argument according to which one is bound by the norms to which one has signed up in freely deciding to join a profession turns against those who would deny HCPs any margin for conscience-based exemptions. Indeed, on the basis of that very argument, can they not claim that they are bound by the old norms, rather than the new ones? In particular, for those very many HCPs in a country such as Canada whose careers overlapped the adoption of new norms according to which it is acceptable under specified conditions to help one's grievously and irremediably ill patients to die, should they not be able to claim exemptions on the basis of the norms that they subscribed to in joining the profession?

Clearly, another argument is required in order to forestall this conclusion. Such an argument could either attack the whole idea of "grandfathering" – that is the idea that it might under certain circumstances be legitimate or even morally required not to impose new norms on those people whose expectations were formed under the norms that are being replaced – or it could attack it specifically in the area of health care. The former strategy would be a difficult one to make for those theorists who would deny a conscience-based claim on the part of HCPs to exempt themselves from medical practices newly made legal, since part of their argument, as we have seen, is itself based on the idea of the legitimate expectations that are formed in choosing to join a profession. And so it is not surprising to find that the argument seeking to block claims to conscience-based exemptions is grounded in putative special features of the health care professions. Specifically, the feature that is pointed to by opponents of exemptions is the "fast moving" nature of the health care sector, that is, the fact that among the second-order norms that one must accept when one enters a health care profession is that the first-order norms to which one is subject will change over time. Thus, Udo Schuklenk writes that "nobody is entitled to a job that does not evolve – *especially in a fast-paced, ever-changing profession like medicine*" (Schuklenk, 2019: 535, my emphasis).

A few remarks seem apposite here. First, though Schuklenk is of course correct in claiming that medicine has changed a great deal over the centuries, and even over the course of the past few years, it has remained remarkably stable and conservative in terms of its fundamental values. Indeed, in what other profession is one of the rites of passage into the professional order the recitation of an oath that was formulated over two millennia ago? The fact that this oath is still part of the introduction of young physicians into the profession is moreover not purely ceremonial. It speaks to the stability over time of the constitutive values of the medical profession.

Now, to be sure, the values and principles expressed in an oath such as the Hippocratic Oath do not ethically rule out MAID. "First, do no harm" does not imply that one should never help one's patient to die, because in some cases continued life can constitute a harm for a grievously ill patient whose suffering cannot be alleviated in ways that they consider to be acceptable. But it is certainly the case that, for generations of physicians and other HCPs, the constitutive values of the profession have been taken by them and by the professional orders to which they are accountable as including a prohibition against the deliberate participation in the steps needed to help a patient to die. The more general point is that there are changes, and then there are changes. It is certainly correct that medicine changes dramatically and quite rapidly in terms of the tools that are available to HCPs, and to the range of procedures that these tools make possible. It is certainly part of the professional responsibilities of physicians that they keep up to date with changes in the science that undergirds their practice, with the instruments that are one of the main results of this rapidly changing science, and with the accompanying new range of practices and procedures. But to say this is not to say that they are duty-bound to simply accept to change their most fundamental values with respect to their profession, values that when they joined the profession were taken to be central to that practice.

We need a more fine-grained set of tools with which to determine whether and when physicians can claim exemptions to changes in their profession on the basis of some kind of a "reasonable expectation" claim. Axel Gosseries and Mathias Hungerbühler (2006) have given us a helpful way in which to think about the circumstances under which moral responsibilities are (or are not) altered by rule changes. According to Gosseries and Hungerbühler, we should assess the changes to our responsibilities on the basis of two variables. The first has to do with the degree to which the prior rule was morally acceptable, and whether reasonable persons could disagree about it. The second has to do with whether the change could be reasonably foreseen. The greater the immorality of the prior rule, and the more change to it was foreseeable, the less the claim of those who would want to be exempted from the new rule has normative weight. Conversely, when a rule about which reasonable persons can disagree changes, and when that change was difficult to foresee, the claim put forward by some that they should be "grandfathered" into the new rule gains normative weight.

I would modify the test proposed by Gosseries and Hungerbühler in the following ways. First, I would give priority to the normative test over the predictability test. That is, if a practice is uncontroversially morally unacceptable, then the fact that it could reasonably be viewed at time t1 as unlikely to change does not exempt an individual from the effect of norm change at time t2. The greater the extent to which reasonable people might disagree about the pre-existing norm, the more the criterion of unforeseeability of change has weight. Second, I would argue that the greater the degree of centrality of a norm to a practice (provided the norm and the practice are not uncontroversially immoral), the greater it is legitimate for a participant in a practice who was brought into the practice under the previous regime of norms to claim exemption from the new norms.

MAID is in my view called for by principles, such as autonomy, that are central to liberal democracies. I was in fact the member of an Expert Panel of the Royal Society of Canada that recommended the changes in Canadian criminal law that ultimately gave rise to Canada's new legal provisions concerning MAID (Schuklenk et al., 2011). But it does not follow from my support for these measures that I think that those who support the previous, blanket prohibition are unreasonable. Many of them, for example, do not prioritise autonomy the way that our panel did. While I believe that in a liberal democracy, the ability to make legally untrammelled choices about fundamental questions of life and death is of paramount importance, it would be an unwarranted leap to claim that those who deny this, in the name, for example, of values to do with the protection of vulnerable persons, are being unreasonable in the same way as, say, someone defending the institution of slavery would clearly be (Beaudry, 2018).

It is also the case, I have suggested above, that the idea according to which HCPs should not be actively involved in ending the life of their patients has been central, rather than marginal or instrumental, to the self-understanding of physicians. That this is a philosophical error based on a misinterpretation of the Hippocratic injunction to "first do no harm", or on an overemphasising of the distinction between killing and letting die, does not detract from the fact that many HCPs entered their professions harbouring the thought, reinforced by professional orders and by law, that they would never be expected to actively participate in the facilitation of the death of a patient. I don't think it is an exaggeration to say that this belief has been central to the practice of medicine, and to the set of expectations on the basis of which generations of HCPs chose to join the profession.

Finally, it is also the case that in a country such as Canada that has recently chosen to legalise MAID, the change was not foreseeable by those people who joined the profession before the Supreme Court of Canada ruled in the matter of *Carter*. The Supreme Court of Canada had in fact already ruled on the matter of MAID in the *Rodriguez* case in 1992. Given the importance of the doctrine and practice of *stare decisis* in the Canadian legal context, it could reasonably be thought by those entering the profession after the Rodriguez decision was rendered that the criminal prohibition of MAID was a matter of settled law in Canada. (Admittedly, as more countries like Canada take the step of legalising MAID, HCPs in other liberal democracies can reasonably foresee that the laws forbidding the practice will eventually probably be called into question, and perhaps overturned, in their own jurisdiction, thus lessening the degree to which they can ground claims to exemptions on considerations of reasonable expectation.)

Thus, there do seem to be reasons grounded in the legitimate expectations formed by physicians and other health care workers who entered their chosen professions when MAID was illegal, and who may not have chosen the profession had it been legal, to exempt them from having to take part in a practice to which they object, either for moral reasons or simply because it does not comport with religious precepts that are central to their identities, about which reasonable people can disagree and with respect to which they could well be excused for having thought that the likelihood of change was slim, a practice that moreover engages with values that are central to the profession, and that have been stably so for a long time.[3]

If any of this is plausible, though, all that I have established is that there is a self-regarding reason to organise the system on the basis of which we regulate access to MAID in a manner that accommodates physicians and other HCPs who entered their profession prior to the judicial decision that overturned the criminal prohibition against MAID. But we have not established that there are "other-regarding" reasons to "grandfather" the prohibition. Arguably, however, such reasons exist. As has been argued by political scientists such as Christopher Leman and by jurists such as Kent Greenawalt, grandfather clauses are often necessary in order to pass legislation that imposes unexpected costs on actors whose opposition can effectively stymie legislative change altogether (Leman, 1980; Greenawalt, 2016). One way of thinking about "grandfathering" is that it attempts to achieve the benefits of legislation in the present while deferring the costs of such legislation to the future. It purchases the support of present stakeholders by telling them that though the costs involved in a new policy will be paid by those who come later to whatever social practice the legislation in question seeks to regulate, and that present generations will be allowed to work within the practice on the basis of whatever rules obtained before. In the case of MAID, grandfathering involves the concern that were the legislation that enables MAID put forward in a manner that precludes exemptions for those HCPs brought into the practice prior to legalisation, they would use their considerable power to block the practice altogether. It thus tells present practitioners that they can opt out of the practice if they so choose, in the hope that by doing so these practitioners will not attempt to block the practice as a whole. Now, there is clearly a balancing act here. If too many HCPs claim an exemption, then the new legislation as a whole is imperilled. But given the numbers of patients who request MAID, it is probably possible in a country like Canada to put in place a regime that recognises the legitimate expectations of present HCPs without threatening access of patients to the procedure. That access might in any event be threatened to an even greater degree were the legislation authorising MAID put forward in a manner that did not carve out any room for exemptions.

The foregoing considerations smack of amoral *realpolitik*. "Rather than having a powerful group make use of its political and social capital in order to block desired legislation altogether", the argument seems to be saying, "let's give in to their blackmail and provide them with a morally unjustified benefit so that they will not get in the way of desired legislation". None of what precedes should be read in this way. My claim is that in certain circumstances, there may be strong normative grounds for acceding to the claims formulated by certain agents who have formed legitimate expectations on the basis of prior legislation. In such cases, acceding to the independently morally justified claims of those claiming a "grandfather" clause may have the extra benefit of turning them into allies of the legislation rather than into potentially destructive foes.

The argument from diversity

The argument just put forward is backward-looking. It only applies to those HCPs who entered their professions before the passing into law of measures that make MAID licit. If it is true, as we have accepted for the sake of argument, that physicians are bound by the norms that govern their profession at the time that they chose to take it up, Canadian physicians who, say, entered medical school after the *Carter* decision in Canada was rendered have formed their legitimate expectations in an environment in which MAID is legally prescribed. They could on the basis of the foregoing argument therefore not reasonably claim that they legitimately expected not to have to aid their patients to die. If the argument from legitimate expectations is the only one that exercises some normative pressure on us to come up with regimes regulating access to MAID that make some room for conscientious refusal, then it is just a matter of time before that pressure disappears completely.

I believe that there are, however, forward-looking normative pressures as well. One of them has to do with ensuring that in the context of a pluralist society, one that is ethno-culturally, religiously and morally diverse, it is important that the cadre of HCPs that serves that population reflect it at least to some degree. I am not claiming that every profession needs to be a perfectly reflective "mirror" of its society, but rather that it be sufficiently reflective of that diversity to fulfil a number of objectives that any modern health care system, and any group of patients dependent on that health care system, appropriately set for themselves.

Let me provide three objectives that seem to me to be relatively uncontroversial. First, it is a truism that medicine serves persons, and not just their bodies. To articulate the claim in slightly less gnomic terms, the clinical encounter is one in which physicians and other HCPs will come across patients who will articulate their sense of their own well-being in ways that are shot through with culturally loaded terms and understandings. The very fact that they use language in order to communicate with physicians means that, if they are not speakers of the same language as their physicians, there is a risk that physician and patient will talk past one another because they are in fact employing different conceptual repertoires (Partida, 2007). While it will in a mass society be impossible to achieve a perfect one-to-one mapping of linguistic patient groups and physicians, it is clear that increasing the linguistic competence within the HCP cadre of a polyglot society will improve communication between the two groups whose successful communication is so important to the success of the clinical encounter.

Second, it has been abundantly documented that trust is key to the success of the medical system (Gilson, 2003; Gille, Smith, and Mays, 2015). Above and beyond questions of communication that can be hampered by linguistic misunderstanding, it has been amply documented that such determinants of positive patient outcomes such as continuity of care improve when they feel trust towards the physicians with whom they interact, and that trust is correlated with ethno-cultural congruity (Waibel, 2018). This may strike some as regrettable, but in a world in which ethno-cultural differences still map out onto patterns of advantage, disadvantage and racialisation, progressive medical practice cannot completely rule out the importance of diversity within the cadre of HCPs as a way of promoting trust with the patient community.

Third, it is not just the case that patients and HCPs in a highly diverse society will come to the communicative context of the clinical encounter with different conceptual repertoires, but also with different values and understandings about health, illness and the role of HCPs. This range of differences will be informed not just by ethno-cultural but also by religious diversity. "Cultural competence" encompasses a wide range of attitudinal and institutional desiderata aimed at reducing the kinds of biases that may inform medical judgement when the medical cadre is too culturally uniform to serve its multicultural constituency, and at increasing the understanding of the way in which different populations understand issues of health and disease (this is of course not to say that HCPs should be servile before these understandings, but that they must have some comprehension of them in order to enter into meaningful communication). Anne Fadiman's classic account of the encounter between a Hmong refugee family and the American health care system provides a poignant illustration of the need for intercultural understanding (Fadiman, 1997).

In sum, it seems plausible to say that communication, trust and understanding are key to the success of the medical enterprise in a religiously and ethno-culturally diverse society. It also seems reasonable to assume that increasing diversity within the cadre of HCPs will serve these goals.

Opponents of accommodations for conscience- and religion-based objections to MAID argue that the fact that performing the procedure is a requirement of medical and of other health care professions should serve as a gatekeeping mechanism at the point of entry into the health care professions, most notably in the application and admission process into HCP schools. Savulescu and Schuklenk, for example, argue that "medical schools and training programmes should carefully outline the nature of the job and screen for conscientious objection where it is relevant to job performance" (Savulescu and Schuklenk, 2017: 163).

The concern with this approach is that while defenders of this filtering mechanism are most probably correct in claiming that it will not prevent societies that implement it from recruiting sufficient *numbers* of physicians and other HCPs (Schuklenk and Smalling, 2016: 239), it might pose a problem from the point of view of recruiting a cadre of HCPs that is sufficiently diverse to satisfy the goals that I have outlined above. Though this claim would obviously have to be substantiated by empirical research, it does not seem outlandish to worry that systematically blocking all applicants to professional schools who have objections to MAID would narrow the range of applicants, even when the numbers drawn from that narrowed range are sufficient to fill a society's quantitative needs. All we need to assume is that there may be fewer members of conservative religious groups that would be accepted were risks of conscientious refusal screened for. It is also possible that opposition to MAID, be it for articulated reasons or for irreducible reasons of cultural and religious identity, is not smoothly distributed across a diverse population, but rather that it is more heavily represented among certain ethno-cultural groups, and that religious people are less likely to be willing to administer the procedure than non-religious people (Falconer et al., 2019). The members of the Expert Panel Working Group on Advanced Requests for MAID of the Council of Canadian Academies recognise that in the context of a highly diverse society such as Canada, attention must be paid to cultural differences in thinking about how to organise end-of-life care. "Culture can be profoundly influential in how people, both patients and healthcare practitioners, view end-of-life medical care, and death and dying in general" (Expert Panel Working Group on Advanced Requests for MAID, 2018: 29).

So the claim is a limited one, and one that needs to be verified by appropriate empirical research. But it is, nonetheless, one to which consequentialists wanting to attend to all manner of ethically relevant consequences of different ways of organising access to MAID should be attentive. The refusal to accommodate HCPs who harbour objections to MAID, ultimately by denying them access to the relevant professional schools through screening, may narrow the field of applicants to such schools in a manner that, though it doesn't threaten the supply of professionals in a purely quantitative sense, makes it less ethno-culturally and religiously diverse than it otherwise might be. This may have a deleterious impact on the cadre of HCPs being able to achieve the requisite levels of communication, trust and understanding in a multicultural and multifaith society. And this is something from which all members of society might suffer, even those who at some point might be inclined to request MAID.

The argument from capacity

In the context of an opinion piece in which he bemoaned the many bureaucratic and legalistic obstacles placed in the way of physicians who have no religious or conscience-based objections to administering MAID, a Quebec-based physician described his experience of the newly legalised practice.

> MAID is infinitely more than just the act of injecting a medication. Accompanying a person who has requested MAID involves that one accepts to live intensely with the dying person for days, and sometimes for weeks, often in their homes, in a context of emotional and stressful family dynamics, and without adequate resources (Viens, 2018, my trans.).

MAID is not a medical procedure like any other, though the actions that must be performed to administer it can be described in a cold, clinical way. A physician who undertakes to help their patient die is, to use the apt term employed by Dr. Viens, "accompanying" the patient. It is a condition of the death that they provide to their patients being a good one that the physician and the other HCPs involved in it engage in it as fully committed persons, rather than as detached professionals administering a procedure.

Given the personal investment that MAID involves, one that has been reported to cause stress and distress even among the HCPs who agree to carry it out (Beuthin, Bruce and Scaia, 2018), it seems plausible to suppose that those HCPs who think that it is morally wrong, or that it offends against religious obligations that are core to their identities, simply will not be able to carry out the procedure well. They will, to be sure, be able to carry out the physical and technical acts that will lead to a patient's death, but the implication of the quote extracted from Dr. Viens' opinion piece is that there is much more to MAID than a sequence of physically describable actions. There is an emotional and personal investment that is involved in “accompanying”, rather than simply administering, that is a condition of an HCP actually providing their patient with the kind of death that they are asking for when they make the request for MAID.

It is hard to imagine that an HCP who feels that MAID is morally wrong, or who believes that in performing it they are violating their personal identity, will be capable of performing the procedure in the right way. The kind of personal investment that physicians have to be willing to make with regard to their dying patients may simply be beyond the reach of those who oppose it as a matter of morality, identity or personal integrity.

Now opponents of accommodation tend to view the unwillingness of some HCPs to carry out MAID as a matter of professional misconduct, to be dealt with through the relevant professional order’s disciplinary mechanisms. Thus, Savulescu and Schuklenk, while acknowledging that “there might be risks in requiring people to provide services they don’t want to provide”, in that those who find themselves in this situation might provide the service “half-heartedly, possibly to the detriment of patient care”, conclude that “doctors who did behave like this would be acting with a gross lack of professionalism and would therefore be subject to censure and appropriate remedies by their professional, statutory bodies” (Savulescu and Schuklenk, 2017: 163–164).

I believe that Savulescu and Schuklenk are making a category error here. Disciplining of the kind that they recommend makes sense when one fails to do something that one had it in one’s power to do. Ought, as Kant maintained, implies can. If I am right about the fact that the kind of accompaniment that is involved in administering MAID well involves a certain emotional tonality and engagement (rather than simply the competent administering of a lethal substance), and if I am right that that engagement may not be available to those who feel that they are committing a grievous wrong in taking part in it, it follows that it is not the case that objecting physicians choose not to carry out MAID in the right way, but that they cannot. And it seems inappropriate to turn a question of incapacity into a disciplinary matter.

More than this, it is not implausible to claim that we would not want HCPs who object to the practice of MAID being forced to administer it, because, though they cannot help it, they are likely to do it badly. It might prove impossible for them, given the kind of personal investment that MAID involves, to do it well, that is, to do it in a manner that does not risk betraying to the patient that the physician thinks that what they are asking for is wrong.

Now, this returns us to the previous point. If religious or conscience-motivated physicians are unable to carry out a procedure that is prescribed by law, then perhaps they should not be practising medicine at all, or at the very least, maybe they should not be practising in specialties that might place them in a position in which they might be asked to carry out MAID. With respect to the prospect of barring potential dissenters from the practice of medicine entirely, I have already suggested reasons for which I think this might be a bad idea. As far as immunising them from the kinds of specialties in which they might be most likely to encounter requests for MAID is concerned, there may be other ways of achieving accommodation that do not involve making specialties in which cultural competence is most needed, like family medicine and general practice, less diverse in their composition than they might otherwise be. Wayne Sumner has in a forthcoming article argued, for example, that as the practice of medicine moves to ever greater degrees, at least in a country like Canada, to medical teams, as opposed to individual practitioners, physicians with objections to MAID might be immunised from requests by having them be addressed to the team as a whole, rather than to individual physicians (Sumner, forthcoming). Accommodations such as this might allow us to achieve both the important goal of ensuring that patients have access to a service to which they have a right *and* that of ensuring that the enforcement of this right does not have the collateral effect of reducing the otherwise desirable ethno-cultural and religious diversity of the health care professions.

Conclusion

I have argued in this chapter for three claims. As jurisdictions that have legalised MAID, or that have started down a path that might lead to legalisation, start thinking about different regimes that might be put in place in order to regulate the practice, there are at least some considerations that militate in favour of accommodating dissenting physicians and other HCPs, not necessarily as a matter of right, but as a matter of what is consequentially optimal. First, legislators seeking to create support for changes in the law might consider grandfather clauses (that are moreover independently morally justifiable) in order to soften what might in some societies be at least initial opposition of powerful HCP groups. Second, as support and opposition for MAID may vary along ethno-cultural and religious grounds, legitimate medical objectives to do with communication, trust and understanding may militate for at the very least monitoring the impact of screening for conscientious objection on the overall ethno-cultural and religious composition of the cadre of HCPs that will be called upon to serve a diverse modern society. And third, those HCPs who have religiously motivated objections to MAID may experience their opposition to the procedure as an incapacity rather than an unwillingness. To the extent that we think it is a good thing for the health care professions to be marked by a certain level of diversity, it might be worth thinking about ways to accommodate such HCPs, rather than about ways to discipline them.

Of course, there are also costs to accommodation that must be considered in an overall consequentialist reckoning. Opponents to accommodation have rightly pointed to, for example, the fact that if too many HCPs take up such accommodations, there may, especially in remote rural areas, be a problem of supply of HCPs willing to provide the service. There may also be deleterious impacts on the workloads of those who do carry out the procedure. As for all consequentialist reasoning, numbers matter here. We want to avoid excess disciplining, that is, disciplining that is above and beyond what is needed to secure adequate supply of the procedure, but we also quite clearly need to avoid insufficient supply. The limited point that I want to make in this chapter is that consequentialist considerations do not all point in one direction. As in most cases of complex institutional design, those who set about constructing institutional mechanisms through which the practice of MAID will be governed will have to face conflicting consequentialist desiderata.

Notes

1 I borrow the term "conscience absolutism" from Wicclair, 2019.
2 Bouthillier and Opatrny (2019) have shown that many physicians who have availed themselves of the right to exempt themselves from the obligation to administer MAID have not done so on the basis of well-articulated reasons.
3 Somewhat surprisingly, Schuklenk and Smalling (2016: 239) do think that accommodation should be sought for those conscientious objectors "who have practiced for a long term under a different kind of contract than doctors who join the profession after particular significant changes to the scope of practice have been made". While I agree with this claim, it is surprising to find it at the end of a section of their paper in which the claim according to which those who choose to join a health care profession should simply accept fast-paced change is made.

Bibliography

Beaudry, J.-S. 2018. "The Way Forward For Medical Aid in Dying: Protecting Deliberative Autonomy Is Not Enough." *Supreme Court Law Review* 2 (85): 335–385.

Beuthin, R., Bruce, A. and Scaia, M. 2018. "Medical Assistance in Dying: Canadian Nurses' Experience." *Nursing Forum* 53 (4): 511–520.

Bouthillier, M.-E. and Opatrny, L. 2019. "A Qualitative Study of Physicians' Conscientious Objections to Medical Aid in Dying." *Palliative Medicine* 33 (9): 1212–1220.

Expert Panel Working Group on Advanced Requests for MAID. 2018. *The State of Knowledge on Advance Requests for Medical Assistance in Dying*. Ottawa: Council of Canadian Academies.

Fadiman, A. 1997. *The Spirit Catches You and You Fall Down*. New York: Noonday Press.

Falconer, J. et al. 2019. "Perceptions and Intentions Toward Medical Assistance in Dying Among Canadian Medical Students." *BMC Medical Ethics* 20: 22.

Gille, F., Smith, S. and Mays, N. 2015. "Why Public Trust in Health Care Systems Matters and Deserves Greater Attention." *Journal of Health Services Research and Policy* 20 (1): 62–64.

Gilson, L. 2003. "Trust and the Development of Health Care as a Social Institution." *Social Science and Medicine* 56 (7): 1453–1468.

Gosseries, A. and Hungerbühler, M. 2006. "Rule Change and Intergenerational Justice." Pp. 106–128 in Tremmel, J. and Elgar, E. (eds.) *Handbook of Intergenerational Justice*. Cheltenham: Edward Elgar.

Greenawalt, K. 2016. *Exemptions: Necessary, Justified, or Misguided*. Oxford: Oxford University Press.

Kramer, M., Simmonds, N. and Steiner, H. 2000. *A Debate Over Rights: Philosophical Enquiries*. Oxford: Oxford University Press.

Leman, C. 1980. "How To Get There From Here: The Grandfather Effect and Public Policy." *Policy Analysis* 6 (1): 99–116.

Maclure, J. 2016. "Conscience, Religion, and Exemptions: An Egalitarian View." Pp. 9–20 in Vallier, K. (ed.) *Religious Exemptions*. Oxford: Oxford University Press.

Maclure, J. and Dumont, I. 2017. "Selling Conscience Short: A Response to Schuklenk and Smalling on Conscientious Objections by Medical Professionals." *Journal of Medical Ethics* 43 (4): 241–244.

Parfit, D. 1986. *Reasons and Persons*. Oxford: Oxford University Press.

Partida, Y. 2007. "Language Barriers and the Patient Encounter." *American Medical Association Journal of Ethics* 9 (8): 566–571.

Savulescu, J. and Schuklenk, U. 2017. "Doctors Have No Right To Refuse Medical Assistance In Dying, Abortion Or Contraception." *Bioethics* 31 (3): 162–170.

Schuklenk, U. 2019. "Conscience-Based Refusal of Patient Care in Medicine: A Consequentialist Analysis." *Theoretical Medicine and Bioethics* 40: 523–538.

Schuklenk, U. et al. 2011. *End-of-Life Decision Making*. Ottawa: Royal Society of Canada Expert Panel on End-of-Life Care.

Schuklenk, U. and Smalling, R. 2016. "Why Medical Professionals Have No Moral Claim to Conscientious Objection Accommodation in Liberal Democracies." *Journal of Medical Ethics* 43 (4): 234–240.

Shapiro, I. 1986. *The Evolution of Rights in Liberal Theory*. Cambridge: Cambridge University Press.

Stahl, R.Y. and Emanuel, E.J. 2017. "Not Conscripts — Conscientious Objection in Health Care." *New England Journal of Medicine* 376 (14): 1380–1385.

Sumner, L.W. forthcoming. "Conscientious Refusal to Provide Medically-Assisted Dying." *University of Toronto Law Journal*.

Viens, P. 2018. "L'objection de conscience, vraiment?" *La Presse*. Retrieved on 5 January 2021. https://plus.lapresse.ca/screens/54739b58-d9d1-44ed-8a4f-b0a3925c6b70%7C_0.html?utm_medium=Ulink&utm_campaign=Internal%20Share&utm_content=Screen&fbclid=IwAR1gF9SKOy3q-yE83-eodw5WYYU9BfiDQ1QekvDos3ebg7q7vDd90ZjzANw.

Waibel, S. 2018. "The Influence of Patient-Clinician Ethnocultural and Language Concordance on Continuity and Quality of Care: A Cross-Sectional Analysis." *CMAJ Open* 6 (3): E276–E284.

Weinstock, D. 2014. "Conscientious Refusal and Health Professionals: Does Religion Make a Difference?" *Bioethics* 28 (1): 8–15.

Wicclair, M. 2011. *Conscientious Objection in Health Care*. Cambridge: Cambridge University Press.

Wicclair, M. 2019. "Preventing Conscientious Objection in Medicine From Running Amok: A Defense of Reasonable Accommodation." *Theoretical Medicine and Bioethics* 40 (6): 539–564.

Part II

Spaces of contestation

4 Freedom of conscience in private companies

An economic or a political problem?

Vincent Valentin

The traditional field for conscientious objection is not in a company or in the workplace but more in the area of the handling of weapons and military action. However slight or marginal the legal reality of conscientious objection in the workplace may currently be, it can be considered that the elements of a future debate of a social, legal and political nature are present in France but also, on a broader scale, in all liberal democracies.

Religious conflicts in companies are increasing, thus presenting many businesses with problems.[1] Whether it is the refusal to perform certain tasks, requests for specific needs concerning the organisation of work or the timing of vacations, to be accommodated or the general attitude of the employee (regarding clothing or gender relations), managers of companies are now facing new types of demands from their employees, which can be linked to the expression of freedom of conscience. At the same time, there is increasing support for the idea that the requirements of religious neutrality that were traditionally imposed on public persons by the French constitutional principle of *laïcité* (secularism) could be extended to private persons. Several companies are thus defining themselves as secular and claiming that they can therefore legitimately impose religious neutrality on their personnel. Bills to this effect have been tabled in France, and some companies are indeed adopting "charters of secularism".[2] Finally, several legislative developments are converging to make the regulation of religious matters in companies a matter of debate. The first development involves finding the balance between freedom of conscience and the freedom to conduct a business, which was destabilised by cases in which female employees were dismissed for wearing the Muslim headscarf, in particular those cases brought before the Court of Justice of the European Union, which handed down two widely publicised judgements in 2017.[3] The second is the recognition of corporations as subjects with fundamental rights (Carpano, 2018: 225; Milano, 2016). This has become a normative resource that allows companies to oppose the legislator, the administration, competitors and their own employees.

Fundamental economic rights are being mobilised against the fundamental rights recognised for employees – as in the *Achbita* case, where the policy of neutrality is justified by the right to conduct business and allows something that is otherwise "prohibited", namely (indirect) discrimination, to be justified by a purely economic objective. In the United States, the *Hobby Lobby* case, which is of a slightly different nature, represents part of the same movement. It illustrates how a company whose purpose is strictly commercial can nevertheless raise a kind of conscientious objection against a legislative provision that gives its employees certain (social) rights.[4]

This development raises the theoretical and practical difficulties that are described and analysed in this book. Not only is the business world being won over by a movement to challenge the law in the name of religion, but the question arises as to whether the solution should be provided by the law or by internal arrangements within a company, with the latter becoming an actor in the challenge. This issue of neutrality arises both for the State in its attitude towards the private sphere and for the employer and employees in their mutual relations.

All these elements point to the possibility of a "Conscience War" (Rosenfeld and Mancini, 2018) being waged in companies. These points certainly deserve our attention not only because of the importance of the political and religious issues they raise, but also because they further modify the very foundations of labour law. Indeed, it is no longer just a matter of regulating the relationship between the economic needs of the company and the rights of employees, but of accompanying a conflict between the freedom of conscience of the employer and that of the employee. This new situation has repercussions not only on the guaranteeing of freedom but also on the principle of non-discrimination. We need to first identify and describe it, as the stakes seem so high, before considering possible ways of easing the religious tensions in the workplace.

A conscience war in private companies?

A private company is therefore no longer merely a place where goods and services are produced, in which the law governs labour relations in such a way as to protect the interests of companies and the rights of employees. In addition, it tends to be the scene of a clash between moral and religious conceptions, which are, if not antagonistic, at the very least divergent. Neither the freedom of the employer and economic necessity on the one hand, nor trade union rights and freedoms or the principle of non-discrimination on the other are sufficient to encompass this new battlefield. In order to gauge this potentially conflicting new configuration, it is probably most appropriate to describe the different actors involved because the main disputes ultimately arise as a result of the definition of a moral agent in the world of work being extended.

Employees are the first moral agents in a company. They are granted two weapons that they can use to counter their employer's demands, that is, freedom of conscience and non-discrimination. The negative protection available to them against discrimination in recruitment or dismissal and in the exercise of their profession can also be considered as facilitating requests for an accommodation to be made in their working arrangements. It can therefore be considered that the law guarantees not only the protection of the employees' internal forum but also the possibility to a certain extent of exercising their freedom of conscience.

When dealing with their employees, companies are gradually also being recognised as moral agents. On the one hand, the status of a legal person with the same rights as a natural person has been extended to companies; on the other hand, the designation "faith-based company" is becoming so flexible that it is debatable whether any company will soon be able to derogate from ordinary legislation in order to declare a form of moral commitment. Indeed, this concept has spread to profit-making commercial companies (such as *Hobby Lobby*), and to activities that are disconnected from any political, moral or religious purpose (Christians, 2018; Delgrange, 2018). It is now sufficient to link it to an ethos, "based on religion or belief", such as a hospital run by a religious order, or to a management technique that is linked to a form of belief or spirituality (such as yoga and mindfulness meditation), or even to a corporate culture. Finally, the trend may also involve an organisational principle, for example through the affirmation of the company's neutrality in its internal regulations.

It can be assumed that clients will also become actors in a conscience war in the world of work. Indeed, from the very moment an employer is authorised to limit the expression of the religious choices of its employees in the name of the assumed or clearly stated expectations of its clientele, the latter becomes the source of conscientious objection in economic contexts. This possibility has been formerly recognised in the case of clothing stores with regard to saleswomen who come into direct contact with customers and whose behaviour or appearance can be expected not to interfere with the commercial relationship.[5] It was revitalised by the *Achbita* and *Bougnaoui* cases, in which the refusal by a customer to "deal" with a (headscarf-wearing) employee is indirectly accepted but seems poorly justified. In the *Achbita* case, it is agreed that the company's brand image is incompatible with the appearance of a headscarf-wearing switchboard operator (a receptionist); in the *Bougnaoui* case, it is indirectly agreed that the client company of an IT company may require that the service engineer does not wear a headscarf during their collaboration (more specifically, the internal regulations may provide for a prohibition on wearing a religious symbol when in contact with customers. But this rule only exists to meet an assumed or anticipated customer request). In each case, it can be considered that it is indeed a question of admitting that the client (a natural or legal person) can assert their own moral, religious or aesthetic conceptions, without having to justify them, against the freedom of conscience of a commercial enterprise.

The final actor is the employee, who is not directly concerned by a limitation of their right to display their convictions, against another employee, a colleague or someone belonging to another company. We are also in the field of hypothesis or conjecture, but the question is in fact raised by the way jurisprudence has evolved. The recognition by the European Court of Human Rights of the extension of the right to privacy in professional and commercial activities provides a basis for the affirmation of the rights of conscience in companies that extend beyond service obligations.[6] While the principle set out in this judgement has not yet generated all its potential effects, it can already be considered as a powerful lever for recognising the rights that employees have not to be subjected to violations of their private lives at work, for example by the obligation to act in a way that offends their conscience or the fundamental choices they make in their private lives.

It can be assumed that an employee may refuse to cooperate with a person whose beliefs or behaviour deeply offend them. It is therefore conceivable that on this basis, in conjunction with freedom of conscience, an employee may refuse to shake hands with a woman but also that another employee may refuse to shake hands with someone who refuses to shake a woman's hand. The *Bougnaoui* case could be linked to this hypothesis, with employees of the service provider's client company refusing to work with a woman whose headscarf would for them be a sign of a religion or a political agenda that they reject. So, the right to privacy within a company could allow me to claim that my convictions prevented me from working with people who follow an antagonistic belief.

The workplace thus seems to have been overrun by a kind of politicisation or "conscientisation", regulated by floating rules that enable it as much (or as little) as they regulate it.[7] This destabilises life within companies and marks a lack of control over the rules that should both allow and limit freedom of conscience at work. It is therefore a question of the legal security of employees and companies, of course, of the risks of discrimination or of the infringement of freedom, and more generally of the fair relationship that freedom of conscience, economic freedom and the common good can maintain in a liberal democracy. It may therefore be necessary to reflect on possible responses to this dual practical and theoretical problem.

Is there a good means of reconciliation?

The solutions outlined here are intended to respect the principle of neutrality of the law with regard to religious or moral convictions. While this principle absolutely protects everyone from direct discrimination by the State, it does not exclude the possibility of indirect discrimination, or of an infringement of freedom of conscience, in the field of social relations.

To be neutral, the State must, to an extent that is admittedly difficult to define, accept a degree of non-neutrality on the part of private persons, insofar as the expression of their free conscience may run counter to the religious, moral, philosophical or political choices of others. It is true that contemporary legislation, driven by the principle of non-classification, tends to support the agenda of a civil society which, like the public authorities, should itself be neutral. It seems to us that this prospect of unlimited extension of the "non-discriminatory" criterion from the public to the private sphere is not self-evident. As Hannah Arendt argued in an article that is certainly highly contested, we may consider that a degree of segregation is a constituent of any individual life and any social order, and that it would be an unbearable attack on human nature to prevent everyone from expressing the discriminatory dimension of any subjectivity (Arendt, 1959). We refer to this text by Arendt only to indicate the spirit of the following proposals. The framework of the conscience war in private companies first requires that the existence and the legitimacy of moral conflict and its social expression be acknowledged.

If we accept this, then three ways of regulating the given religious and moral situation in a company are emerging. The first is to make employers' economic justifications more flexible in order to absorb the religious and moral issue into the dynamics of entrepreneurial freedom (and the market). The second pleads for the recognition of secularism-based (as opposed to faith-based) companies. The third argues for the possibility of a company operating on a secular basis. Though based on different philosophies, these three approaches would make it possible to confront the current situation, where an ordinary company cannot counter employees' demands without committing discrimination (is not sufficient to justify their rejection on the grounds of proper functioning or of the activity to be performed) even when these demands create serious problems.

Relaxing the accepted economic justifications

A first way to legally resolve the issue of religious demands in a company would be to submit them to an economic logic.

Although it is not exactly how the CJEU acted in this case, it is arguably the path that was opened up by the *Achbita* case: The ban on wearing the headscarf is justified by a customer request, and therefore by the need to adapt to the request in order not to lose business. In the end, it is not the employee's requirement of neutrality for herself that is legitimate, but the requirement of conduct in the company's interest – and this takes precedence over indirect discrimination or the restriction of religious freedom. The request not to wear religious symbols in front of customers is an "essential and determining professional requirement" based on the right to operate a business, a fundamental right of the legal person that is the company.

The conscience war has shifted to another field, that of profit. A company is a neutral place, where no one has the opportunity to assert their faith in order to escape from economic logic. In a way, the fact that religion is subsumed by economic factors means that a kind of secularism is practised. In other words, a company operates in ignorance of religion. It is only indirectly, or secondarily, that a company encounters religion, namely when the latter wishes to exist within the company. Religion is not contested when it remains outside the interests of the company.

However, this interest may turn against religious freedom, as in the *Achbita* case, or against any right that may be challenged by customers' preferences. Indeed, what obstacle could impede the recognition by a supplier of prejudices or discriminatory principles of demand, when seen from a perspective that is supported only by economic logic? What would prevent the restitution of the "separate but equal" doctrine established by the United States Supreme Court in 1896 (*Plessy v. Fergusson*),[8] by defending the lawfulness of companies' expression of consumers' discriminatory expectations and values? Similarly, on a different note, would *Achbita* not echo the far-distant *Lochner* judgement[9] by placing the primacy of freedom of contract above any other consideration, in particular with regard to an objective fundamental right?

The relaxation of economic justifications is in contradiction with the requirement of fundamental rights and the principle of non-discrimination cannot be circumvented by the need to adapt to the discriminatory prejudices of customers. In this case, the employer would no longer be neutral but would be an actor in the discrimination. And yet, conversely, the idea that the company should be taking an active part for the implementation of fundamental rights can only have a very thin legal basis (Wolmark, 2009). In support of this solution, it could also be argued that the employee's religious freedom remains protected by the need for the employer, on the one hand to declare an objective disorder (even if it is extended at the risk of losing a customer) and, on the other hand, to incorporate in the company's internal regulations the principle of possible restrictions on the expression of religious freedom. Thus, the employee is not discriminated against during the recruitment process and remains protected from any invasion of their privacy.

Finally, therefore, the choice of this solution is confronted with the possibility of limiting the expression of an objective fundamental right by opening it up to the subjectivity of market players, who are by definition free and arbitrary. While this constitutes a purely liberal/libertarian logic, it does not fully satisfy the framework of an entitlement to guarantee certain values and rights.

Operating a secularism-based company

Another possibility is to allow the company to channel the religious demands of its employees or customers no longer through the economic needs of its development, but through the affirmation of its own axiological identity. If such a possibility has already been recognised for companies with links to a substantial religion or philosophy that forms the basis of their activities or permeates their operations, the point here is to consider whether this scheme could be extended to companies who would choose to claim that their particular identity is secular rather than faith-based (Valentin, 2017; Gaudu, 2011: 1186).

Two objections are generally made to the hypothesis of operating a secular company. The first emphasises that secularism is not a conviction but a principle that involves the coexistence of convictions and is not a trend but the absence of a trend. In a way, it would have no other content than to arrange respect for religious choices. It would be a rule but not a philosophy of life. Strictly speaking, a secular company would then have no real purpose (Mouly, 2014: 65).

The second objection is based on the idea that secularism is a rule that applies only to the organisation of the State in its relationship with religions and that it cannot be transposed into the private sphere or into civil society without being totally distorted. Secularism would therefore only exist within the context of the State, as the National Consultative Commission on Human Rights has observed.[10]

These two objections seem rather unconvincing, insofar as they limit the scope of secularism to its implementation in institutions. While the secular nature of the State cannot as such be extended to private persons (this would not make sense and would even negate the distinction between the private and public spheres on which it is itself based), there is nothing to prevent private persons from freely appropriating the concept in order to organise themselves according to a chosen model. Thus the idea that secularism is an unsubstantial rule cannot hold water. The rule separating politics and religion contains a philosophy of separation, which is a philosophy of life in society that offers a model for relationships with others.

As Gwénaëlle Calvès has it, secularism can be considered as "a philosophy of silence on religion" (2013), one that is thus perfectly applicable to a private structure (an association, a company, a club and so on). The idea that social life benefits from neutralising antagonisms and conflicts related to religious issues is indeed a personal belief on the one hand, yet it can be the operating principle of a private group on the other.

However, one practical difficulty remains: What would the constitutive activity of a secular enterprise consist of? Indeed, if we accept secularism in principle, we may be perplexed by the ambiguity inherent in its implementation: Should a secular enterprise be closed or open to the expression of religions? Should it accept or refuse all accommodations? How will the display of their own secular conviction allow the employer to rigorously supervise the expression of their employees' beliefs? Moreover, what would the company's secular activity consist of? The category of faith-based company was created to grant a derogation to companies whose raison d'être, whose very activity involves the service of a conviction, which is offered as a good or a service. How could we define a company that "sold" secularism?

The Baby-Loup crèche, whose application to call itself an "*entreprise de tendance*" was refused by the French Cour de cassation, provides us with a good example that highlights this difficulty. The Court's refusal was based on the argument that the purpose of the crèche was not secularism but childcare, which in itself is neutral regarding any trends. We might consider the findings of the Court on the one hand as being a little insubstantial and as being harried by conventional law on the other. While it is true that initially the designation "trend enterprise" originated from the need to grant a derogation to religious bodies and that it was a category reserved for companies directly serving a moral or spiritual truth, it is gradually being interpreted in a much broader way. For instance, a denominational hospital was recently recognised as a faith-based company, although its activities themselves are far removed from any conviction (Christians, 2018; Delgrange, 2018).

The Baby-Loup crèche could therefore have been described as based on a "belief" – as supported by its lawyers. Indeed, its internal regulations did include a rule prescribing that "the principle of freedom of conscience and religion of each member of staff must not interfere with the principles of secularism and neutrality which apply in the exercise of all the activities developed by Baby Loup". The crèche's claim that its identity was not merely business-oriented but also socially and politically motivated is perfectly admissible intellectually. It submitted that the activity of childcare was performed with the aim of transcending community and religious tensions. Unlike the *Hobby Lobby* company, which was allowed to derogate from federal law in the name of religious values unrelated to a purely commercial activity as a result of the recognition of freedom of conscience for a legal person, the Baby-Loup crèche was able to highlight that the choice of secularism permeated its childcare activity, in the way it took care of children and welcomed parents in order to overcome a particular territorial and socio-economic situation that was very much marked by cultural and religious diversity.

Moreover, nothing conceptually prevents anyone from being opposed to what is valid for a religious belief yet is not valid for a conviction of another nature, but which expresses a substantial and real axiological choice, such as that of secularism, that is, a conception of human relations that is free from religion. To refuse to accept this would establish a discrimination that is difficult to justify between philosophical and religious beliefs (and we are not convinced by the idea that religious choice runs deeper and is more important for human beings).

The legal movement referred to earlier in this chapter is therefore calling for the recognition of the designation "faith-based company", but with an indeterminate link between the activity and this conviction. The European Court of Justice has opened the door by accepting as a criterion of conviction not only the activity but also the ethos of the company (that is, based on religion) (Christians, 2018; Delgrange, 2018). The French Constitutional Council, by defining secularism as a guaranteed "right and freedom", is authorising a subjectification that allows appropriation by individuals and natural or legal persons.[11]

As the law stands, even if it becomes more flexible, the activity must be commercial and secular – which is difficult to determine in substance and to implement in practice (that is, prohibiting or accepting religion). Another problem with the extension of the concept of a trend-oriented company is the protection of employee rights. Traditionally, this concept has made it possible to limit an individual's rights, in particular through an obligation of loyalty, which can extend to private and family life well beyond the professional task to be performed. While it is understood that the activity itself may require it, it seems that the infringement of the employee's freedom is excessive as long as the choice of trend does not permeate the good or service offered. It is therefore necessary to consider another approach, which is intellectually bolder but less restrictive of employee rights: the possibility of designating a company as secular by assuming that this has no link with its business activity.

A company that operates as a secular organisation

The aim here is to outline a hypothetical situation, which is scarcely supported by French law.[12] The company could make a political choice, disconnected from its activities, and concerning only the way its operations are organised. The manifestation of employees' convictions would be regulated by how the employer conceives the correct relationships within the company, without having to justify it other than by their own will. The novelty would be that the justification would not be linked to economic reasons (market demand) or to the nature of the activity. To highlight the originality of this approach, we might speak of a "company policy".

Before going any further, it should be noted that this solution to the religious problem may be supported by very different political sensitivities. Alain Supiot, with a view to extending employee rights, defends this possibility in the name of the idea of a "political community within a company" (Supiot, 2016: 296). We might also consider how very well this fits in with the liberal-libertarian perspective of extending entrepreneurial freedom.

It would be a matter of viewing the secular company in the same way as the secular state, maintaining the same relationship with the religious beliefs of its employees as the state does with its citizens. Freedom of conscience would be perfectly protected, and employees would be free in the internal world, free in private life and outside the company, and restricted only by the "law", that is, by how social relations function within the company. No discrimination would be accepted during recruitment or in the organisation of work since the employer would be required to be oblivious to the religious belief of the employee, who could not use it to obtain any accommodations. Company rules would be required to remain agnostic vis-à-vis religions. Secularism would be understood as neutrality from a perspective that is closer to John Locke than to Roger Williams, the internal regulation being justified by the life of the company taking precedence over the prescriptions of the different religions of the employees.[13] No accommodation would be justified by the mere mention of religious freedom. It is of course conceivable that derogations would be granted to some, particularly with regard to taking holidays, but the religious argument would not be more worthy than an argument on personal grounds relating to family or sporting obligations. In this context, the right to manifest one's religion is overruled by the operational interest of the company. The rules of procedure must be precise in order to avoid discrimination and arbitrary decisions. Restrictions on the expression of a conviction must be clearly explained at the time of recruitment and included in the employment contract.

This organisational model cannot be mandatory or perceived as a logical consequence of secularism. The principle of a secular state does not require the extension of secularism to all private companies. It is therefore not in the name of secularism as traditionally defined as a rule of the State that it would be possible to promote this type of enterprise, but in the name of the freedom to operate a business, correlated with the employer's freedom of conscience. The neutrality imposed by the legislator cannot be imposed on the latter, only proposed.

Such a model would, however, be worth experimenting with because it represents the most balanced response to the affirmation of religion in the world of work. Compared to the first model, which prioritises economic necessity over employee rights, it proposes less arbitrary protection, and is closed to the expression of discriminatory demands by the market. Compared to the second model, it does not subject the employee to any control of their private life outside the company. The main, if not the only, reservation that could be considered, from the point of view of "neutrality", is that in order not to discriminate between different beliefs, this model cannot be reserved for secularism and should be open to other beliefs and values, and should also allow companies to organise themselves according to religious prescriptions (within which non-believing employees could be hired and protected, just as non-believers are in a religious enterprise). Some will find the idea of a society that is divided into different communities, and of a regulation system that is undermined by particular claims, a depressing prospect. However, the solution offered by this chapter does not have such a broad scope. It merely represents an adjustment of existing legislation, or the development of a potentiality that it already contains. The possibility for an entrepreneur to affirm a moral or religious belief as a principle underlying the foundation of their company does not jeopardise most of the guarantees granted to the employee, in the workplace and outside. The risk of discrimination is controlled, and the infringement of freedom of conscience is limited or non-existent. After all, it would only be a matter of agreeing, on the basis of a voluntary commitment, not to manifest one's religion during working hours – which is not incompatible with assuming one's identity of conscience. This is the most neutral solution conceivable in order to resolve a potential conscience war.

The advantage, in addition to finding a solution to the problem posed by religious demands within a company, is that this establishes a new freedom. It would in fact be a question of injecting political freedom into a place driven solely by economic logic. It would be a mistake to reject this freedom, which could benefit the entire working community, not just the employer, because of an absolutist conception of freedom of conscience or the principle of non-discrimination. The proposed relaxation of labour law seems both necessary and desirable.

Notes

1 See, with regard to France, the study by the *Observatoire du fait religieux en entreprise* and the Randstat Institute (http://groperandstat.fr/étude-le-travail-l'entreprise-et-la-question-religieuse/).
2 Paprec is a pioneer in this field, having adopted a "charter of secularism and diversity" in 2014. Retrieved on 23 September 2020, see https://www.paprec.com/fr/groupe/ressources-humaines/charte-laicite-diversite. Since the EL Khomri law of 2016, companies have been able to include the principle of neutrality in their internal regulations.
3 CJEU, 14 March 2017, C-157/15 *Achbita, Centrum voor Gelijkheid van kasen en voor racismebestrijding/G4S Secure Solutions,* et C-188/15 *Bougnaoui et Association de défense des droits de l'homme/Micropole Univers*. Among other comments, see Calvès, 2018; Gonzalez, 2017; Hennette-Vauchez, 2017; Bribosi and Rorive, 2017.
4 US Supreme Court, 30 June 2014, *Burwell, Secretary of Health and Human Services, and al. v. Hobby Lobby Stores, INC.* No. 13–354. See Morri, 2014.
5 C.A. Saint Denis de la réunion, 9 September 1997. This case law was applied again to a saleswoman in the shopping centre "La Défense" who, in contact with a diverse clientele, refused to tie her headscarf into a hat. (CA Paris, 16 March 2001).
6 ECHR, Niemietz, 16 December 1992, 13710/88.
7 It should also be noted that while in France life in public administrations or companies is regulated and simplified by the principle of secularism and therefore the neutrality of public officials, tensions exist around the same problem.
8 *Plessy v. Fergusson*, 163 US, 537 (1896).
9 *Lochner v. New York*, 198 US 45 (1905).
10 See opinion of 26 September 2013, § 25.
11 Decision No. 212-297, QPC, 21 February 2013.

12 Since the so-called El Khomri law of 8 August 2016, the Labour Code has stipulated that "the internal regulations may contain provisions enshrining the principle of neutrality and restricting the expression of employees' convictions if these restrictions are justified by the exercise of other fundamental freedoms and rights or by the requirements of the proper functioning of the company and if they are proportionate to the desired purpose" (art. 1321-2-1).

13 For a contemporary perspective, see Nussbaum, 2012.

Bibliography

Arendt, H. 1959. "Reflections on Little Rock." *Dissent* , winter, 45–56.

Bribosia, E. and Rorive, I. 2017. "Affaires Achbita et Bougnaoui: entre neutralité et préjugés." *Revue trimestrielle des droits de l'homme* 112: 1017–1037.

Calvès, G. 2013. "La chambre sociale de la Cour de cassation face à l'affaire Baby Loup: Trois leçons de droit, et un silence assourdissant". *Respublica*. Retrieved on September 24th, 2020. www.gaucherépublicaine.org/respublica/la-chambre-sociale-de-la-cour-de-cassation-face-à-laffaire-baby-loup-trois-leçons- et-un-silence-assourdissant/6149.

Calvès, G. 2018. "Le critère "religion ou convictions", même sens et même portée à Luxembourg et à Strasbourg?" *Droit Social* 13 (4): 323–329.

Carpano, E. 2018. "La charte, une constitution de la liberté économique des entreprises?" *Revue des Affaires Européennes* 2: 225–240.

Christians, L.-L. 2018. "Les mutations du concept d'entreprise de tendance. Essai de prospective juridique sur les futures entreprises postséculières". Pp. 253–271 in Callebat, B., Courrèges, H. and Parisot, V. (eds.) *Les religions et le droit du travail. regards croisés d'ici et d'ailleurs*. Bruxelles: Bruylant.

Delgrange, X. 2018. "L'entreprise de tendance, c'est tendance!" *Revue Trimestrielle des Droits de l'Homme* 119: 655–686.

Gaudu, F. 2011. "La notion d'entreprise laïque." *Droit Social* 12: 1186–1189.

Gonzalez, G. 2017. "Vade-mecum pour interdire les signes religieux au travail." *Revue de l'Union européenne* 609: 342–347.

Hennette-Vauchez, S. 2017. "Equality and the Market: The Unhappy Fate of Religious Discrimination in Europe." *European Constitutional Law Review* 13: 744–758.

Milano, L. 2016. (ed.) *CEDH et droit de l'entreprise. L'influence des droits de l'homme dans les affaires*. Limal: Anthemis.

Morri, J. 2014. "Une pilule dure à avaler: La Cour suprême des Etats-Unis consacre l'entreprise de tendance à but lucratif." *La revue des droits de l'homme*. Retrieved on September 23rd, 2020. https://journals.openedition.org/revdh/871#quotation.

Mouly, J. 2014. "L'affaire Baby Loup devant la Cour de renvoi: la revanche de la laïcité?" *Recueil Dalloz* 1: 65–71.

Nussbaum, M. 2012. *The New Religious Intolerance: Overcoming the Politics of Fear in an Anxious Age*. Cambridge, MA: Havard University Press.

Rosenfeld, M. and Mancini, S. 2018. *The Conscience War. Rethinking the Balance Between Religion, Identity and Equality*. Cambridge: Cambridge University Press.

Supiot, A. 2016. "Commentaire sur l'avis sur la laïcité." P. 293 in Lazerges, C. (ed.) *Les grands avis de la Commission nationale consultative des droits de l'homme*. Paris: Dalloz.

Valentin, V. 2017. "La notion d'entreprise de conviction laïque." in Callebat, B., Courrèges, H. and Parisot, V. (eds.) *Les religions et le droit du Travail*. Bruxelles: Bruylant.

Wolmark, C. 2009. "L'entreprise n'est pas un établissement scolaire." *Revue de droit du travail* 9, 488.

5 Should conscience clauses in Belgian health care be institutionalised?

Xavier Delgrange and Hélène Lerouxel[1]

In medical cases, the conscience clause is generally understood in its individual dimension. It is the prerogative of the physician and the medical staff (Proeschel, 2016; Leigh, 2018). In Belgium, this clause is included in laws with a strong ethical content, such as the law of 3 April 1990 on the termination of pregnancy, the law of 28 May 2002 on euthanasia and the law of 6 July 2007 on medically assisted reproduction (MAR) (Delgrange and Koussens, 2019).[2] As a result thereof, the Belgian legislator recognises the ethically controversial nature of abortion, euthanasia and medically assisted reproduction. The existence of such legislative clauses did not affect the implementation of a democratic public space. As the product of a political transaction, they were even a tool for the secularisation of Belgian society.

These laws offend Catholic doctrine. As soon as he took office, the new Primate of Belgium, Archbishop Jozef De Kezel, widely regarded as a progressive, declared: "I think we have the right at an institutional level to decide that we do not do it (euthanasia and abortion, ed note). I am thinking, for example, of our hospitals" (Blogie, 2015). In his wake, authors are campaigning for the institutionalisation of the conscience clause, which would allow Catholic institutions (hospitals, rest homes or family planning centres) to refuse to perform acts contrary to their ethos (abortion, euthanasia or assisted reproduction) under their roof (Montero, 2012, 2016).[3] They invoke Resolution 1763 of the Parliamentary Assembly of the Council of Europe adopted in 2010, "The right to conscientious objection in lawful medical care", which begins with these words:

> No person, hospital or institution shall be coerced, held liable or discriminated against in any manner because of a refusal to perform, accommodate, assist or submit to an abortion, the performance of a human miscarriage, or euthanasia or any act which could cause the death of a human foetus or embryo, for any reason.

In order to justify the fact that an institution may refuse to perform an abortion, euthanasia or MAR, and prohibit a physician from performing such acts, these authors must demonstrate that none of these acts constitute a patient's right, nor do they constitute a medical act. Without these characteristics, the disputed act could not be claimed by the patient or protected by the physician's therapeutic freedom.

In Resolution 1763,

> the Parliamentary Assembly stresses the need to affirm the right of conscientious objection together with the responsibility of the state to ensure that patients are able to access lawful medical care in a timely manner. The Assembly is concerned that the unregulated use of conscientious objection may disproportionately affect women, notably those with low incomes or living in rural areas.

Thereupon, "in view of member states' obligation to ensure access to lawful medical care and to protect the right to health", the member states are invited "to develop comprehensive and clear regulations which", among other things, "ensure that patients receive appropriate treatment, in particular in cases of emergency".

In its institutional dimension, the conscience clause is not only a simple incursion of ethics or of specific ethical issues into the law, especially in Belgium where the Catholic Church manages more than 50% of health institutions. In this case, it is also an incursion of religious arguments into the public space. Moving from the individual to the institutional dimension, the conscience clause has to reinvent a balance between a secularised society and religious demands.

The possible recognition of a conscience clause for health institutions therefore requires adjustments in order to guarantee patients' right to receive care such as abortion or euthanasia and to safeguard the therapeutic freedom of physicians.

The characteristics of abortion, euthanasia and MAR

Abortion, euthanasia and MAR are also medical treatments to which patients are entitled if they meet the legal conditions for claiming them to be acts protected by therapeutic freedom.

Abortion, euthanasia and MAR are patients' rights

By its decision *Roe v. Wade* of 22 January 1973, the United States Supreme Court recognises a genuine "right to abortion", based on the right to privacy. The European constitutional courts did not venture onto that ground, because generally in European laws, abortion was only decriminalised and not legalised. European states can be grouped into three categories in their abortion regulations: countries that set a time limit during which the decision belongs only to women; those that adopt "indications" where the decision belongs to third parties (physicians) and those that have very restrictive legislation (Mastor, 2017).[4]

The Belgian law of 3 April 1990 on the termination of pregnancy does not explicitly enshrine the right to abortion. After heated parliamentary debates, the law partially decriminalised abortion, which remained in the Criminal Code. When strict conditions were met, two types of abortion were allowed (Article

350 of the Criminal Code). Until the 12th week of conception, abortion was only possible if the physician noticed that the pregnant woman was in a "state of distress". Beyond that period, only therapeutic abortion was possible:

> The abortion can be performed only when the continued pregnancy severely endangers the health of the woman or when it is certain at the time of diagnosis that the unborn child is suffering from a particularly serious disease that is recognised as incurable.

In both cases, a six-day reflection period was imposed on the pregnant woman after the first consultation.

In 1990, abortion was therefore partially decriminalised. It remained a criminal offence located in the Criminal Code among "crimes against families and against public morality". Abortion was only allowed on the basis of a medical diagnosis. The woman did not have control over her body.[5] The title of the law was clear in that respect; it related to the termination of pregnancy without any reference to the potentially voluntary nature of that act.[6]

The law of 15 October 2018 was a game-changer. It bore the title "voluntary termination of pregnancy and repealed Articles 350 and 351 of the Criminal Code". This meant that a "voluntary" termination was now permitted. The recognition of a genuine right to abortion was clearly expressed in the parliamentary debates. The author of the proposal which was to finally be adopted as a law stated that, with that proposal,

> the right to abortion is becoming a fact, subject to certain conditions. It is necessary … to respect the balance between, on the one hand, the undeniable right of women to dispose of their own bodies and the freedom to decide when to become a mother, and, on the other hand, the ethical dimension.[7]

From then on, and this was the most spectacular step forward, the termination of pregnancy was regulated in an autonomous law, outside the Criminal Code. According to Article 2 thereof, a "pregnant woman may ask a physician to terminate her pregnancy under the conditions (enumerated)". The "criterion of a state of distress" disappeared in favour of the pregnant woman's "determination". The decision to abort is the result of a dialogue between her and her doctor. She expresses her determination and the doctor informs her of the options and of the risks associated with her pregnancy. The woman thus moves from the status of a simple object of care to that of a subject who is an actor in her treatment.

The 2018 law was the result of a compromise between the parties of the governing majority that included parties close to Catholic circles. Since its adoption, the Government has fallen, and elections have been held. Until a new federal government is formed, Parliament is free to find a majority to amend abortion legislation once again. A secular majority in favour of extending the time limits and completely decriminalising abortion, both for women and for doctors, even if the time limits are exceeded, is taking shape. Abortion will be considered exclusively as a medical act, which will strengthen the woman's right to use it. The Bishops of Belgium are highly critical of the fact that abortion will become an ordinary medical act and therefore a woman's right. They fear that it will be much more difficult for the physician to invoke his conscience clause, which was easier when abortion was only (partially) decriminalised (Durré, 2019b).

International law is moving in the same direction. In 2008, the Parliamentary Assembly of the Council of Europe stated that "the ultimate decision on whether or not to have an abortion should be a matter for the woman concerned, who should have the means of exercising this right in an effective way".[8] While the European Court of Human Rights has not yet recognised the right to abortion, the UN Human Rights Committee did so in its Communication *Mellet v. Ireland* of 31 March 2016, where "the Committee considers that the interference in the author's decision as to how best cope with her non-viable pregnancy was unreasonable and arbitrary in violation of Article 17 of the Covenant"[9] which enshrines the right to privacy (Willems and Cohen, 2017).

The Belgian parliamentary discussions on euthanasia which led to the law of 28 May 2002 focused on the right to self-determination (Leleu and Genicot, 2004). However, Members of Parliament agreed that the law would not enshrine a right to euthanasia. The chairman of the Justice Committee of the House of Representatives said that the draft law

> does not grant the patient any subjective right to humane killing: the patient may make a request for euthanasia, but the physician is not obliged to grant the request. The request does not create any contractual relationship between the physician and the patient.[10]

The Belgian Advisory Committee on Bioethics was also unanimous in 2014, stating that

> the law does not create a right to euthanasia and, in general, the patient cannot compel the physician to perform acts which are not medically appropriate in his or her case (therapeutic freedom), or are inconsistent with the physician's personal convictions in the case of actions with significant ethical implications.[11]

However, perceptions changed with the law of 28 February 2014, which extended euthanasia to minors. Several members of the Belgian Senate alluded to the extension of the "right to euthanasia", while others were highly critical of this expression and accused those who proposed the bill of wanting to enshrine this right.[12]

The Constitutional Court ended the debate with its judgement dismissing the appeal against the law of 28 February 2014:

> The contested law is based on the right balance between, on the one hand, the right to end his life in order to avoid an undignified and arduous end of life, which stems from the right to respect for private life, and, on the other hand,

> the right to measures aimed at preventing abuse in the practice of euthanasia, which is derived from the right to life and physical integrity[13] (Bioy, 2016: 775–800; Pâques, 2019: 22–23).

The Constitutional Court relies on the European Court of Human Rights, which stated in its judgement of 20 January 2011, *Haas v. Switzerland*,

> that an individual's right to decide by what means and at what point his or her life will end, provided he or she is capable of freely reaching a decision on this question and acting in consequence, is one of the aspects of the right to respect for private life within the meaning of Article 8 of the Convention.[14] (Genicot, 2019)

However, the Court recognises "that the States enjoy a considerable margin of appreciation" in the end-of-live regulation and may impose procedural conditions. In this case, Switzerland may require that the supply of lethal substances be subject to a medical prescription.

In 2007, Belgium adopted a law regulating MAR (Genicot, 2009). In the parliamentary discussions, the question of the right to have a child was raised, but it was the medical problem of infertility that was the subject of debate. The law does not enshrine a right to have a child or even a right to MAR. It simply imposes on applicants certain obligations of transparency and monitoring.

However, shortly after the law of 2007, the European Court of Human Rights ruled "that the right of a couple to conceive a child and to make use of medically assisted procreation for that purpose is also protected by Article 8, as such a choice is an expression of private and family life".[15]

Abortion, euthanasia and MAR are medical acts protected by therapeutic freedom

According to some of the legal literature, euthanasia is not a medical act, since such an act must have a therapeutic purpose, which seeks to improve the quality of life (Montero, 2016: 3–4).

It is true that the Belgian legislation was not free from ambiguities. According to the law on the practice of health care professions, "the healing art covers the medical art, including the art of dentistry, practised on human beings, and the pharmaceutical art, in the form of preventive or experimental, curative, continuous and palliative care".[16] It is difficult to argue that, from the point of view of the moribund or the embryo, abortion or euthanasia is part of the healing art. In 2002, two related laws were adopted. The first, of 28 May 2002, was on euthanasia, and the second, of 14 June 2002, concerned palliative care. The latter modified the definition of the healing art to include palliative care. The first law failed to extend the definition of the art of healing, which therefore does not include euthanasia.

However, the ambiguity was removed by the law of 22 April 2019 on the quality of health care practice, which defines health care as "services provided by a healthcare professional in order to promote, determine, preserve, restore or improve a patient's state of health, to change his body appearance for aesthetic purposes or to accompany it at the end of his life".[17]

Under what conditions could the conscience clause be institutionalised?

If, under Belgian law, the conscience clause is designed in accordance with individual logic, some elements already give it an institutional dimension. The figure of the ethos-oriented enterprise could help to strengthen institutional freedom in this area. However, the enterprise's freedom should be balanced against the patient's right to abortion or euthanasia and the physician's therapeutic freedom.

The conscience clause, personal with institutional elements

The conscience clause is implemented by means of an accreditation system: If the institution does not apply for accreditation, it does not obtain the right to perform the act that is disapproved of. The question of the implementation is for hospitals in relation to abortion and euthanasia and for nursing homes in relation to euthanasia.

In relation to abortion, only the individual stance of the medical personnel is taken into account by law. The conscience clause is regulated. The physician consulted must inform the person concerned during the first visit that he or she refuses to conduct an abortion. Since the law of 15 October 2018 came into force, they have also had to give "the contact details of another physician, a pregnancy termination centre and/or a hospital service", by forwarding the medical file. However, they are not required to ensure that the colleague informed actually takes care of the patient.

In addition to the individual clause, Belgian legislation allows family planning centres to decide whether or not to conduct an abortion. In the Walloon Region, for example, the legislation distinguishes between compulsory activities, such as medical, psychological, legal and social consultations, and voluntary activities, such as abortion.[18] However, any family planning centre must guarantee access to abortion: "No request or distress can be left unanswered by a family planning centre". If the centre does not conduct an abortion itself, it will direct the patient, or even accompany them, to a centre or other facility that performs abortions. If a family planning centre decides to carry out abortions, it must obtain specific accreditation. The centres receive an additional subsidy. Out of the 71 centres accredited by the Walloon Region, 15 are authorised to conduct abortions.[19] Family planning centres therefore already benefit from an institutional conscience clause.

In the case of MAR, the conscience clause is not available to physicians, but only to "fertility centres": "Fertility centres shall be the most transparent about their options as regards accessibility to treatment; they are free to invoke the conscience clause in relation to applications addressed to them".[20]

This legislative provision originates from an Opinion of the Belgian Advisory Committee on Bioethics. While the members of the Committee were divided into three groups with regard to general ethical options, they unanimously recommended recognising that the centres had

> the right to refuse to contribute to situations which they consider to be too problematic. They considered that the medical teams should be recognised as being free to decide whether to treat people (whether by donating their gametes or another indication of assisted reproduction) when they consider that the risk to the child of being confronted with major difficulties is excessive.

Therefore, it seemed "necessary that the medical teams which carry out assisted reproduction retain the freedom to refuse it to persons who do not seem to be likely to ensure the proper development of the child".[21]

If the conscience clause is not conceived here in its individual dimension, it is clearly because MAR is always conducted in a team, within the "fertility centres".[22] A hospital may decide to set up a "fertility centre", which will be able to choose which type of "reproductive medicine"[23] it will practice (Schiffino, 2017: 18–20).

In the area of euthanasia, the conscience clause is individual and is regulated in the same way as that applicable to abortion:

> If the physician consulted refuses to perform euthanasia, he or she must inform the patient in good time, stating the reasons for doing so. If the refusal is justified by a medical reason, this is recorded in the patient's medical file. A physician who refuses euthanasia shall, at the request of the patient, be required to communicate the patient's medical file to the doctor appointed by the patient.[24]

Should an institutional conscience clause be enshrined alongside the individual conscience clause, currently the only one recognised in law? This issue is controversial (Van Assche, 2016-2017). The Belgian Advisory Committee on Bioethics has been unable to reach a unanimous decision. Those who opposed the institutional conscience clause relied on the MAR law, stating "where the legislators intend to give a health institution the right to invoke the 'conscience clause', they do so expressly".[25] Those who were in favour of this clause relied on ethical considerations.[26]

Since euthanasia does not require any particular infrastructure, the legislator did not have to deal explicitly with this issue by setting out the conditions for the accreditation of hospitals or rest homes.

However, most Catholic hospitals and rest homes impose a "palliative filter" procedure on patients who request euthanasia. The decision to perform or not to perform euthanasia is not made by the doctor alone but by an interdisciplinary team. This team assesses whether, in the case in question, palliative care is an acceptable alternative to euthanasia[27] (Van Assche, 2016-2017: 344–345). Some Catholic rest homes do not permit euthanasia in their establishments.[28]

An ethos-oriented enterprise

After some hesitation (Delgrange, 2019a), the bodies administering the European Court on Human Rights recognised that

> a church is an organised religious community based on identical or at least substantially similar views. Through the rights granted to its members under Article 9, the church itself is protected in its right to manifest its religion, to organise and carry out worship, and to teach its practice and observance, and it is free to act out and enforce uniformity in these matters.[29]

The result is that if a person who is linked contractually to a church is in disagreement with the institution, their freedom of religion is preserved by the possibility of dispensing with their services: "to submit or to dismiss is the choice offered to the rebel" (Gonzalez, 2014). However, the Guide to Article 9 of the Convention drawn up by the Court, in its version of December 2018, states: "Although a legal entity can claim to be a victim of a violation of its freedom of thought and religion, it cannot exercise, as such, freedom of conscience".[30]

The European Court of Human Rights borrows from European Union law the concept of an "ethos-oriented enterprise". This is an enterprise whose ethos is based on religion or belief, as enshrined in Article 4 (2) of Directive 2000/78/EC. Since 2009, the Court has relied on that provision to assess restrictions on the fundamental rights of employees that are imposed by enterprises in the name of their ethos.[31] The Directive begins by prohibiting direct or indirect discrimination based on, inter alia, "religion or belief in the field of work" (Article 1). The Directive allows an exception for "occupational activities within churches and other public or private organisations the ethos of which is based on religion or belief". Such enterprises may discriminate during recruitment and may also "require individuals working for them to act in good faith and with loyalty to the organisation's ethos" (Article 4).

In its initial versions, the Directive reserved the status of an enterprise for those

> which pursue directly and essentially the aim of ideological guidance in the field of religion or belief with respect to education, information and the expression of opinions, and for the particular occupational activities within those organisations which are directly and essentially related to that aim.[32]

The final version of the Directive no longer refers to the purpose of disseminating a doctrine, but rather to any activity "which is based on religion or belief". As a result, a Christian hospital can claim the status of an ethos-oriented enterprise (Christians, 2017).

If, therefore, in the eyes of the European Court of Human Rights, a legal person has no conscience, an ethos-oriented enterprise has an ethos, which it can impose on its employees.

In the current state of Belgian law, the question arises as to whether an institution whose ethos is based on a religion can prohibit its medical staff from conducting an abortion or euthanasia. Article 4 (2) of the Directive states that Member States may maintain in their legislation the authorisation given to such an institution to discriminate or impose on its staff an attitude of good faith and loyalty to its ethos. There are two consequences. On the one hand, it is merely an option left open by the Directive, which it is up to the State to implement or not, on the condition that its national legislation had already made provision for this before the Directive came into force. On the other hand, there is no doubt that a State may waive that right, which is an exception to the fundamental aim of the Directive, that is, to eliminate discrimination against workers.

The "anti-discrimination" law of 10 May 2007, which transposes the Directive 2000/78/EC, introduces the concept of an ethos-oriented enterprise into Belgian legislation.[33] The law makes use of the possibility granted by Article 4 (2) of the Directive to "provide in future legislation setting out national practices existing at the date of adoption" of the Directive. Even if such practices have been confirmed in Belgian law (Delgrange and El Berhoumi, 2017; Delgrange, 2019b), it is not obvious that they apply to enterprises whose purpose is not to disseminate an ethos but merely to comply with it, such as a hospital (Christians, 2011: 644).

How can we reconcile the institutional awareness clause with patients' rights and therapeutic freedom?

As seen in the introduction, Resolution 1763 of the Parliamentary Assembly of the Council of Europe suggests extending the right to invoke the conscience clause to institutions. However, it must be ensured that another requirement of the Resolution is guaranteed:

> There is a comprehensive and clear legal and policy framework governing the practice of conscientious objection by health-care providers ensuring that the interests and rights of individuals seeking legal medical services are respected, protected, and fulfilled (3).

This soft law recommendation was applied immediately by the European Court, and therefore cast in marble by hard law, in its judgement of 26 May 2011, *R.R. v. Poland*, which was adopted less than one year after the recommendation:

> Once the State, acting within the limits of the margin of appreciation, referred to above, adopts statutory regulations allowing abortion in some situations, it must not structure its legal framework in a way which would limit real possibilities to obtain it. In particular, the State is under a positive obligation to create a procedural framework enabling a pregnant woman to exercise her right of access to lawful abortion (§ 200).

Therefore,

> "States are obliged to organise the health services system in such a way as to ensure that an effective exercise of the freedom of conscience of health professionals in the professional context does not prevent patients from obtaining access to services to which they are entitled under the applicable legislation", in this case the right to abortion under the conditions defined by Polish law.
> (§ 206)[34]

Resolution 1763 "invites Council of Europe member states to develop comprehensive and clear regulations that define and regulate conscientious objection with regard to health and medical services" (4). The Resolution, therefore, assigns three objectives for the legislation of the Member States:

4.1. to guarantee the right to conscientious objection in relation to participation in the medical procedure in question;
4.2. to ensure that patients are informed of any conscientious objection in a timely manner and referred to another health-care provider;
4.3. to ensure that patients receive appropriate treatment, in particular in cases of emergency.

These three recommendations give rise to three considerations. Firstly, conscientious objection must be related to a medical activity, which must necessarily be carried out with respect for the physician's therapeutic freedom. Secondly, the State organises its health care system such as to ensure that all patients have effective access to the medical services to which they are entitled, despite the exercise of the conscience clause that would be exercised by individuals or institutions. Finally, the institutional conscience clause, like the individual one, must be carried out in the most transparent manner.

The freedom of institutional conscience in the face of the physician's therapeutic freedom

A hospital or a rest home which invokes its status as an ethos-oriented enterprise may in principle discriminate during recruitment and, during the employment relationship, impose on its staff an attitude of good faith and loyalty towards its ethics (Delgrange, 2019a).

While discrimination on recruitment may be permitted provided that the conditions set out in Article 4 (2) of Directive 2000/78 are met, the requirement of loyalty to the organisation's ethos in the context of employment relationships comes into conflict with the physician's therapeutic freedom, which is inherent in the duties of the physician and is already at the heart of the Hippocratic oath (Leurquin and Kaiser, 2010).[35]

This diagnostic and therapeutic freedom is defined in the law on compulsory health insurance: The physician appreciates "conscientiously and freely the care provided to patients" and ensures "the provision of medical care with devotion and competence in the interests of, and respect for, patients' rights and taking into account the overall resources made available to them by society".[36]

On several occasions, the law prohibits the undermining of therapeutic freedom. The law on hospitals and other health care establishments applies to all hospitals, public or private.[37] It makes provision that "in each hospital there shall be drawn up general rules governing the legal relationship between the hospital and physicians, the conditions of organisation and the working conditions, including the financial conditions of work". It states that such "general regulation may not contain provisions which would call into question the professional autonomy of the individual hospital physician in terms of establishing the diagnosis or carrying out the treatment".[38]

The law of 22 April 2019 on the quality of health care practice makes the following provision:

> The healthcare professional freely chooses, within the limits of the powers conferred on him by or under the law, the resources which he implements in connection with the provision of healthcare. No regulatory restrictions can be imposed on it in this context.
>
> The healthcare professional shall be guided in his choice by relevant scientific data and his or her expertise, while taking into account the patient's preferences.[39]

The Belgian government specifies that

> freedom of diagnosis and treatment is indeed the starting point for any quality practice. However, the healthcare provider must exercise that freedom in accordance with the principle of prudence and without in any way infringing the patient's right to informed consent for each provision of care.[40]

While the "anti-discrimination" law of 2007 recognises the entity of the ethos-oriented enterprise in Belgian law, the legislation enshrining therapeutic freedom very clearly prohibits the limitation of that freedom from being imposed by a hospital or a rest home, even if it is an ethos-oriented enterprise. These institutions will be able to select their medical staff but may not interfere in the staff's therapeutic relationship with their patients.

An effective right to medical services, beyond the conscience clause

Belgium, like Germany or the Netherlands, is a consociative democracy, which systematically seeks compromises between the different worlds which segment society (Dumont, 2011; Andeweg, 2019). Care establishments are organised according to this logic, based on two pillars. The first pillar consists of the Catholic health care organisations, traditionally very active. The second pillar brings together secular, mainly socialist, organisations. Philosophical secularism is also based in the public sector, which consists of institutions that are in principle neutral.

Belgium, and in particular Flanders, has a majority of Catholic hospitals.[41] Family planning centres are mostly secular.[42] Rest homes are characterised by the presence of a large number of commercial enterprises (Rosenfeldt, 2014).

To institutionalise the conscience clause and thus allow health care institutions to refuse to participate in abortion or euthanasia, the Belgian legislator should organise its health system in such a way that these rights can be effectively exercised by all those who wish to benefit from them.

The Italian Constitutional Court ruled back in 1997 with respect to individual freedom of conscience, which cannot be considered to be unlimited or unconditional. It is primarily for the legislature to establish a balance between, on the one hand, individual awareness and the rights deriving therefrom, and on the other, all the duties of political, economic and social solidarity which the Constitution requires (Article 2), so that public policy is preserved and the resulting burdens are distributed fairly among all, without privilege.[43]

The European Committee of Social Rights also recalls that

> the implementation of the Charter requires state parties not merely to take legal action but also to make the resources available and introduce the operational procedures necessary to give full effect to the rights specified therein. … The provision of abortion services must be organised so as to ensure that the needs of patients wishing to access these services are met. This means that adequate measures must be taken to ensure the availability of non-objecting medical practitioners and other health personnel when and where they are required to provide abortion services, taking into account the fact that the number and timing of requests for abortion cannot be predicted in advance.[44]

It is already up to the State to take into account the effects of the individual conscience clause in order to ensure the effectiveness of the right to abortion,[45] euthanasia and MAR across the whole of its territory.[46] The recognition of an institutional conscience clause would require the legislator to review its entire system of approval and provision in the field of health care, and to take into account institutions that refuse to participate in certain medical acts.

On the basis of the third target set out in Resolution 1763, namely to "ensure that patients receive appropriate treatment, in particular in cases of emergency", it may be considered that the granting of a conscience clause to institutions to which the citizen chooses to turn with full knowledge of the facts and by having a reasonable choice, such as a rest home, would be admissible provided that their freedom of choice is guaranteed by adequate programming of health services. However, it is hardly conceivable that a hospital, in which citizens can find themselves without having chosen it and in circumstances where they may not express their own will, benefit from this clause. If, in the logic of Belgian consociative democracy, a private hospital intends to participate in the public service of the provision of care and receives public funding for that purpose, it must offer patients all the services provided under the law. If an institution intends to make use of a conscience clause, it must remain outside the public health service, with regard to the act to which the institutional conscience clause applies.

For institutions of choice, an obligation for a high level of transparency

Institutions "of choice" are those institutions which the citizen enters in full knowledge of the facts, such as a rest home or a family planning centre. On the contrary, a hospital, especially its emergency department, is not an institution of choice. Only institutions of choice could apply an institutional conscience clause, under two conditions, however.

The first condition affects the State, which has a positive obligation to guarantee the freedom of choice of the citizen, by ensuring diversity and by taking charge of neutral institutions that offer an appropriate service.

The second condition affects the ethos-oriented enterprise itself, which must be as transparent as possible, both to the beneficiary of the service and to its own employees.

The person who turns to an ethos-based institution must immediately be informed of the conscience clause and of its exact scope. The law of 22 August 2002 on the rights of patients lays down a general obligation for the physician to provide information and ensure transparency. Under Article 2 (7) of the law of 15 October 2018 on the voluntary termination of pregnancy,

> the physician consulted shall be required to inform the person concerned, as from the first visit, of their refusal to intervene. In this case, they indicate the contact details of another doctor, a termination centre or a hospital service that she can consult for a new pregnancy termination request. The physician who refuses to conduct the voluntary termination shall send the medical file to the new physician consulted by the woman.

The euthanasia law also requires doctors who refuse euthanasia to inform the patient "in good time". Finally, the MAR law makes provision that "fertility centres shall be as transparent as possible about their options as regards access to treatment" and requires them to notify "the applicant(s) of their refusal to comply with the request, within one month following the decision of the doctor consulted".

In cases where the conscience clause is institutionalised, this information and the obligation for transparency should be extended to the care institution so that the (future) patient has full knowledge that certain medical acts will be refused. The institution should also ensure that its personnel carefully takes into account and deals with any request for abortion or euthanasia and that the patient is directed in good time to a service that can grant the request, the medical file being forwarded.

The health professional must know, prior to making any commitment, what part of their therapeutic freedom and their individual freedom of conscience they will have to relinquish in favour of the enterprise's ethics. Thus, in the Rommelfanger case, the European Commission of Human Rights pointed out that the physician's contract "contained a clause according to which the employment relationship was to be governed by the guidelines issued by the umbrella organisation of Catholic charities in Germany". The Commission notes that

> by entering into contractual obligations vis-à-vis his employer the applicant accepted a duty of loyalty towards the Catholic church which limited his freedom of expression to a certain extent. … In principle, the Convention permits contractual obligations of this kind if they are freely entered into by the person concerned.[47]

The Commission then considered the dismissal by a Catholic hospital of a physician who was in favour of abortion to be legitimate.

Conclusion

The Belgian Catholic Church continues to fight against the secularisation of society and the secularisation of the law brought about by the abortion and euthanasia acts,[48] yet it seems to do so without having too many illusions. It gives the impression of withdrawing into its positions in order to create a bastion where its values can be preserved. The Church is mobilising the "Catholic pillar", in particular in hospitals and rest homes, which are urged to refuse to practise abortion, euthanasia or MAR.

But today there is no longer any concurrence between the size of this pillar, which includes more than half of public hospitals, and the number of Belgians who still declare themselves practising Catholics (less than 10% according to the Church itself).[49] In the Belgian context, it is virtually impossible for Catholic institutions to scrupulously and openly observe the doctrine of the Church when that doctrine is in contradiction with civil law, since they are financed by the State to participate in the public health service.

Two difficulties accompany this statement. First, Catholic institutions are in competition with secular or official institutions. An institutional conscience clause would cause them to lose significant market shares. These institutions therefore tend to avoid any explicit reference to Catholicism. Many have relinquished names that showed their Catholic affiliation in favour of a more neutral designation.[50] Second, the legislator is increasingly requiring these institutions to adopt stringent standards of care provision and is compelling them to merge.[51] Institutions of Christian origin are thus encouraged to join institutions with another ethos, which dilutes the strength of their convictions.

Like academic freedom (Delgrange, 2019b), therapeutic freedom must now be addressed at three levels: the physician, whose conscience must be preserved in his therapeutic relationship with the patient; the institution, which is part of a highly competitive market and needs to take into account both its philosophical ethos and the personal freedom of the medical staff; and the Church, which intends to maintain its doctrine and to impose it on the institutions that claim to be part of the Church.

Caught in a vice between the logic of the market and the doctrine of the Church, a Catholic institution is likely to sacrifice its duty of transparency on the altar of economic realism. However, this duty of transparency is vital to safeguard the rights of patients and the therapeutic freedom of the medical staff. This transparency must therefore be ensured in respect of patients as soon as they plan to enter the institution. Transparency must be guaranteed to the staff as soon as they consider going to work for the institution. Finally, transparency must be ensured with regard to the State, which must be able to run the public health service such as to ensure the effectiveness of the right to abortion, euthanasia and MAR.

Notes

1 The authors would like to thank Frédéric Vanneste, a member of the Belgian Council of State (Conseil d'État) and Professor of Human Rights Law at the University of Antwerp, and Samuel Pétrequin, a journalist at Associated Press, for their attentive and positively critical reading of this article.

2 Belgian legislation can be consulted on the "Conseil d'État" website, via the "refLex" database. Retrieved on 9 September 2020, http://reflex.raadvst-consetat.be/reflex/?page=chrono.

3 According to its Charter, "The European Institute for Bioethics (EIB) is independent of all parties or groups of a political or religious nature. It is non-denominational and adheres to the principle of the secular state, respectful of and attentive to religious traditions" (European Institute for Bioethics, 2001). For Henri Bartholomeeusen, President of the Centre for Secular Action (Centre d'action laïque), the EIB is nothing more than a Belgian association of activists from conservative religious circles. Its founder, Étienne Montero, Honorary Dean of the Faculty of Law at the University of Namur, defended the theses of Opus Dei (Bartholomeeusen, 2015). He became an Opus Dei priest and is now regional vicar of that congregation (Durré, 2019a).

4 The author classified Belgium in the first category, considering that the condition of distress is defined only by the woman. For another point of view, see Vansweevelt, De Meyer, Van Assche, 2018.

5 An action for annulment of the law of 3 April 1990 was brought before the Constitutional Court. The Court rejected it but avoided commenting on a woman's possible right to abortion. However, an argument put forward by the applicants criticised the self-determination granted to women (judgement No. 39/1991 [1991] Constitutional Court). Retrieved on 9 September 2020. www.const-court.be/en/common/home.html) (6.A.2). See Pâques, 2019: 15–16.

6 The French law of 17 January 1975 bears the title "voluntary termination of pregnancy", while the Belgian law of 1990 bears the title "termination of pregnancy".

7 Documents parlementaires, Chambre, 2017–2018, No. 54-3216/003, 14 – keynote speech by the main author of the proposition, David Clainval. Retrieved online on 9 September 2020 (www.lachambre.be).

8 Resolution 1607 (2008) on access to safe and legal abortion in Europe. Retrieved on September 9th, 2020. http://assembly.coe.int/nw/xml/XRef/Xref-XML2HTML-en.asp?fileid=17638.

9 Human Rights Committee, Views adopted by the Committee under Article 5 (4) of the Optional Protocol, concerning communication No. 2324/2013, CCPR/C/116/D/2324/2013, § 7.8. Retrieved on 9 September 2020. http://docstore.ohchr.org/SelfServices/FilesHandler.ashx?enc=6QkG1d%2FPPRiCAqhKb7yhsukPtYsnxNH1DBeueuCbK4iM7LfcZ49JWRwflq07QFTX3yW0YS8VLYGR0RQhwv5RZ89fncjj

zOC4SIwckjpt%2FU2Z1qQ5BbCFmPD4GJANJdPox9jnOHXVRg%2B1jGEqnFAP6w%3D%3D.

10 Rapport de la Commission de la Justice de la Chambre, 2001–2002, No. 50-1488/9, 176. Retrieved on 9 September 2020 (www.lachambre.be/FLWB/PDF/50/1488/50K1488009.pdf).

11 See Belgian Advisory Committee on Bioethics, Opinion No. 59 of 27 January 2014 on ethical aspects of the application of the law of 28 May 2002 on euthanasia (27 January 2014), 13. Most of its opinions may be consulted in English on the site of the Federal Public Health Service. Retrieved on 9 September 2020. www.health.belgium.be/en/belgian-advisory-committee-bioethics. The Committee emphasised that "attention is paid to a balanced representation of the various ideological and philosophical movements, to a balanced number of men and women, and to an equal number of Dutch- and French-speaking members, in the composition of the Committee. The same applies to a balance between members from the scientific and medical communities, on the one hand, and those from the philosophical, legal and life science communities, on the other hand". Due to its philosophically balanced composition, the Committee may not be able to express a common opinion. This was the case in Opinion No. 27 about MAR and in Opinion No. 59 on the institutional conscience clause.

12 Rapport des Commissions réunies de la Justice et des Affaires sociales, *Documents parlementaires*, Sénat, 2013–2014, No. 5-2170/4, 30 and 42–44. Retrieved on 9 September 2020 (www.senate.be).

13 Judgement No. 153/2015 [2015]. Constitutional Court, B.26 and B.41. Retrieved on 9 September 2020 (www.const-court.be/en/common/home.html).

14 *Haas v. Switzerland* [2011] ECHR 51.

15 See *S.H. and Others v. Austria*, [2011] ECHR (Grand Chamber) 82. See, Gallus, 2016; Willelms, 2018: 13–14.

16 Art 1er de la loi relative à l'exercice des professions des soins de santé, coordonnée le 10 mai 2015 (Art. 1 of the law of 22 April 2019 relating to the practice of the healthcare professions). Retrieved on 9 September 2020. https://www.ejustice.just.fgov.be/cgi_loi/change_lg.pl?language=fr&la=F&cn=2015051006&table_name=loi.

17 Art. 2, 3°, de la loi du 22 avril 2019 relative à la qualité de la pratique des soins de santé (Art. 2 and 3 of the law of 22 April 2019 relating to the practice of the health care professions). This law will come into force on 1 July 2021. Retrieved on 9 September 2020. http://www.ejustice.just.fgov.be/cgi_loi/change_lg.pl?language=fr&la=F&cn=2019042220&table_name=loi.

18 Art. 192, Code wallon de l'Action sociale et de la Santé (Walloon Code for Social Action and Health), introduced by a *decreet* (regional law) of 23 January 2014.

19 See Court of audit, 'Le subventionnement des centres de planning et de consultation familiale et conjugale', 25. Retrieved on 9 September 2020 (www.ccrek.be/Docs/2012_17_CentresPlanFam.pdf, 2012).

20 Art. 5, loi du 6 juillet 2007 relative à la procréation médicalement assistée et à la destination des embryons surnuméraires et des gamètes (law of 6 July 2007 relating to medically assisted procreation and to the use of surplus embryos and gametes). Retrieved on 9 September 2020. https://www.ejustice.just.fgov.be/cgi_loi/change_lg.pl?language=fr&la=F&cn=2007070632&table_name=loi.

21 See Belgian Advisory Committee on Bioethics, avis No. 27 'relatif au don de sperme et d'ovules', not available in translation. Retrieved on 9 September 2020. https://www.health.belgium.be/sites/default/files/uploads/fields/fpshealth_theme_file/7970404/Avis%20n%C2%B027%20du%208%20mars%202004%20relatif%20au%20don%20de%20sperme%20et%20d%E2%80%99ovules.pdf.

22 See Belgian Advisory Committee on Bioethics, Opinion No. 6 "concernant les bases éthiques pour l'optimalisation de l'offre et des critères de fonctionnement des centres de fécondation *in vitro*" (8 June 1998) 5, not available in translation.

23 Arrêté royal du 15 février 1999 "fixant les normes auxquelles les programmes de soins "médecine de la reproduction" doivent répondre pour être agréés" (Royal decree of 15 February 1999, "setting the standards that reproductive medicine treatment plans have to meet to gain certification"). Retrieved on 9 September 2020. http://www.ejustice.just.fgov.be/cgi_loi/change_lg.pl?language=fr&la=F&table_name=loi&cn=1999021541.
24 Art. 14, loi du 28 mai 2002 relative à l'euthanasie (law of 28 May 2002, relating to euthanasia). Retrieved on 9 September 2020. https://www.ejustice.just.fgov.be/cgi_loi/change_lg.pl?language=fr&la=F&cn=2002052837&table_name=l. See Lossignol, 2016.
25 Opinion No. 59, 21. See Tack, 2012–2013.
26 Opinion No. 59, 35–41.
27 See Flemish Palliative Care Federation, "Dealing with euthanasia and other forms of medically assisted death", 6 September 2003. Retrieved on 9 September 2020. www.consciencelaws.org/dutch/assist008-007(14).aspx.
28 In one specific case, such a home was ordered to pay damages for refusing to allow euthanasia within its walls. The judgement does not rule on whether the conscience clause is institutional or not. See Tribunal de première instance de Louvain, 29 June 2016 (*Tidschrift voor gezondheidsrecht/Revue du droit de la santé*, 2016-17) 341–343.
29 See *X. v. Denmark* [1976] E Comm. HR, No. 7374/76.
30 *Guide on Article 9 of the European Convention on Human Rights 8 (No. 13)*. Retrieved on 9 September 2020 (www.echr.coe.int/Documents/Guide_Art_9_ENG.pdf).
31 See *Lombardi Vallauri v. Italy [2009]* ECHR 23 and 41; *Schüth v. Germany* [2010] ECHR 40 and 70; *Obst v. Germany* [2010] ECHR 27 and 51; *Siebenhaar v. Germany [2011]* ECHR 46; *Sindictul "Păstorul cel BUN" v. Romania*, [2013] ECHR 60 and 142; *Fernández Martínez v. Spain* [2014] ECHR (Grand Chamber) 66 and 138; *Travaš* v. *Croatia* [2016] ECHR 46.
32 Proposal for a Council Directive establishing a general framework for equal treatment in employment and occupation, OJEC, 27.6.2000, C 177 E/42, Art. 4.2. Retrieved on 9 September 2020.
33 Art. 13, loi du 10 mai 2007 tendant à lutter contre certaines formes de discrimination (Art. 13, law of 10 May 2007, which aimed to combat certain forms of discrimination). Retrieved on 9 September 2020. http://www.ejustice.just.fgov.be/cgi_loi/change_lg.pl?language=fr&la=F&cn=2007051035&table_name=loi.
34 See, *R.R. v. Poland* [2011] ECHR 200. See further *P. and S. v. Poland* [2012] ECHR 99. See Larralde, 2012.
35 In Belgium, see also Conseil national de l'Ordre des Médecins, "commentaire de l'article 7 du *Code de déontologie médicale commenté*" 19–20. Retrieved on 9 September 2020. https://www.ordomedic.be/ethics2018/pdf/download/fr/?compendium=1&XMLHttpRequest=1.
36 Art.73, §1er, de la loi relative à l'assurance obligatoire soins de santé et indemnités coordonnée le 14 juillet 1994 (Art.73, §1 of the law relating to mandatory health care insurance and compensation coordinated on 14 July 1994). Retrieved on 9 September 2020. http://www.ejustice.just.fgov.be/cgi_loi/change_lg.pl?language=fr&la=F&cn=1994071438&table_name=loi.
37 Art. 1er de la loi du 10 juillet 2008 sur les hôpitaux et autres établissements de soins (Art. 1 of the law of 10 July 2008 on hospitals and other health care establishments). Retrieved on 9 September 2020. http://www.ejustice.just.fgov.be/cgi_loi/change_lg.pl?language=fr&la=F&cn=2008071090&table_name=loi.
38 Id. Art.144, §1er.
39 Art. 4, loi du 22 avril 2019 relative à la qualité de la pratique des soins de santé (Art. 4, law of 22 April 2019 relating to the quality of health care practice). Retrieved on 9 September 2020. http://www.ejustice.just.fgov.be/cgi_loi/change_lg.pl?language=fr&la=F&cn=2019042220&table_name=loi.

40 See *Documents parlementaires*, 2018–2019, No. 54-3441/001, 16. Retrieved on 9 September 2020 (https://www.lachambre.be/FLWB/PDF/54/3441/54K3441001.pdf).

41 In 2013, Zorgnet Vlaanderen, the federation of Christian hospitals in Flanders, would bring together more than 70% of the general hospitals of Flanders (*Jaarverslag 2013*, 40). Retrieved on 9 September 2020. www.zorgneticuro.be/sites/default/files/2014__Zorgnet_Jaarverslag_1kolom%20def.pdf). In Wallonia, the Federation of Christian Hospitals, UNESSA, brings together 46% of the accredited beds in Walloon hospitals (*2018 activity* report, 8). Retrieved on 9 September 2020. www.unessa.be/getattachment/Actualite/Documents-Communiques/RA2018/RA2018-(2).pdff.aspx.

42 The secular federation brings together 20 centres, the federation of female socialist, also secular, 17, the pluralist federation, 17 and the Catholic federation, 15 (Court of Audit, 21, quoted in note 19).

43 Judgement No. 43, §49, quoted by (Larralde, 2015: 407–408).

44 See *International Federation for Family Planning – European Network (IPPF EN) v. Italy* (2013). European Committee of Social Rights (Complaint No. 87/2012) 162–163.

45 Regarding the current situation in Belgium, see Luong, 2015.

46 Conscientious objection may be refused to a pharmacist if it compromises the availability of contraceptive products: "As long as the sale of contraceptives is legal and occurs on medical prescription nowhere other than in a pharmacy, the applicants cannot give precedence to their religious beliefs and impose them on others as justification for their refusal to sell such products, since they can manifest those beliefs in many ways outside the professional sphere" (*Pichon and Sajous v. France* [2001] ECHR 898). The McFarlane case is also interesting. Employed by a private enterprise with a policy of requiring employees to provide services equally to heterosexual and homosexual couples, he had refused to commit himself to providing psycho-sexual counselling to same-sex couples. He was fired. The European Court took into account the fact that the employee knew of the enterprise's anti-discrimination policy: "The State authorities therefore benefitted from a wide margin of appreciation in deciding where to strike the balance between Mr McFarlane's right to manifest his religious belief and the employer's interest in securing the rights of others. In all the circumstances, the Court does not consider that this margin of appreciation was exceeded in the present case" (*Eweida and Others v. the United Kingdom* [2013] ECHR 109).

47 See *Rommelfanger v. Germany [1989]* EComm. HR No. 12242/86.

48 With regard to euthanasia, the Church, with the backing of the political parties of Christian origin (see El Berhoumi and Pitseys, 2016), tried to avoid the extension thereof to minors and is campaigning to prevent its application to the insane (see Durré, 2015). Furthermore, the "Citoyens pour la vie" Association brought an action against the 2018 abortion law before the Constitutional Court and called for a suspension of the discussions on proposals for its full decriminalisation, pending the decision of the Constitutional Court. See Granier, 2019.

49 Rapport annuel, "L'Église Catholique en Belgique" (Annual report, The Catholic Church in Belgium) (*Cathobel*, novembre 2018). Retrieved on 3 September 2020 (https://www.cathobel.be/eglise-en-belgique/rapport-annuel/).

50 For example, in Brussels, the Saint-Elisabeth and Saint-Michel clinics merged to become "Europe Hospitals". When they set out their vision and values, no reference was made to religion. Retrieved on 9 September 2020 (www.cliniquesdeleurope.be/en/mission-vision-values). Similarly, the federations of hospital institutions set up in Caritas Catholica have adopted titles which no longer show their Catholic affiliation (Zorgnet Vlaanderen; Fédération des Institutions Hospitalières de Wallonie; Coordination Bruxelloise d'institutions sociales et de santé).

51 A law of 28 February 2019 requires hospitals to be grouped together in a network of 25 local hospitals (loi du 28 février 2019 modifiant la loi coordonnée du 10 juillet 2008 sur les hôpitaux et autres établissements de soins, en ce qui con-

cerne le réseautage clinique entre hôpitaux) (law of 28 February 2019 modifying the coordinate law of 10 July 2008). Retrieved on 9 September 2020. http://www.ejustice.just.fgov.be/cgi_loi/change_lg.pl?language=fr&la=F&table_name=loi&cn=2019022807.

Bibliography

Andeweg, R.B. 2019. "Consociationalism in the Low Countries: Comparing the Dutch and Belgian Experience." *Swiss Political Science Review* 25 : 408–425.

Bartholomeeusen, H. 2015. "Des assassins à l'hôpital ?" *Centre d'action laïque*. Retrieved on September 2nd, 2020. www.laicite.be/des-assassins-a-lhopital.

Bioy, X. 2016. "Moi aussi, aujourd'hui, je rentre chez moi…" *Revue Trimestrielle des Droits de l'Homme* 107: 775–800.

Blogie, E. 2015. "De Kesel sur l'euthanasie: 'Ce n'est pas un révolutionnaire'." *Le soir*, décembre 28.

Christians, L.-L. 2011. "Diversité au travail. Entre cultures et consciences, entre identité et éthique. Enjeux juridiques des recompositions postmodernes du religieux." Pp. 623–657 in Ringelheim, J. (ed.) *Le droit et la diversité culturelle*. Bruxelles: Bruylant.

Christians, L.-L. 2017. "Les mutations du concept d'entreprise de tendance. Essai de prospective juridique sur les futures entreprises postséculières". Pp. 253–270 in Callebat, B., de Courrèges, H., and Parisot, V. (eds.) *Les religions et le droit du travail. Regards croisés, d'ici et d'ailleurs*. Bruxelles: Bruylant.

Delgrange, X. 2019a. "L'entreprise de tendance, c'est tendance !" *Revue Trimestrielle des Droits de l'Homme* 119: 655–686.

Delgrange, X. 2019b. "Qui la liberté académique délivre-t-elle de qui?" *Journal des Tribunaux* 6769: 293–305.

Delgrange, X. and El Berhoumi, M. 2017. "Le droit de tendance des pouvoirs organisateurs." Pp. 83–88 in Delgrange, X., Detroux, L. and El Berhoumi, M. (eds.) *Les grands arrêts du droit de l'enseignement.* Bruxelles: Larcier.

Delgrange, X. and Koussens, D. 2019. "Les nouveaux arc-boutants de la laïcité belge pilarisée." Pp. 83–100 in Bruyère, L., Crosetti, A.-S., Sägesser, C. and Husson, J.F. (eds.) *Piliers, dépilarisation et clivage philosophique en Belgique*. Bruxelles: Éditions du CRISP.

Dumont, H. 2011. "Le modèle de la loi du Pacte culturel a-t-il encore une pertinence aujourd'hui ?" Pp. 167–204 in Ringelheim, J. (ed.) *Le droit et la diversité culturelle.* Bruylant: Bruxelles.

Durré, J.-J. 2015. "Les évêques belges réaffirment la dignité de la personne humaine, même démente." *Cathobel*, March 2. Retrieved on September 3rd, 2020. https://www.cathobel.be/2015/03/les-eveques-belges-reaffirment-la-dignite-de-la-personne-humaine-meme-demente/.

Durré, J.-J. 2019a. "Belgique: L'abbé Etienne Montero, nouveau vicaire régional de l'Opus Dei." *Cathobel (Official website of the Belgian Catholic Church)*. Retrieved on September 2nd, 2020. www.cathobel.be.

Durré, J.-J. 2019b. "Nouvel élargissement des conditions de l'avortement." *Cathobel (Official website of the Belgian Catholic Church)*. Retrieved on September 2nd, 2020. https://www.cathobel.be/2019/11/nouvel-elargissement-des-conditions-de-lavortement-declaration-des-eveques-belges/.

El Berhoumi, M. and Pitseys, J. 2016. "L'obstruction parlementaire en Belgique." *Courrier hebdomadaire du Crisp* 2289–2290: 35.

European Institute for Bioethics. 2001. "Charter of the EIB." *European Institute for Bioethics*. Retrieved on September 2nd, 2020. www2.ieb-eib.org/en/about-ieb/charter-of-the-eib-3.html.

Gallus, N. 2016. *Filiation*. Brussels: Bruylant.

Genicot, G. 2009. "La maîtrise du début de la vie : la loi du 6 juillet 2007 relative à la procréation médicalement assistée." *Journal des Tribunaux* 2: 17–27.

Genicot, G. 2019. "Vulnérabilité et intégrité physique en droit belge - Entre protection renforcée et autonomie encadrée." *Revue de Droit de l'Université de Liège* 1: 111–147.

Gonzalez, G. 2014. "L'autonomie ecclésiale au risque relatif des droits de l'homme." *Revue Trimestrielle des Droits de l'Homme* 100: 803–818.

Granier, P. 2019. "Réforme de l'IVG : Les Citoyens pour la vie demande de suspendre l'examen des projets de loi." *Cathobel*, October 29. Retrieved online on September 3rd, 2020. https://www.cathobel.be/2019/10/reforme-de-livg-les-citoyens-pour-la-vie-demande-de-suspendre-lexamen-des-projets-de-loi/.

Larralde, J.-M. 2012. "La Cour européenne des droits de l'homme et le droit à l'avortement entre avancées prudentes et conservatisme assumé." *Revue Trimestrielle des Droits de l'Homme* 91: 609–624.

Larralde, J.-M. 2015. "Le Comité européen des droits sociaux face aux dysfonctionnements des interruptions de grossesse." *Revue Trimestrielle des Droits de l'Homme* 102: 403–420.

Leigh, I. 2018. "The Legal Recognition of Freedom of Conscience as Conscientious Objection: Familiar Problems and New Lessons." Pp. 390–395 in Ahdar, R. (ed.) *Research Handbook on Law and Religion*. Cheltenham: Elgar.

Leleu, Y.-H. and Genicot, G. 2004. "L'euthanasie en Belgique et aux Pays-Bas. Variations sur le thème de l'autodétermination." *Revue Trimestrielle des Droits de l'Homme* 57: 5–50.

Leurquin, X. and Kaiser, M. 2010. "La liberté diagnostique et thérapeutique: un principe juridique à soigner." Pp. 889–914 in Melchior, M. (ed.) *Liège, Strasbourg, Bruxelles : parcours des droits de l'homme. Liber amicorum*. Limal: Anthémis.

Lossignol, D. 2016. "L'euthanasie et le détournement de la clause de conscience." *Revue médicale de Bruxelles* 9: 384–389.

Luong, J. 2015. "L'IVG plaide toujours coupable." *Le Vif*, August 2. Retrieved on September 3rd, 2020. www.levif.be/actualite/belgique/l-ivg-plaide-toujours-coupable/article-normal-408467.html.

Mastor, W. 2017. "L'embryon en droit comparé." *Journal international de bioéthique et d'éthique des sciences* 28 (4): 152.

Montero, É. 2016. "La liberté des institutions de soins eu égard à la pratique de l'euthanasie." *Dossiers de l'Institut Européen de Bioéthique*. Retrieved on September 2nd 2020. www.ieb-eib.org/ancien-site/pdf/20161024-euthanasie-liberte-des-institutions.pdf.

Montero, É. 2012. "La loi contre la conscience: réflexions autour de l'objection de conscience." Pp. 163–198 in Fierens, J. (ed). *Jérusalem, Athènes, Rome, Liber amicorum Xavier Dijon*. Bruxelles: Bruylant.

Pâques, M. 2019. "Avortement, euthanasie et Cour constitutionnelle." *Open Repository and Bibliography*. Retrieved on September 2nd, 2020. https://orbi.uliege.be/handle/2268/237393.

Proeschel, C. 2016. "L'objection de conscience pour motifs religieux: un impossible défi démocratique." *Religiologiques* 34: 215–239.

Rosenfeldt, M. 2014. "L'hébergement des personnes âgées en Wallonie: état des lieux." *Centre d'Education Populaire André Genot*. Retrieved on September 3rd, 2020. www.cepag.be/publications/etudes/2014/hebergement-personnes-agees-wallonie-etat-lieux.

Schiffino, N. 2017. "La régulation publique de la biomédecine. Procréation médicalement assistée, recherche sur embryons, gestation pour autrui." *Courrier hebdomadaire du CRISP* 23 (2348–2349): 5–64.

Tack, S. 2012–2013. "Recht op (uitvoering van) euthanasie? Instellingsbeleid en de professionele autonomie van de arts." *Tijdschrift voor gezondheidsrecht/Revue du droit de la santé* 1: 7–22.

Van Assche, K. 2016–2017. "Refus d'une maison de repos et de soins d'autoriser l'euthanasie dans ses murs, même lorsqu'un médecin externe accepte d'y procéder." *Tijdschrift voor gezondheidsrecht/Revue du droit de la santé* 5: 344–353.

Vansweevelt, T., Meyer, F.D. and Van Assche, K. 2018. "De Abortuswet 2018 : over symbolische verbeteringen en openstaande knelpunten." *Tijdschrift voor gezondheidsrecht/Revue du droit de la santé* 19: 220–232.

Willems, G. 2018. *Droit des personnes et des familles 2011–2016*. Brussels: Larcier.

Willems, G. and Cohen, L. 2017. "Regards croisés de la Cour européenne des droits de l'homme et du Comité des droits de l'homme des Nations Unies sur le droit à l'avortement." *Revue Trimestrielle des Droits de l'Homme* 111: 557–583.

6 Advocating in ecology through meditation

A case study on the Swiss "inner transition" network

Christophe Monnot and Alexandre Grandjean

Introduction[1]

In Europe and North America, actors claiming to be involved in religious interests bring about moral arguments to contest many progressive political projects, such as access to civil marriage (Tricou, 2015; Béraud and Portier, 2015) or medically assisted procreation for homosexual couples (Mathieu, 2017). As noted by Claude Proeschel and David Koussens (Introduction), these contestations have mainly fostered around normative secularist legal framework or new rhetoric of pluralistic individual freedom of conscience. In their complete review of situations in which public contestation occurs through religious actors or motives, they interestingly observe the "emergence of new areas of contestation, both in the locations where contestation is expressed and in the causes that it champions" (Introduction). Indeed, though religious contestation can easily be affiliated only with conservative political and ontological agendas, religious or spiritual argumentative registers are twofold. For instance, religious/spiritual actors and rhetoric are also used to support political or citizen-based projects related to ecology, alter-globalism, the introduction of new "green" technologies, and the struggle against climate change (Gottlieb, 2010; Kearns, 2012; Koehrsen, 2018; Veldman et al., 2014). The latter thus being contestation topics usually attributed to progressive and politically left-oriented social actors (Becci et al., 2021).

Yet, this twofold public contestation by religious actors is to be reconsidered, notably in the light of a general movement involving a blurring of conventional political maps, divided between progressives and conservatives, which Anthony Giddens already analysed in his book *Beyond Left or Right: The Future of Radical Politics* (1994). For instance, the contribution of religious actors to ecological issues is equally intertwined. Noteworthy is the example of Pope Francis's Encyclical *Laudato Si* (2015) and his proposal for "integral ecology". Indeed, while taking up the broad lines of the scientific debate and the current activists' rationale for "the care of the Creation", the encyclical statements remain, however, in line with the bio-power stakes supported by the magisterium and previous popes (Turina, 2013).

In this chapter, we focus on the "new areas of contestation" Claude Proeschel and David Koussens wrote about, thus following on politically oriented left-wing or progressive contestation originating with religious and spiritual actors. We will do so through a case study grounded within a network of religious and spiritual ecoactivists in Switzerland. The latter particularly drew our attention, because in their discourses two action registers intersect in a virtuous *continuum*. First, these religious and spiritual actors claim a posture of advocacy has relevance on environmental issues. Second, the posture of meditation is equally raised so as to seek a so-called harmony with the inner dimension of the "self" and its relation with the environment and consumerist Western societies. More precisely, we will follow a case study we conducted on the *Laboratory for Inner Transition* (*Laboratoire de la transition intérieure*), a newly created programme by the Swiss Protestant Church's humanitarian NGO, "*Bread for All*" (BFA).[2] It all began in 2016, when the international cooperation organisation *BFA* commissioned Michel Maxime Egger (MME),[3] a well-known actor on account of his books and lectures on ecospirituality and ecopsychology (2012, 2016). This laboratory is of particular interest to us, because it is one of the influential nodes of an identified network of actors that calls for an "inner transition". This situation is innovative in that it addresses both an audience of social Christians and actors active in the holistic milieu, besides those engaged in more secular forms of sustainable militancy.

By means of this structure – unique in Switzerland – the Laboratory, its founder (MME) and his employee have access to resources and enjoy institutional credibility, hence anchored in the continuity of this renowned organisation in Switzerland. The latter is situated at the intersection between the sustainable and humanitarian development advocated by Switzerland's major development aid programmes and the Christian social tradition supported by the Swiss Protestant Church. With the case study of *the Laboratory for Inner Transition*, we will show how this programme operates a set of junctions, "binding" different social worlds and rhetoric together (religion/spirituality, the economy, politics, ecology, bottom-up alternatives, etc.). We will examine the contextual origins, social dynamics, successes and limitations of this strategy that strives to bind together advocacy and meditation in new modes of contestation. Indeed, is BFA's political and humanitarian programme being renewed in its public expression throughout these innovative spiritual motives? Does this new form of advocacy through meditation reach or federate new audiences? In this context, what types of actors are engaged by the "inner transition" trope? Are these the one support by the Christian social base originating from BFA? Or are they members already active in ecological militancy, or leaders and decision-makers in the established Churches? In short, does the model of militancy proposed by MME bear political offspring or does it remain confined to alternative publics and individuals?

We assess these questions by discussing the results of a participant observation survey that we conducted over several years in Switzerland. After describing the general context of our investigation, we will first detail the founding of the Laboratory. We will highlight from which authors and approaches its founder, MME, shapes its "meditator-advocator" motto, and how this in turn resonates with BFA's new institutional orientations and objectives. Second, we will situate the Laboratory's activities in the context of the "inner transition" milieu that we observed between 2016 and 2019. In the third part, these observations will enable us to outline the successes and limitations of the "meditator-advocator" promoted by BFA and the Laboratory. We will note, in conclusion, that the "inner transition" trope, while it succeeds in uniting several audiences around a commitment linking the "inner self" and ecology, modifies communication modes without influencing the substance of BFA's advocacy work. As a result, the Laboratory and the "inner transition" trope benefit from BFA's aura. Yet, this institution remains the sole legitimate and audible interlocutor when it comes to interacting with ecclesiastical, economic and political institutions in Switzerland. In a sense, it does not activate new forms of political militancy in the milieu of climate justice and calls in support of sustainability.

The context of the survey: eco-activism and the "inner transition" milieu in Switzerland

In summer 2015, and in the wake of the Paris COP21 summit, actors and references associated with the religious and the spiritual domain were gaining increasing visibility in public discourse: For example, the World Council of Churches (WCC) was fully involved in the many mobilisations and petitions submitted to political leaders. Likewise, a group of civil society organisations were working together on climate change, focusing in particular on religious symbols such as the "Fasting for Climate" days, which brought together both religious and secular actors. In the French-speaking world, the success of cultural productions such as the film *Demain* (Tomorrow, 2015) participated in disseminating models of local bottom-up alternatives (Becci and Monnot, 2016; Grandjean et al., 2018). In these approaches, the notion of "inner transition" repeatedly accompanied the leitmotif of "sustainable transition". Overall, these actors took up one of the central arguments by one of the "greening of religion" forerunners, Lynn White Jr (1967). In a widely mediated conference in front of the AAAS,[4] this author argued that, if the "root" cause of the environmental crisis had obvious religious origins, then its resolution was also to be religious: either by founding a new religion (or spirituality) or by rethinking the contours of current religious traditions (1967: 1206–1207).

During an early survey in Switzerland, investigating the relation between religion, spirituality, and the energy transition,[5] we first identified an emerging network of actors claiming to be part of the "inner transition" (Grandjean et al., 2018 ; Becci and Monnot, 2016). The feature we observed is notably their ability to link different social worlds (ecological, political, technological, religious, etc.) with that of the ecological sphere. Under "holistic" motifs that place different dimensions in a network of interrelationships, these actors express themselves during round tables, practical workshops at festivals advocating a "sustainable transition", or through their publications. From their perspective, the idea of transition would have two dimensions: one "external" (technological and political) and the other "internal", tinged with "deep ecology" (Naess, 2008), which envisions a radical surpassing of these dimensions. The way they articulate these two perspectives challenges the common approaches and languages of dominant sociotechnical environmental paradigms (White et al., 2016).

The data presented here were collected in Switzerland between 2015 and 2019, through two qualitative surveys: one supported by the University of Lausanne's Volteface platform (2015–2017) and the other which directly followed as part of the Swiss National Science Foundation (2017–2021).[6] Our successive surveys bring together two dimensions generally separated by the study of the religious domain and ecology (Berry, 2013; Taylor, 2016): on the one hand, the process of greening "established" religious traditions and, on the other hand, the elective affinity between the contemporary spirituality movements (Fedele and Knibbe, 2012) and the trope of "nature" (Taylor, 2010; Bloch, 1998). In our field of investigation, it turned out that the foundation of a *Laboratory for Inner Transition* was an unprecedented innovation, at the junction between the institutional religious domain and more diffuse demands for ecospirituality. Moreover, the inclusion of this dimension in a religious NGO associated with political lobbying adds many potentialities to this innovation. Through its founder's (MME) personality and life history, we have considered the establishment of the Laboratory as a case study, yet one that was representative of the general dynamics of the "inner transition" trope in Switzerland (Yin, 1994). We consider it as representative as it tends to be one of the central nodes of a wider network of activists and self-proclaimed therapists that encounter in numerous activities and gathering such as urban festival, public conferences, de-growth and ecopsychology meeting groups, or in collective ecoritualisation and "healing" sessions of one's relation toward a so-called "relation toward nature".

Two semi-directive interviews were conducted with MME. One in 2016,[7] when he had just been hired by BFA and the other, two years later,[8] at the time of an initial assessment. We also collected the textual documents produced by BFA, and met with its director[9] in order to better understand the institutional issues of that Laboratory for Inner Transition. In parallel, we have attended and recorded more than a dozen public interventions by MME, both during debates, festivals related to sustainability and in church-related events. In addition, we participated in activities that he organised under the Laboratory's flag. One of us participated in two intensive ecospirituality weekends where other important "inner transition" actors in Switzerland were invited to participate. MME's media appearances, as well as those various writing about ecospirituality, have been taken into account. The diversity of the collected data reflects the strategy of dissemination and "binding" different social worlds, the "inner transition" actors operate at various analytical levels (individual, institutional, cultural, etc.).

The coding and analysis of the material collected made it possible to highlight the main themes, but also the limits of this strategy that were highlighted discursively by the actors.[10] We were also able to point out the mobilisation of different social worlds in all these public interventions. Interestingly, it has not always been easy to settle a coding procedure that demarcates "religious", "spiritual", and "ecological" worlds, precisely because the "inner transition" milieu seeks to correlate them together, in a way that exceeds formal institutional boundaries. We have therefore integrated a number of codes that clarify and analyse the connection modalities "transition" actors operate in terms of boundary-making.

An "incidental encounter": when ecospirituality is bound to a Christian humanitarian NGO

The BFA organisation holds a special place on the Swiss NGO scene. It is known to the general public through its awareness-raising and lobbying campaigns[11] on topics related to social justice, also including climate justice. Every year, it supports more than 300 projects worldwide.[12] This facet is especially well known to the Protestant Church, as BFA represents its main social lever toward the Global South. However, it is perceived by the general public through its involvement in fair trade,[13] its commitment and lobbying in Switzerland's development policy and for raising public awareness on issues integrating North-South relations. During Lenten Campaigns, BFA cooperates with the Catholic organisation *Fastenopfer*.[14] For its political lobbying, BFA notably collaborates with other NGOs, many of which have a Christian social orientation, within a working community called *Alliance Sud*. One of the key actors in our case study was found in this umbrella NGO at federal level whose aim is "to influence Swiss policy in favor of poor countries".[15] Indeed, MME was a member of the management team, responsible for multinational regulation politics until 2016, when he was hired by BFA to found the *Laboratory for Inner Transition*.

In its policy, BFA faces several challenges. First, the Christian-social-oriented generation is ageing, thus shrinking the reservoir of relays within parishes. Second, actions and campaigns concerning social issues are no longer closely linked to religious themes. In addition, the hit campaign formulas no longer seem to appeal to the population as much as it used to. It is in this context that BFA, under the aegis of a new director, Bernard DuPasquier, is beginning a process of overhauling its operating mode and seeking new audiences. BFA director explained–during an interview conducted in the small private park next to the Lausanne office – how, during a meeting with MME, "something was given" in the form of a "win-win" situation:

> Ultimately something actually emerged. Michel [MME] had worked for BFA, and at the time was also involved in development policy at *Alliance Sud*. He lacked [professionally] this very aspect of the meditator. Only the advocator aspect existed, and he saw we were striving for, uh, coherence to say, "no, we have to be both meditators and advocators". That is when we had that impulse to say, "why not connect MME's private commitment and BFA's public engagement". I mean, a win-win situation, you know.[16]

An idea developed in the wake of this "incidental" meeting: a laboratory for the exploration and experimentation of the inner dimensions (psychological, spiritual, and cultural) of the sustainable transition. Currently, it presents itself as a way of "contributing to the transition towards a more equitable world that is respectful of nature, in synergy with the alternatives that are emerging in every corner of the world".[17] It also encourages individuals to combine the two facets described above, namely, the figures of the "meditator" and of the "advocator". The discourse related to the hybridisation of different social worlds finds a unique anchoring here. It should be noted that MME's militancy and the foundation of the *Laboratory for Inner Transition* do not radically depart from *BFA*'s North-South social and mutual aid programmes. Notwithstanding, this laboratory is part of an institutional renewal strategy that aims both to reinvigorate spirituality and to "revive it with its spiritual roots"[18] in an increasingly secularised Christian social milieu; and renew their audience as well as embark in new processes that, alongside exposing injustice, proposes a positive approach to sustainable transition. Based on an initial assessment coupled with our field observations, we will appraise the dynamics and limits of this configuration. However, a more in-depth analysis of MME's background, along with the content of the "inner transition" claims, seems essential to us in order to better situate what "has actually emerged".

"Binding" social worlds: the ability of cultural mobility

The key actor in our case study, MME, proves to be a "circumstantial" man for both BFA and the "inner transition" network. We have already mentioned its intra-institutional mobility within the Swiss Christian NGOs constellation. We will return here to his life's path, from which we can postulate that he developed one of his special features in this milieu: that of, within his current position, articulating two commitments, being as much of a "meditator" as an "advocator". This part aims to demonstrate that this strategy of "linking" or hybridising between two normally separate poles implies, for some actors, being multi-situated and acquiring different referential languages, which guarantees their cultural mobility between several milieus.

It is during a trip to Southeast Asia that MME inaugurated his role as a "meditator", when he shared with us a narrative of the spiritual experience he had at that time. This early biographical departure led him to approach Zen Buddhism at first, though he returned to Christianity following a second spiritual experience, and committed to the Orthodox tradition. He became a deacon for an Orthodox parish in Switzerland and had to leave this position after ten years, following a divorce. This other biographical rupture led him to distance himself from religious institutions. He is currently pursuing his career as a guest speaker or "free preacher" in Protestant Reformed and Catholic "liberal" circles, where his speeches on ecospirituality encounter a favourable response.

At the same time, his professional career gradually brought him into the role of the "advocator". After working in journalism, he joined the world of activist NGOs in 1993. He collaborated for the first time with *BFA* in their Lenten Campaigns to raise awareness among the Swiss public against anti-personnel landmines and for ethical clothing. In 2003, he joined *Alliance Sud*, where he continued his militancy through a commitment to parliamentary lobbying, especially to reinforce regulation on multinationals operating in Switzerland. Committed to the emergence of alter-globalisation assertions in the early 2000s, he developed an early work of hybridisation between these two – political and religious – dimensions. For him, self-transformation and world transformation were envisioned as inseparable. During the same period, he participated in the emergence of an alternative "spiritual" scene marked with the stamp of ecology (Bloch, 1998). In MME's discourse, it is then a matter of linking three worlds: (1) engaging a dialogue between various spiritual traditions or quests for meaning, (2) ecology, and (3) the major contemporary socioeconomic issues.

His progressive involvement in various ecospirituality networks from the 2010s onward encouraged him to develop a central notion in his work: "the path of the meditator-advocator". In other words, an approach that would combine "contemplation and action in the creation of local alternatives and resilient territories".[19] Through the figure of the meditator-advocator, MME evoked the possibility of becoming a "weaver", an expression he borrowed from the French philosopher Abdennour Bidar (2016). On the website[20] he is currently running, readers can observe how MME situates his commitment within the values promoted by BFA, while assuming this position as a "weaver":

> BFA sees itself as a "weaver" driven by the desire to contribute – in synergy with others – to the "paradigm of a well-connected life" emerging all over the world. Tomorrow's civilization will be more equitable, collaborative, united and meaningful, or it will not be.[21]

His "weaver" status is part of a militant logic of networking the various existing actors and ongoing projects at the time of this *laboratory*'s creation. In an interview, MME stated his intention to set up, in French-speaking Switzerland, a "hub" greatly inspired by the *Transition towns* network, initiated by Rob Hopkins in Totnes, England (Boudinot Garrett and Le Vasseur, 2016). In addition, he collaborated in a cosmopolitan French-speaking network (Beck, 2006) of associations sharing the same objectives as the *Laboratory for Inner Transition*. All of them openly profess they pertain to English-speaking authors on ecospirituality and ecopsychology, or to organisations centred around Pierre Rabhi, a charismatic figure and one of the main promoters of "voluntary sobriety" in France. This dynamic of "binding" is directly in line with the advocacy and meditative postures BFA has invited him to infuse into his institutional renewal strategy.

The path of the "meditator-advocator": from the English-world counterculture to a polymorphic French-speaking audience

As illustrated by the case study of MME's involvement in *BFA*, a more internalised – if not spiritualised – approach to ecology is being promoted. The "self" becomes, so to speak, one of the places reinvested to envisage "tomorrow's" world. The ecological crisis and its religious or spiritual aspects are thereby highlighted by these networks. However, in this "meditator-advocator" approach, the spiritual is not essentially contemplative, but must be part of a set of societal actions and postures:

> Basically, it is the psychological, spiritual, and cultural dimensions – what I call "inner transition"– ... that are embodied in alternatives such as presented in [the film] *Tomorrow.* With subsidiary currencies, with energy, with urban agriculture and whatever you want.[22]

A life-path analysis is instructive of the great social mobility MME has exhibited. His religious journey was marked by several distancing stances and conversions. In his political commitment, he displays a degree of social mobility that places him at the crossroads between several social worlds and as a "mediator" between them. His ecospiritual posture and commitment position him in-between Christian circles, contemporary spiritualities spheres, as well as ecological and alter-globalist advocates. Intriguingly, in his public interventions, MME adapted his discourse – or rather translated it – according to audiences, summoning in turn theology and the Church Fathers when addressing religious audiences, or ecopsychology and the notion of "interiority" with more secular publics:

> Admittedly, if I want to reach people in a Christian environment, I must be able to show them that all this has to do with their faith. And that in reality, there are actual foundations in theology to give meaning and language, to translate it into a [transitional] language. But then I can talk to other people. [For] me, the important thing is this inner reconnection work from which we enter into concrete actions and changes in our lifestyles.[23]

Such ambivalence between ecospirituality and ecopsychology does not implicate the substance of the Laboratory's message regarding "transition". The latter is mainly based on the writing, lectures and workshops of English-speaking authors involved in counterculture, such as Theodore Roszack or Joanna Macy, two American activists who embody the ecospiritual and ecopsychological aspects of an "inner transition" (Macy and Brown, 2014). In particular, Joanna Macy is at the origin of the *Work That Reconnects* (WTR) technique, promoted by MME. It consists of a series of practical exercises and rituals designed to "(re)connect" individuals to their feelings, to others and to nature. Specifically, MME shares with these two authors a critique of the constant "economic growth" ideology of (post)industrial societies. The state of ecological and social crisis attributed to it is said to lead individuals to a state of despair, helplessness and anxiety about the future, which WTR exercises seek to mediatise. The approach advocated by Johanna Macy and Molly Young Brown shared by MME is presented as acting on inner foundations, if not directly as being of spiritual and sacred nature:

> Now, in our time, three rivers – anguish for our world, scientific breakthroughs and ancestral teachings – flow together. From the confluence of these rivers we drink. We awaken to what we once knew: we are alive in a

> living Earth, the source of all we are and can achieve. Despite our conditioning by the industrial society of the last two centuries, we want to name, once again, this world as holy.
>
> (Macy and Brown, 2014: 14)

By taking up English-world countercultural actors' approaches, and colouring them with an ecospiritual perspective based, among other things, on the writings of the Church Fathers, MME induces an innovation. He proposes a particular version of the idea of "inner transition" in a French-speaking and religious context: It could take place both in traditional churches circles and among ecological activists. By embarking on this path, *BFA* is also involved in this vision and is emerging as one of this movement's key players. He considers that, through a demand for ecospirituality, religious faith/activity in Switzerland could become ecological, and conversely. However, in the next section, we will submit that this "binding" strategy and the emerging new category of the meditator-advocator, while it involves remarkable transformations within the field of religion in Switzerland, remains limited in its implications: Neither environmentalist circles nor religious institutions reinvest this approach by basing it on the idea of "transforming oneself to change the world".

The achievements and limits of the "inner transition" in Switzerland: "binding" worlds, for whom and why?

MME's commitment within *BFA* is, as it has been noted, the result of a strategic change in the organisation. We will analyse here the constitution of the *Laboratory* from *BFA*'s institutional perspective. Faced with a pool of employees and sympathisers that is increasingly falling into a profile "distanced" from religious commitment (Stolz et al., 2016), the *Laboratory* "spiritualises" the organisation. From this point of view, the "meditating advocacy's" action instilled by MME can be considered a success. This organisation is better known to the public on account of its militancy than through its links to Churches; it can therefore be reintegrated into a meditative path by organising meetings, conventions and spiritual challenges in the midst of the transition milieu. To underline this point, let us simply mention an initiative, led by MME in particular.

On the premises of a sociocultural centre actively involved in the ecological and internal transition, he brought together several partners[24] around a more than 12-conference cycle in Lausanne, entitled "everything can (still) change", dealing with themes ranging from "inventing a new education" to "meditation as a social transformation driver" and "tools to nourish our civic commitment". They attracted nearly 200 people – each time. *BFA* then proved to be a key player with a spiritual and inner dimension, which is conceived as necessary in the transition movement. The NGO, renowned for its public activism, can then stand out for its flexible or "meditative" spiritual approach.

This "transition spirit", as MME puts it, goes beyond that. BFA's entire public action has also been transformed under its influence. The 2018 Lenten Campaign

"Let's take part in change, let's create tomorrow's world together!" is a perfect example of this. It instils a positive spirit and does not mark out commitments between North and South as a way to transform the world. Moreover, it proved an instant success: On 22 February 2018, the 200-seat *Welle 7* auditorium in Bern proved too small to cater to the success of the "day dedicated to transition" event that launched this campaign: It was sold out more than three weeks before the event. The NGO, known for raising questions about the consequences of North-South relations, can therefore re-embark into a larger militant path of action, since it also involves actions in the North while instilling a spiritual and positive movement outside the Churches, thus reaching the population distanced from religious institutions.

It should be noted, however, that though MME's path oscillates between contemporary spiritualities and theologies, thanks to access to institutional resources provided by BFA, MME's Laboratory has strengthened the link with parish groups involved in social and fundraising actions for the Global South. Following the review of his activities in 2018, MME's list of supports are indeed already established but "tired" groups. However, new interregional groups joined the supportive programme. In this sense, the action of the *Laboratory for Inner Transition* reactivates the network of ageing Christian social activists that follows *BFA*'s usual activities. It attracts new, younger, people, who are "in a spiritual quest" and interested in getting involved in sustainable transition. *BFA*'s strategy seems to be bearing fruit, although MME would like to place it even more at the centre of "transition" networks. However, the networking carried out by the Laboratory supports other citizen-based initiatives, such as conventions and participation in festivals related to sustainable alternatives, the creation of a French-speaking ecopsychology group in Switzerland and the organisation of intensive ecospirituality weekends, where speakers claim to be as much Buddhists as (neo)shaman practitioners. Academic actors were also invited to express themselves. On this point, it can therefore be noted, as shown in Figure 6.1, that *BFA*'s action through MME exhales a fresh spirit in the classic militancy world. By integrating a spiritual dimension, *BFA* can position itself as a positive and holistic NGO: It can also take into account human beings' so-called deep needs, including spiritual ones, in both southern and northern countries. Second, MME's work renews the spiritual world by blurring the boundaries between the classical Christian social environment and the holistic one. The inner transition offers a conceptual bridge both to Christians concerned with environmental or social causes and to the holistic environment followers, who are interested in well-being and also concerned about their environment. MME's meditative profile assessment is a success, both for *BFA* and for the internal dynamics of the Swiss ecological transition network.

Notwithstanding, this hybridisation between spiritual and ecological also displays its limits from the "advocator's" perspective. The Laboratory does boast collaborations with committed ecological and social groups such as environmental conservation associations, permaculture networks, citizen-based festivals and sociocultural centres, but these collaborations are *ad hoc* only. It is only when

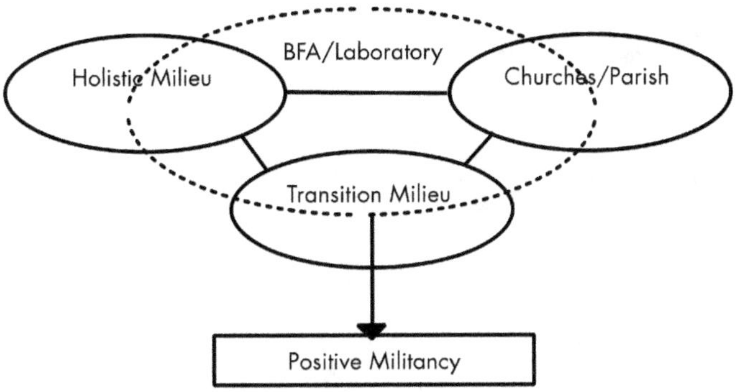

Figure 6.1 Hybridisation of holistic, parish and transition environments by the BFA Laboratory. This figure represents three circles tending toward positive militancy represented by ellipses connected to each other by straight line segments. On the right, the ellipse of the parish or church milieu, on the left an ellipse of the holistic milieu and lower, centred, the ellipse of the transition milieu. A large dotted ellipse representing the field of action of BFA and the Laboratory for Transition. It partially covers the other three ellipses. An arrow starts from this ellipse at the transition milieu to point toward positive militancy.

these communities seek to address the spiritual issue in their own actions that collaboration is possible. Otherwise, neither MME nor *BFA* are perceived as partners. In other words, in the ecological milieu, MME'S renowned expertise rests with the facet of the meditator and not of the ecology advocator. This is particularly evident in the events programme such as the Alternatiba Festival in Geneva, or federated actors' demands during mobilisations such as the "Climate Marches" where spiritual and religious tropes are poorly represented, whereas anti-capitalist criticism of ecology takes pride of place. We indeed observed no seminars given in these kinds of events; at most, stands are set up jointly with other Christian actors, who will present some of the Laboratory's efforts. The hybridisation promoted by MME does not seem to be catching on in ecological militancy circles, where its place has already been taken by experts in environmental science or policy. However, the institutional base provided by *BFA* still enables MME, although marginalised, to endure over time within these militant networks. As shown in Figure 6.2, through its focus on linking the ecological world with the spiritual one, it may be invited to events or mobilisations, with a view to producing a positive image of spirituality, which is consensual for a significant proportion of activists, but never to achieve a credible form of ecological militancy.

We have observed another limitation to this hybridisation work: It concerns established Churches. As Jens Koehrsen (2018) has observed, Churches' commitment to sustainable development competes with other thematic objects usually attached to them in Switzerland, such as mutual solidarity and justice issues. This means that commitment to "transition" is not part of Churches' programmes, but

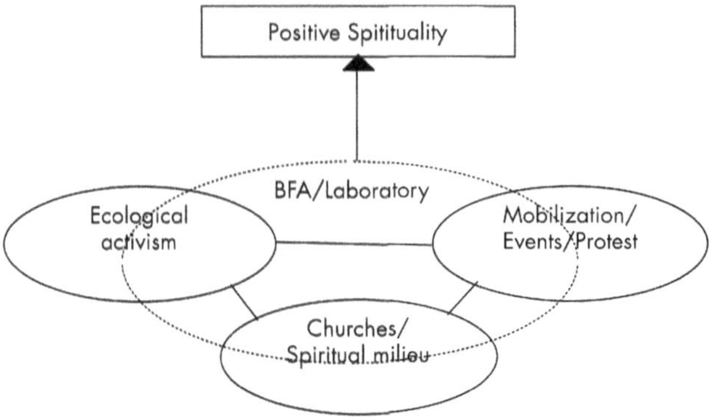

Figure 6.2 Hybridisation of the ecological and religious/spiritual world through the BFA Laboratory's work. This figure represents three milieus of activism that point toward positive spirituality. The ellipses are connected by straight line segments. On the left is the ellipse of ecological activism milieu, on the right is the ellipse of protest movements, mobilisations, and events, and at the bottom, centred, is the ellipse of the churches and the spiritual milieu. A large dotted ellipse representing the field of action of BFA and the Laboratory for Transition with an arrow pointing from this ellipse at the level of the ellipse Church/holistic milieu toward positive spirituality.

rather of parish communities or places of retreat run by the Church. "Spiritualised" approaches to transition do not reach decision-making structures and do not imply a reversal of ecclesial agendas. Indeed, when ecology is called into the Church, other theological approaches and actors are privileged. Whether it is Pope Francis's Encyclical *Laudato Si* or the initiatives of the World Council of Churches' Program "Justice, Peace and the Integrity of Creation", these theological languages sound more audible to religious institutions when it comes to defining an environmental or ecological platform. *BFA* remains one of the Christian works Churches support institutionally through agreements established by the synods of cantonal Churches. Yet, the Laboratory has no impact on these agreements. In the same way as in the world of ecological militancy, the Laboratory is still a bottom-up initiative that has little bearing on ecclesial structures. Indeed, no synod has appropriated part of the discourse or perspectives promoted by MME.

In short, the Laboratory shares bottom-up militant dynamics with the other "transition" movements, whether linked to Christian works or not. They then struggle to break through an institutional glass ceiling. Hence, while actors close to political or economic circles might have sympathies or use "interiorised" approaches to ecology, the institutions they represent remain alien to these discourses, calibrated as they are around individual transformation and citizen-based initiative. In this sense, despite the institutional resource provided by *BFA*, MME can hardly access the institutions' milieu, or at best is not invited as an expert. Spiritual discourse, centred on experience and feeling, is therefore one that does not mix with those of rational legal authorities embraced by public, synod and diocesan councils or companies' administrations. Nevertheless, *BFA*'s institutional foundation provides the benefit of ensuring that the Laboratory's actions for transition are sustained over time. The hybridisation work promoted by MME can then boast some success, even if the transition milieu invites him to express himself under the label of the meditator more than of the advocator. *BFA* thus remains the main representative of the organisation's "advocacy" posture, but its initial platform is not being radically renewed behind spiritual motivations. The Laboratory, for its part, represents the "meditating" posture and, in line with its transformation programme, seeks to act on individuals (collaborators, network members, publics of distanced social Christians) without structurally reaching institutions.

Conclusion

We have analysed the activities of the *Laboratory* and the networks mentioned by MME twice and two years apart – both focusing on *BFA*'s direct organisation and observing some lack of access to the institutional levels of the "internal transition" tropes. These various observations lead us to answer the chapter's initial questions as follows. First of all, it should be noted that the "win-win" contract described by *BFA*'s director shows the winner is indeed the Christian NGO. Through support of the *Laboratory for Inner Transition*, it is able to reactivate its base and broaden it to new, younger audiences interested in ecological and inner issues. In this sense, we are dealing with the "spiritualisation" of a segment of the religious milieu through the ecological question. This mainly affects a sub-milieu of distanced Christians or the reconfiguration of Christian social commitments. It is being aggregated with another sub-milieu of environmental militancy advocating an "inner transition". In that sense, it demonstrates "new areas of contestation" by religious and spiritual actors, as already noted by Claude Proeschel and David Koussens.

Behind this hybridisation strategy, the *Laboratory* is part of the Swiss scene as a particular religious innovation. On the one hand, it shows that the modalities of protest are rooted in progressivist axes and prioritises a demand for an "alternative" and "critical modernity" (Knauft, 2002). This means it achieves a practical renegotiation between references to tradition and progress – between local and global scales, external and internal transitions, meditation and militancy or even between religious milieus and institutional religion, secularity, and "holistic" spirituality movements. MME also establishes a link between the Anglo-American countercultural movements and its adjustment to French-speaking political contexts and traditions. In doing so, and in an intriguing way, he manages to go beyond the circles *BFA* usually reaches, by getting involved in ecospirituality circles, as well as in networks of the French-speaking sustainable transition movements. However, he does not manage to link the actors active in local environmental policy, neither at Swiss institutions level nor with more specific institutions such as the Churches. Indeed, contesting on religious and spiritual grounds proves to have its limitations when it comes to addressing institutions that do not consider hybridisation through the same modalities – or do, but in more conservative ways.

One of the aspects we have not addressed in this chapter (and it would be worth analysing separately) is the particular impact of the "inner transitions" concept on the cultural production community. Actors like MME have chosen a stance and discourse that are critical of the failings of modernity (Beck, 2016), and their "linking" capacity have found grounds for dissemination. However, in this context, the "inner transition" actors present themselves as virtuosos between meditation and advocacy postures, and in the end prove to be relegated to mere inspiring figures: These inspired figures do disseminate ecospiritual or "inner ecology" tropes, whether through the publication of books on ecospirituality and ecopsychology published in mainstream publishing houses, or by leading lecture cycles, roundtables and workshops at festivals. Thereby, they "popularise" (Knoblauch, 2008) these hybrid registers in the public space, and more precisely within a cosmopolitan sub-milieu (Becci et al., 2020), concerned with taking care of themselves (well-being, personal development, etc.) and the earth (clear ecological conscience, degrowth posture, etc.). Contesting through a spiritual motif, in the framework of progressive agendas, would therefore seem to have a powerful discursive dimension, even though it is part of an already established – but secular – activist movement whose modes of action are not necessarily renewed by the "inner transition" trope.

Notes

1 We thank Salomé Okoekpen for the data transcription and analysis; Irene Becci for comments on a previous version; and Dominique Macabies for academic English.
2 The annual budget for this NGO is 18 mio Swiss francs, 38 staff members in Switzerland.
3 We would like to thank MME for his confidence and comments on a previous version of this chapter. A second part-time staff member is working for the Laboratory.
4 American Association for the Advancement of Science.
5 Project PI: Irene Becci and Christophe Monnot. Survey duration: 2015–2017. Grant: Université de Lausanne *Volteface* Platform. Retrieved on 21 September 2020. http://www.volteface.ch/contenu/spiritualit%C3%A9-et-religion-les-nouveaux-carburants-de-la-transition-%C3%A9nerg%C3%A9tique-en-suisse.
6 Project PI is Irene Becci. Survey duration: January 2017 to January 2021. Grant SNSF.
7 Interview conducted on 7 June 2016 in the University of Lausanne.
8 Interview conducted on 3 July 2018 in the Lausanne *BFA* premises.
9 Interview conducted on 15 August 2017 in the Lausanne *BFA* premises.
10 For the analysis, the various conferences, interventions and interviews were transcribed and cross-referenced with the other texts and observations in the MAXQDA software.
11 Approximately 12% of the annual budget is allocated to these campaigns. The fundraising during these campaigns brings in about 35% (decreasing intake) of the annual budget.
12 More than 50% of the annual budget.
13 She is one of the cofounders of Max Havelaar, Claro, STEP, Clean Clothes Campaign and TerrEspoir.
14 www.cidse.org/lent-2019-learning-to-change-our-attitude-towards-others. Retrieved on 29 September 2019.
15 www.alliancesud.ch. Retrieved on 9 September 2018.

16 Interview with Bernard DuPasquier, 15 August 2017.
17 *Source:* Presentation flyer by *BFA*, heralding the *Laboratory for Inner Transition.*
18 Conversation with MME, on 30 March 2019.
19 Presentation flyer by the *Laboratory of Inner Transition.*
20 www.trilogies.org. Retrieved on 21 September 2020.
21 http://www.trilogies.org/blog-notes/creation-dun-laboratoire. Retrieved on 2 August 2018.
22 Interview on 3 July 2018, conducted in the Lausanne *BFA* offices.
23 A quotation drawn from the 3 July 2018 interview.
24 Coorganized between *BFA* (*Protestant*) – *Action de Carême* (*Catholic*), the *Theofil* University chaplains association (*œcumenical*) and *Pôle Sud* Vaudois trade union' socioultural center (secular, committed to ecology), http://polesud.ch/activite/tout-peut-encore-changer/ consulted on 7 November 2018.

Bibliography

Becci, I. and Monnot, C. 2016. "Spiritualité et Religion: Nouveaux Carburants vers la transition énergétique?" *Histoire, monde et cultures religieuses* 40: 93–109.

Becci, I., Monnot, C., Wenli, B. 2021. "Sensing 'Subtle Spirituality' among Environmentalists: A Swiss Study," *Journal for the Scientific Study of Religion, Nature and Culture*. Forthcoming.

Beck, U. 2006. *Cosmopolitan Vision*. Cambridge: Polity Press.

Beck, U. 2016. *The Metamorphosis of the World: How Climate Change is Transforming our Concept of the World.* Cambridge: Polity Press.

Berry, E. 2013. "Religious Environmentalism and Environmental Religion in America." *Religion Compass* 7 (10): 454–466.

Bidar, A. 2016. *Les Tisserands.* Paris: Les liens qui libèrent.

Bloch, J.P. 1998. "Alternative Spirituality and Environmentalism." *Review of Religious Research* 40 (1): 55–73.

Boudinot Garrett, F. and Le Vasseur, T. 2016. "'Grow the Scorched Ground Green' : Values and Ethics in the Transition Movement." *Journal for the Study of Religion, Nature and Culture* 10 (3): 379–404.

Dion, C., Laurent, M., 2015. *Tomorrow (Demain)*. Move Movie.

Egger, M.M. 2012. *La Terre comme soi-même: Repères pour une écospiritualité*. Geneva: Labor et Fides.

Egger, M.M. 2016. *Ecopsychologie: Retrouver notre lien à la Terre*. Geneva: Labor et Fides.

Fedele, A. and Knibbe, K. 2012. *Gender and Power in Contemporary Spirituality: Ethnographic Approaches*. London: Routledge.

Gottlieb, R.S. 2010. *The Oxford Handbook of Religion and Ecology*. Oxford: Oxford University Press.

Grandjean, A., Monnot, C. and Becci, I. 2018. "Spiritualités et Religions: Des 'facilitateurs' pour la transition énergétique ?" Pp. 157–175 in Niwa, N. and Frund, B. (eds.) *Volteface, la transition énergétique: Un projet de société*. Lausanne: Éditions d'en bas et Charles Léopold Mayer.

Kearns, L. 2012. "The Role of Religions in Activism." Pp. 414–428 in Dryzek, J.S., Nordgaard, R.B. and Schlosberg, D. (eds.) *The Oxford Handbook of Climate Change and Society*. Oxford: Oxford University Press.

Knauft, B.M. 2002. *Critically Modern: Alternatives, Alterities, Anthropologies*. Bloomington: Indiana University Press.

Knoblauch, H. 2008. "Spirituality and Popular Religion in Europe." *Social Compass* 55 (2): 140–153.

Koehrsen, J. 2018. "Religious Agency in Sustainability Transitions: Between Experimentation, Upscaling, and Regime Support." *Environmental Innovation and Societal Transitions* 27: 4–15.

Macy, J. and Brown, M.Y. 2014. *Coming Back to Life: The Guide to the Work That Reconnects*. Gabriola Island: New Society Publishers.

Mathieu, S. 2017. "Quelle nature du désir? Assistance médicale à la procréation, désir d'enfant et transmission." *Anthropologie et Sociétés* 41 (2): 121–138.

Naess, A. 2008. *Ecology of Wisdom*. Berkeley: Counterpoint.

Pope, F. 2015. *Laudato Si. On Care for our Common Home (Encyclical Letter)*. London: Catholic Truth Society.

Portier, P. and Béraud, C. 2015. *Métamorphoses catholiques*. Paris: Edition de la Maison des sciences de l'homme.

Stolz, J. et al. 2016. *(Un)believing in Modern Society : Religion, Spirituality, and Religious-Secular Competition*. London: Routledge.

Strauss, A. and Corbin, J. 1994. "Grounded Theory Methodology: An Overview. Handbook of Qualitative Research." Pp. 273–285 in Denzin, N.K. (ed.) *Handbook of Qualitative Research*. London: SAGE.

Taylor, B. 2016. "The Greening of Religion Hypothesis (Part one): From Lynn White, Jr and Claims That Religions Can Promote Environmentally Destructive Attitudes and Behaviors to Assertions They Are Becoming Environmentally Friendly". *Journal for the Scientific Study of Religion, Nature and Culture* 10 (3): 268–305.

Tricou, J. 2015. "La "cathosphère", montée en puissance de nouvelles autorités religieuses?" *Tic & société* 9 (1–2): 1–29.

Turina, I. 2013. "L'Église catholique et la cause de l'environnement." *Terrain* 60: 20–35.

Veldman, R.G., Szasz, A. and Haluza-DeLay, R. 2014. *How the World's Religions Are Responding to Climate Change*. Oxon: Routledge.

White, D.F., Rudy, A.P. and Gareau, B.J. 2016. *Environments, Natures and Social Theory: Towards a Critical Hybridity*. New York: Palgrave-Macmillan.

White, L. 1967. "The Historical Roots of our Ecological Crisis." *Science* 155: 1203–1207.

Yin, R.K. 1994. *Case Study Research: Design and Methods*. London: SAGE.

7 "We don't wanna be outlaws"

Hasidic Jews and their allies contest municipal bylaws in a Montreal neighbourhood

Valentina Gaddi

As is well illustrated in this book, when we think about objection in the name of conscience, our minds go almost directly to what are often considered the "classic cases": reproductive rights, the end of life, marriage or education and parenthood, and the complicated and sensitive entanglements of their legal, ethical and social implications.[1] This chapter addresses the phenomenon of conscientious objection from an unexpected – and seemingly more trivial – angle. The moral dilemmas I will consider deal with mundane questions like where to park a car, what we are allowed to build on our private balconies and how, or where it is permitted to open a new place of worship. Municipal bylaws are thus involved, or more precisely, to quote Mariana Valverde,

> the little-understood agglomerations of laws, ordinances, bylaws, rules, policies, inspection practices, and regulatory fines that cities have, and which do not seem to be known, in their totality, to anyone [but] that do, in fact, shape the experience of urban life to a great extent.
>
> (Valverde, 2012: 6-7).

While Valverde considers "diversity" in all its multiple dimensions, for the sake of this chapter I will focus on religious diversity, its relationship with municipal bylaws and the conflicts and contestation that may sometimes arise from their interaction. Following Valverde, I consider municipal bylaws and, I add, the place where they are debated in order to offer a propitious space in which to investigate and observe how contestation in the name of religion may unfold on a local scale in our contemporary society, allowing us to document new locations and new issues around which such contestation is expressed.

The bulk of this chapter will be devoted to an analysis of the controversies which took place between 2013 and 2016 around the public discussion of three municipal bylaws dealing with zoning and traffic in the Montreal neighbourhood of Outremont. More precisely, I will focus on the objection to these bylaws by the Hasidic Jews and their allies living in the borough. Who were these actors contesting the bylaws in question? How did the objection(s) take place? What kinds of actions were deployed? What arguments were invoked? What were the responses of the local borough council to these acts of contestation?

Hasidic Jews form a relatively small minority compared to other minority groups in Montreal.[2] However, the spatial implications of their lifestyle, in particular the concentration of the Hasidic population, together with the community's infrastructures,[3] in addition to their dress code, contribute to making their presence strongly felt in Outremont. Walking through the neighbourhood, one cannot help noticing the Hasidic men with their beards and sidelocks (*payes* in Yiddish), dressed in their long black coats from which the *tsitsit* dangle down (i.e. the knotted white tassels of their *talit*[4]) and the large fur hat (*shtreimel*) that they wear on holidays. As for the women, their behaviour and also their dress code are governed by the precepts of *tsinius*,[5] or modesty, which can be discerned from the dark clothes they wear that conceal their shoulders, upper arms and legs above the knee. Once married, their hair is covered with a kerchief, a headscarf or a wig. Speaking in general terms, Shauna Van Praagh describes Outremont's urban landscape as being comprised of sophisticated, secular French-speakers on the one hand, and traditional, religious Yiddish-speakers on the other (2008: 22). Gagnon, Dansereau and Germain are somewhat more nuanced in asserting that within the borough of Outremont, French Canadians along with ultra-orthodox[6] and Hasidic Jews constitute two large, identifiable groups and that this situation "tends to highlight linguistic, cultural, and religious differences" (2004: 62).

The data upon which this text is based was collected by means of an ethnographic study that followed the development of three controversies, referred to here as Purim, Sukkot and synagogues.[7] The first part of the text will be devoted to an explanation of the above, along with a brief outline of our analytical framework. The second part, which is more empirical in nature, will explore more closely how these controversies played out on a day-to-day basis, focusing on the multiple stages, or settings, where the borough residents discuss these issues. Finally, I will draw on these empirical extracts to advance some thoughts on the options for contestation that are available to pious citizens in our so-called secular societies and, more generally, on the place of devout citizens in the public spaces that our democracies offer us. This chapter may not provide straightforward answers to the possibility and the challenges of creating a common standard in a pluralistic society. Rather, I will adopt a sociological approach, outlining how a particular norm – in this case, a municipal bylaw – comes to be proposed and implemented in a pluralistic neighbourhood, and how such bylaws are contested by concerned citizens, pious or not, in the name of religion or, as we will see, for other reasons. Moreover, our approach will reveal how this contestation is expressed in different ways, depending on the public that is being addressed. All of this will hopefully allow us to suggest several new avenues for reflection, not only on the manner in which (by)laws are produced, but also on the conditions for public debate in our pluralistic and democratic societies.

The controversial bylaws and the analytical framework

In my account of the three controversies that took place in Outremont between 2014 and 2017, I propose to describe how events unfolded simultaneously in several different settings: on *front-stage* at the borough council and on *back-stage* at the council, but also in informal discussions that I had with Hasidim and non-Hasidim in the course of my fieldwork.[8] *Front-stage* and *back-stage* establish the Goffmanian theoretical framework that will allow us to account for what Lemieux (2007) calls "the laminated composition of controversies", or their multi-level nature. Following Eliasoph (1998), I adopt Goffman's terminology to describe the principal interactions that took place *front-stage* at the borough council, as well as the more peripheral interactions that took place *back-stage*, i.e. those that were considered marginal by the participants themselves, uttered away from the microphone or *sotto voce*. Goffman convincingly demonstrated that the ways of communicating are very different when people are on stage and when they are behind the scenes:

> Speaking on stage and speaking behind the scenes are not the same thing. There is a sharp distinction in the way situations are framed that corresponds to the extent to which they are public, i.e. depending on whether people are giving a public performance or chatting in private among friends."
>
> (Cefaï, 2007: 575; our translation).

The norms that govern conversation change depending on who is listening. Warner describes the phenomenon like this: "When appearing in a *public* field, genres of arguments and polemic must accommodate themselves to the spatial conditions of public address" (Warner, 2005: 90).

Three municipal bylaws are at the heart of the controversies that interest us. First, the application of the traffic and parking bylaws[9] was the focus of attention in discussions involving the celebration of the Purim holiday. During Purim, which commemorates a miracle that happened to the Jewish people in ancient Persia, children and young boys in the Hasidic community don disguises and go from house to house collecting money for the poor in exchange for a little gift, generally cakes or candy. To ensure the children's safety, the Hasidic schools hire small buses to shuttle boys between the ages of 12 and 16 around the neighbourhood. The bylaw mentioned above came into effect in 2003 and was originally adopted to prevent large inter-city buses from driving through the streets of Outremont.[10] It was never intended to interfere with the celebration of Purim, although this turned out to be one of its effects. In 2012, Céline Forget, one of the borough councillors, took it upon herself to monitor the celebration, because she suspected that buses considered illegal under the 2003 bylaw were being used by community schools. This degenerated into a direct confrontation between the councillor and the Hasidim, which was widely viewed on YouTube.[11] Similar tense scenes were repeated in subsequent years, creating conflict between the schools, who were concerned about ensuring that the holiday was celebrated safely, and certain residents, who demanded that the buses be monitored and fines imposed. The conflict eventually made its way to the borough council, where representatives of the Hasidim asked that the bylaw be modified, or at least not applied during Purim, whereas those residents who opposed their request insisted that the bylaw be strictly enforced and the celebration of the holiday carefully monitored, given the disturbances it had caused in the streets of the borough.

The next controversy involved the holiday of Sukkot,[12] and led to a proposal to change the zoning bylaws governing temporary shelters.[13] Sukkot are small wooden cabins that some Jews temporarily install on their balconies during the holiday bearing the same name. Outremont has a specific bylaw regulating their installation: zoning bylaw 1177. Section 6.1 of this bylaw allows Sukkot to remain in place for a maximum period of 15 days.[14] However, whenever the urban planning department sought to apply the bylaw, this wording turned out to be problematic for, since nowhere is it indicated when the 15-day count is to begin. In the autumn of 2014, the employees of the department therefore requested that the borough council modify the bylaw, adopting a wording based on that used by the borough of Côte-des-Neiges–Notre-Dame-de-Grâce, which allows soukkot to be erected seven days before the holiday and requires them to be dismantled seven days after the holiday. During the discussion at the council meeting, Councillor Céline Forget succeeded in amending the new wording so that it became more restrictive: "three days before and three days after". It was with this wording that the borough council undertook to amend the bylaw,[15] and it was along these lines that the ensuing argument took shape. On one side there were those who supported the "three days before and three days after" version, while the other side supported the version of "seven days before and seven days after".

The final controversy we will consider was also caused by a change to the zoning bylaws, which in this case was meant to prohibit the construction of places of worship on the borough's commercial arteries.[16] The notice of the motion to modify the zoning bylaw was tabled in the autumn of 2015. What it proposed was the banning of places devoted to "worship and religion" on Laurier Avenue and Bernard Avenue, while allowing such places in a zone designated as C6, north of Van Horne Avenue between Hutchison and Querbes streets. Although synagogues are not mentioned explicitly, the motion was perceived by many Hasidim and non-Hasidim alike as directly targeting the Hasidic community. The population of all the Hasidic congregations that make up the community was growing, and each wanted to be able to have its own synagogue within walking distance, where their members could regularly pray. The proposed change to the bylaw would prevent them, for all intents and purposes, from opening any new place of worship within the borough. Indeed, building permits are not generally granted on residential streets, and since 2003 another bylaw has prohibited the construction of places of worship on the one remaining commercial artery, Van Horne Avenue. On the other hand, those who supported the proposed change to the bylaw were convinced that banning places of worship was the only way to revitalise local businesses, whose volume of sales had been declining in recent years.

A number of important factors are clearly intersecting here, including the legislative framework, the spiritual domain, people's intimate lives and the manner in which such issues are publicised. In what follows, I will explore the very specific experience that these controversies gave rise to within the borough, tracing their trajectory and focusing on the manner in which the municipal bylaws were contested. Before turning to the issues of that contestation and the dissonance we observed between what people said front-stage versus back-stage, I will briefly describe the individual and collective protagonists who were implicated in this contestation and the range of actions they deployed to show their disagreement.

Contestation by Hasidim and their allies both front-stage and back-stage

We will now consider the two stages where the controversies unfolded and where the *publicity* was widely different: first, the borough council, a public space *par excellence*, where these divisive subjects were debated by borough residents and elected officials; second, the more intimate discussions I had with some residents – Hasidim and non-Hasidim. The majority of my respondents consisted of people who, in various ways, supported the Hasidic community and questioned the adoption or application of the regulations, which they considered to be targeting the Hasidic minority. More precisely, when asked, my respondents called themselves "activists" and "concerned citizens". The word "activist" was employed by the Jewish Hasidic men I met as a translation of the Hebrew word *askan* (עסקן), which is derived from the word "esak", which means "affair"; but also, from *asuk*, which means "occupied" or "involved". Spielman and Goldberg (1998) describe *askanim* (plural) as "indigenous paraprofessionals", while Mitnick (1999) speaks rather in terms of "community activists". Lightman and Shor offer us a more complete definition:

> Within the ultra-Orthodox world, askanim attempt to address and resolve a variety of personal problems of individuals and families, as well as other social and financial difficulties within their communities. As necessary, they also serve as a "bridge" between the ultra-Orthodox families and the world outside.
>
> (Lightman and Shor, 2002: 316)

As for the non-Hasidic respondents, they were mostly women, between 25 and 45 years old, who describe themselves as "concerned" about the situation in Outremont and are willing to help their Hasidic neighbours defend their rights. On front-stage, their actions covered the conventional democratic ways of expressing dissent with a municipal bylaw in Canada, from participating and speaking during question time in the borough council or in public consultations, getting together in order to ask for a referendum when permitted, and talking to local newspapers and media.

On front-stage: the municipal framework and the results of alignment with this framework

The contextualisation of the controversies outlined above shows their "municipal" matrix; for it was around the three municipal bylaws that the controversies emerged and played out in the public space of the neighbourhood. To use a more sociological terminology, we could maintain that when controversies take place in public, on stage at the borough council, the actors align themselves with a typical framework (Goffman, 1974), which crystallises around municipal regulations. This "master framework" (Snow and Benford, 1992: 138–140), which we refer to as municipal, is set and imposed by the council, and in particular by the chair of the meetings (generally the mayor) when draft regulations are presented. When they speak at council meetings, citizens are often reminded that the debate is taking place within the field of municipal laws.

When citizens expressed themselves "on stage" at council meetings in order to contest the controversial bylaws, they placed themselves within this dominant framework. Questions or comments made by residents often revolved around regulations for buses, temporary shelters and places of worship. This was the case, for example, of one woman who questioned the council about the celebration of Purim. After briefly explaining the context of her presence and that of her family within the borough, and stating her appreciation of the "cultural contribution" made by her Hasidic neighbours, she went on to speak of the history of the bylaw:

> For over twenty years, the Hasidic community has used minibuses to safely transport their children during the festival, without any conflict. Even after 2003, when By-law AO-20 was adopted to restrict the circulation of buses, these same minibuses were used without incident. It was only in 2009 that the Hasidic community was suddenly accused of breaking the law. It was decided to give tickets for the use of these same minibuses during the Purim festival, a practice that occurred only in Outremont. However, these vehicles had never been a problem before. So, what changed in 2009? It seems that what changed is that Outremont applied a new interpretation of the regulation, making the use of these minibuses illegal. According to this new interpretation, these vehicles were treated as being in the same category as buses. The council makes insignificant distinctions in the application of the regulations. For example, you make a distinction between single-wheeled and double-wheeled minibuses. But in bus rental agencies in Quebec, all of these vehicles are identified as "minibuses".

As we can see, the woman displayed an extremely detailed knowledge of the bylaw, as well as of the technical issues that made its application problematic during the celebration of the festival, and it is on this basis that her contestation was presented. Placing herself within the same framework, another woman asked the council to review the bylaw, recognising that sometimes the laws simply do not work anymore and need to be changed. In the case of the controversy involving the synagogues, the bylaw on places of worship was the subject of several questions put to the council between the spring of 2015 and the autumn of 2017, both by people requesting that the proposed zoning change be abandoned and by people congratulating the council and encouraging it to go ahead with the idea. Questions were often formulated using the official grammar of bylaws, sometimes adopting the "opinion mode", and sometimes the "criticism mode", in an effort to convince the council not to adopt the bylaw (in the case of Sukkot, and synagogues), or to change it or not apply it (in the case of Purim) (Cardon, Heurtin, and Lemieux, 1995).

Answers were provided by councillors or the mayor immediately after questions or comments from the public and were limited to technical issues, thus promoting alignment with this municipal framework. When a Hasidic man asked the council, during a council meeting, to drop the bylaw on places of worship, councillor Gremaud, who occasionally assumed the role of Acting Mayor, replied that the draft bylaw was not addressed "specifically at the Hasidic community", but that it "will indicate places for worship, for all places of worship, regardless of religious denomination". The rule "is not directed against one community; it is a rule that will apply to all communities", she stated. The ultimate goal of the bylaw was to protect commercial avenues because "in Outremont, we care about their economic development". Secondly, she reminded him that, by following the legislative process for all changes in the zoning bylaw, the bylaw would also be discussed in a public session. On this point, councillor Potvin echoed her, saying:

> With the public meeting, you will have the right to express yourself with all due respect ... and if there are changes to be made, we will make them at that time, but you have a public meeting to express your requests and your specifics. ... that is why there is all this legal procedure ... and I will be happy to hear you, to hear the members of your community ... and that is what the *vivre-ensemble* is.[17]

As with the Purim festival, where police surveillance of the celebration was to be interpreted as a precaution that one would take for any event of this kind (cf. Halloween), the goal here was not to apply a restrictive and specific regulation to one community. For places of worship, again, the council was not specifically targeting Hasidim: It was not a question of synagogues, but of places of worship, and the regulation was aimed in the same way at all religious communities. Moreover, the focus of the discussion was reoriented towards the objective of the regulation, namely to revitalise commercial arteries, thus avoiding any discussion of the consequences that the adoption of such a regulation could have on the Hasidic communities.

During public consultations, the mayor often explicitly invited the speakers to position themselves within a binary municipal framework, choosing "seven days or three days" for the Succot bylaw; and "for or against" for the bylaw on places of worship. This binary logic also manifested itself at council meetings. During one particularly animated session on the question of places of worship, the mayor decided to make an exception to the borough bylaw which limits the number of questions on the same subject to three, instead of allowing three interventions for, and three against, the bylaw. Finally, it was not uncommon for the speakers in public consultations to "anticipate" this same framework, in order to make their comments clearer. This was the case with one Hasidic man who, after asking his question about places of worship, thanked the mayor for her answer and, before retiring, wished to specify that "of course, I will vote against the change in the zoning". Shortly afterwards, in the same manner, another Hasidic man took leave of the councillors and the mayor with similar words: "Thank you for your time and I am opposed to this bylaw".

By focusing on the regulatory issues alone, the debate becomes not only polarised but also highly technical, ignoring the practical implications for the Hasidic population. We are no longer talking about Hasidim, but about the buses whose presence must be regulated in relation to safety issues; not just about synagogues, but about all places of worship; not about the holiday of Sukkot, but about the number of days that temporary shelters are to be allowed. Any religion would fit into this discursive style of reasoning and the issues of cohabitation between Hasidim and non-Hasidim, as well as the needs of the Hasidic communities, are thus set aside. Debates over these rules and the technical details thereof "absorb" the contesting speakers, who remain caught up within this framework or are constantly brought back to it (Goffman, 1974: 345). Since it is shared by all participants in the conversation, the framework becomes invisible and yet continues to constrain residents' interventions, often leaving them dissatisfied and with the impression that "we are not talking about the real issues" (Berger, 2009).

Contestation back-stage

Behind the scenes, people's conduct is less inhibited (Goffman, 1963: 198) and the discourse is quite different: It is more often whispered than loudly proclaimed. For example, halfway through the presentation of the reasons for the proposed regulation to prohibit the opening of new places of worship on commercial avenues, one Hasidic man sitting in front of me whispered: "This is the typical pattern of anti-Semitism: Our business is not doing well, let's blame the Jews!" This was also the case with a Hasidic woman who, following the second adoption of the draft regulations on places of worship, commented to me in exasperation: "Why they don't like us? Why? It is so obvious!"

The back-stage discourse gradually moved away from municipal bylaws and technical issues to address the general situation in Outremont as it relates to the relationship between Hasidim and non-Hasidim, as well as the behaviour of the borough council. Some people alluded in a nuanced way to a "certain animosity" that permeates the attitude of non-Hasidim towards the Hasidim. One commonly heard view is that "it is not convenient to have a Hasidic neighbour because if something ever happened to you, for example, he would not help you". Shortly after arriving in Outremont, one woman I met during my fieldwork overheard this idea bandied about by her neighbours while she was gardening. She didn't expect it, but many of them "had it in for the Hasidim". For her, however, this remained of secondary importance when compared to the more "serious" issue of the council's behaviour.

Janine, another woman I met, incorporated both these two dimensions in our discussion of the controversies, that is, the presence of regulations which, according to her, target the Hasidic communities, and the attitude of some Outremontais[18] towards this minority. In particular, she mentioned another bylaw that she had discovered by chance while conversing with her Hasidic neighbour across their balconies. Under this bylaw, her neighbour, and also other Hasidic families, had been fined for putting up trellises on their balconies to prevent their children from falling. Janine found the idea of the trellises clever and did not understand the coercive reaction of the borough, which, after investigation, she discovered was aimed exclusively at Hasidic families. Moreover, she added that the behaviour of some non-Hasidim she observed in the park when she went there with her children both disturbed her and alerted her:

> There are things I had been hearing since I was a mother in Outremont. I would go to the park and hear people saying stuff like "Oh the Jewish families are messy"; "the Jewish kids were running out of control ..." and you know, "they leave garbage everywhere ...", "their yards are messy ...", I was like, really? Are you really like ... really? Again? This is not cool!

As we continued our conversation, she confided to me that, in her view, there is no doubt that what is happening in Outremont is anti-Semitism. However, she acknowledged the impossibility of using that term in public. Others had reminded her of this: "Oh, they told me so many times not to say it ... just not use it in public ... but, you know, it should be used in ... you know, one to one conversations. It's a word that scares people".

Another woman, Lucy, put aside the question of neighbourhood relations to talk about the existence of systemic racism in the neighbourhood, placing the responsibility on the borough council:

> I think there is a big problem of racism in Outremont. What the council is doing, they are using systemic racism, institutional racism, because they are creating laws. ... they are using the institutions. ... it's an institutional racism. ... the institution of the council is used to target the Jewish community, you see ... that's racism. I think there is a problem of discrimination, of targeting this community, they want to stop their practices, they see them as "the other", "they have to speak French, they have to act like us, they have to integrate". There is no concept that we can live with diversity! There is intolerance!

Although she never employed the term anti-Semitism, she referred to people who don't like the Hasidim, who are anti-Hasidim: "The people who don't like the Hasidim, who are anti-Hasidim". Like Janine, she remarked on the difficulty of mobilising these arguments in the public spaces of the neighbourhood: "If I go to the council tomorrow and say 'You are all guilty of systemic racism', oh they will just get mad at me and throw me out and deny it".

In back-stage contestations, during the long conversations that constituted our interviews, some Hasidim used the word racism and more often anti-Semitism in referring to a "very small minority" of Outremont residents. However, they remain sceptical about the use of these words to describe the more global situation in the neighbourhood, meaning the day-to-day interaction and innocuous neighbourly relationships. During our interview with Simcha, a young Hasidic man, for example, he explained to me that "I have never felt any anti-Semitism, hate, or any dislike in the streets of Outremont". The same was true for his friends, he said.

> I ask them if they have ever felt a real threat to their … you know, who they are, anti-Semitism, hate, towards them, if they were ever attacked physically. Nobody, nobody could tell me that they were actually physically threatened. I asked them, if they go to other towns, other cities, North, and Laurentians and Mauricie, wherever we go we feel … you know, people look at us sometimes, it's interesting and different, but we don't feel any physical threat.

When he talked about the council and the bylaws, which he believed were specifically aimed at the community, Simcha also talked about "attitudes": "It's about the attitude the council has toward the Hasidic community". He described as anti-Semitic only a small group of people who were born to hate, although they didn't develop this "psychology of hate" by radicalising themselves when faced with others who were different, like some of Outremont's non-Hasidic residents. While a man called Yidel described the council's actions in a whispered comment as anti-Semitic, when he was talking with me sitting at the table in the kindergarten at his synagogue, he widened the conversation to the entire borough. He first gave me a more nuanced portrait of the neighbourhood. He acknowledged that there were racist persons, who were in a minority in Outremont; but also some "positive" people, meaning allies who were ready to speak up for them; and then a majority whom he considered "neutral", some with a favourable prejudice towards Jews ("neutral-in favour persons"), others with an unfavourable prejudice ("neutral-negative persons"). In his opinion, these "neutral people" did not harbour any specific attitude towards their Hasidic neighbours, but once a controversy arose, they were in a way forced to choose their side. Even more interestingly, he quickly abandoned the "municipal framework" in order to share with me a few anecdotes that in his opinion were the real core of the controversies. For example, Yidel shared with me the following vignette, which he witnessed while sitting in his car one day in the autumn:

> A 13-year-old boy was raking out the leaves from his yard, and he put them next to the sidewalk. So it became a big big pile … and he felt that it's gonna be difficult for the cars to park, or for people to cross the street, because it was a big, big pile. So, in his mind he thought, "you know what? I'll go on the street, I'll spread it out, so the cars are gonna drive by and it's gonna go away!" He started doing that and a neighbour, a non-Jewish neighbour, saw it, and he got upset. … I saw him looking at the kid for five to ten minutes and starting to get angry. Now he had two ways out of this: either you stay angry and when the next public meeting comes you bash all the Hassidic Jewish; or, as I said, you go to the kid and talk to him! So he went to the kid, he spoke to the kid, I was in my car, I don't even know what the conversation

> was, and the kid said, "ok, I didn't think about it, I am sorry ..." and he took it back! That's it! Not a big deal! His point of view was like this, that it's better like this, you disagree, tell him! ... That's the way neighbours should live!

Yidel's anecdote illustrates very well the connection between everyday "failed interactions" (Amiraux and Araya-Moreno, 2014) between Hasidim and non-Hasidim and the radicalisation of the situation in Outremont, which materialises in controversies that take place at the borough council. However, there seems to be no place where such matters can be discussed in Outremont's public space, where all the conversations revolve around municipal bylaws and technical issues.

Conclusion

What can we learn from these controversies about religious contestation in Quebec today? First of all, our observations confirm the initial intuition that it is not exclusively those laws which touch on major moral issues (life, death, or the education of children) that are being challenged. Bylaws which at first glance may seem quite innocuous, like those we have discussed here, are contested just as vigorously and passionately by pious individuals who feel their lifestyle is being threatened. Moreover, and this is our second finding, it is not only religious people who are contesting the bylaws. The Hasidim who live in the neighbourhood in question are supported in their demands by non-Hasidim: citizens, and particularly women citizens, who feel the need to engage individually and collectively in support of their Jewish neighbours. This refutes the idea that was widely disseminated in the media that the controversies in Outremont set Hasidim against non-Hasidim. Third, the ethnographic description briefly provided above challenges the basic premise put forward in this book, namely the idea that contestation is engaged "in the name of religion". Indeed, the protests we described were shaped principally by the dominant municipal framework, leaving aside "questions of religion", whether they relate to daily worship (what one might call "everyday religion"), theological explanations or even to a demand for religious freedom. While this may be due to the realisation on the part of those involved in the protests that religious matters are non-intelligible (Amiraux, 2014), our account underscores how certain mechanisms of *avoidance* operate in public discussions of the issues connected with religion: in this case, avoidance of the needs of a growing religious community, avoidance of the requirements of cohabitation between Hasidim and non-Hasidim and avoidance of the experience of anti-Semitism. This avoidance is imposed by the dominant municipal framework, responsibility for which lies with the municipal council, but those actors in the protests, that is, those who actively contest, are also participating in that framework when they speak in the public arena, demonstrating thereby a detailed understanding of what I have called the "grammar of Outremont".

This does not mean that certain "mistakes" – or, to once again employ Goffman's terms (1974: 201), "out-of-frame" activities – never occur when the contestation is taking place on stage. However, as in all grammars, these errors only serve to better highlight the presence of the framework, reminding us of its vulnerability, as well as the consequences of its breakdown. The most eloquent case was that of a citizen who spoke at the public consultation around the Sukkot, presenting a petition in favour of the initial version of "seven days before, seven days after" and suggesting that the vote on this bylaw offered the council an opportunity to establish a real dialogue between all the communities in the borough. Some people sitting behind him started grumbling. The speaker then turned to them and said that his "message of hope" was also addressed at those fellow citizens "who do not like the Hasidim". The comments grew louder and louder: Booing was added to the voices that rose from the front rows. A visibly angry citizen sitting in the front row turned to the man with the microphone and accused him of calling him an anti-Semite. The mayor then intervened, repeatedly calling for silence. "We don't want that! We don't want to stop talking, sir. I must ask you to leave the room". With an embarrassed smile on his face, the speaker sat down, evidently upset, and then tried to awkwardly add something over the microphone. A policeman then arrived, asked him to stand up and escorted him out of the room to the applause of the crowd, while other Hasidic men stopped him to thank him and shake his hand. When this citizen stated that his "message of hope" was also addressed at his fellow citizens "who don't like Hasidim", the framework broke down (Goffman, 1974: 345). The booing in the room signalled an alert. The tone of his speech was clearly not appreciated. The punishment was heavy, a sign that his conduct was not acceptable not only to the mayor, but also to the whole assembly.

Finally, this chapter invites us to think more deeply about contestation in the name of religion, in ways that go beyond conscientious objection. In particular, this means questioning the manner in which we construct norms and laws, as well as reflecting on the conditions for dialogue in our democratic societies. Indeed, one could very well ask: Who conceived the regulations in question? To meet whose requirements? In order to develop what kind of neighbourhood and for whom? These are questions which have already been raised by the critical urban studies of the 1990s (Sandercock, 1998), but we can extend their scope beyond the urban dimension in order to include all normative dimensions. All these questions came together in the words of one Hasidic woman with whom I discussed these controversies, when she exclaimed: "We don't wanna be outlaws, but we are forced to!" She was referring to the fact that, in her view, certain regulations were specifically designed to force a part of the population, i.e. the Hasidic population, into violating the law. At which point the larger question becomes how to truly include minority and minoritised populations in the decision-making and law-making processes. The modalities of contestation in Outremont effectively highlight certain limitations in our democratic institutions, particularly those practices involving participatory democracy (e.g. question times, public consultations), which are not always capable of ensuring respect for the rights – but also the needs – of minorities in our pluralistic societies.

Notes

1 I would like to thank Elliott Macklovitch for his help in translating this chapter.

2 There are around 5200 Hasidic Jews in the borough of Outremont and in the adjacent borough of the Plateau Mont-Royal (Mile End sector). For more demographic data, see Anctil, 2019.

3 It is forbidden for Hasidic Jews to drive or use public transport on Shabbat and other religious holidays; consequently, they need to live close to their synagogue. For practical reasons, they also prefer to live near stores that sell kosher food. Moreover, the different Hasidic communities each have their own schools and other facilities, like the *mykvoth* (ritual baths) or *yeshivot* (talmudic schools).

4 A fringed undergarment passed over the head and worn under the shirt (*talit katan*). The word *talit* also designates the prayer shawl in which men wrap their upper body (and sometimes their head) during morning prayers (*talit gadol*).

5 The conventions stemming from the concept of *tsinius* (modesty or decency, in Yiddish) apply both to men and to women, as well as to the relations between people of the opposite sex. *Tsinius* also governs the choice of books and images to which Hasidim allow themselves to be exposed, along with the leisurely activities they can engage in. For more details, see Fader, 2009.

6 The term "ultra-orthodox" is often employed in the English and French literature to refer both to Hasidic Jews, whose distinguishing characteristic is their loyalty to a spiritual master who can trace his roots back to the *rebbes* of Eastern Europe, as well as to Jews who may be strictly observant in following the laws and traditions of Judaism but who are not affiliated with a particular spiritual master (Shahar et al., 1997). In this text, however, I prefer to use the terms "Hasidim" and "Hasidic Jews", for two reasons. Many religious Jews consider the term "ultra-orthodox" to be pejorative (King, 2003: 312). What is more, the Hasidic Jews that I interacted with while conducting my research employed the term very rarely, preferring instead to speak simply of "Jews", or *Yidn* in Yiddish.

7 For a complete analysis of these three controversies and of the methodology employed, see my Master's dissertation (Gaddi, 2016).

8 All the names that appear below are invented, in order to protect the identities of those who participated in my research.

9 Most municipal bylaws in Outremont are only published in French. This one, the *Règlement relatif à la circulation et au stationnement*, No. 1171 AO-20, Chapter XI (2013-02-28), sets the rules – among other things – for buses and minibuses that drive through the streets of the borough.

10 Particularly those large buses that members of the Hasidic community take to travel back and forth between Montreal and New York, which were blocking traffic in the streets of Outremont.

11 http://www.youtube.com/watch?v=I5g71VACYw0. Retrieved on 19 September 2020.

12 Celebrated in the autumn, this holiday, also called the Feast of Tabernacles, lasts eight days, during which Jews who wish to do so eat their meals outside, in a temporary wooden cabin. Sukkot commemorates the precarious conditions the Israelites lived in when they crossed the desert after fleeing Egypt, as well as the divine protection that God afforded them.

13 Arrondissement d'Outremont, *Règlement modifiant le règlement de zonage*, No. 1177 AO-271-P1, Article 6.1 (2014-10-29), henceforth referred to as the Bylaw on Sukkot.

14 Arrondissement d'Outremont, *Règlement de zonage* No. 1177 AO-271-P1 (2014-10-29), Article 6.1. Retrieved on 19 September 2020. http://ville.montreal.qc.ca/pls/portal/docs/PAGE/ARROND_OUT_FR/MEDIA/DOCUMENTS/1177-REGLEMENT-ZONAGE-2013.PDF.

15 The Quebec government's Act Respecting Land Use Planning and Development imposes a very rigorous process for adopting changes to zoning regulations. After an initial adoption, public consultations are required so that the opinions of all residents can be heard, and then the bill must be adopted a second time by the borough council. Even then, voting residents have the right to call for a referendum if they feel that the proposed change requires further debate. The results of the referendum are binding; and if no referendum is requested, the borough council must approve the new bylaw a third time. *Loi sur l'aménagement et l'urbanisme* (L.R.Q. c. A-19.1). Retrieved on 19 September 2020. http://legisquebec.gouv.qc.ca/fr/pdf/cs/A-19.1.pdf.

16 Arrondissement d'Outremont, *Règlement modifiant le règlement de zonage*, No. 1117 concernant l'usage relié au culte (2015-05-24), henceforth referred to as the By-law on Places of Worship.

17 *Vivre-ensemble* (literally "living together") is a normative term often employed in the political and administrative lexicon of Quebec (at all levels) in order to describe the ideal of a pluralistic society where all members live together peacefully and respectfully, regardless of their differences.

18 The French term used to designate people living in Outremont.

Bibliography

Amiraux, V. 2014. "Visibilité, transparence et commérage: de quelques conditions de possibilité de l'islamophobie... et de la citoyenneté." *Sociologie* 5: 81–95.

Amiraux, V. and Araya-Moreno, J. 2014. "Pluralism and Radicalization: Mind the Gap!" Pp. 92–120 in Dawson, L.L. and Bramadat, P. (eds.) *Religious Radicalization and Securitization in Canada and Beyond.* Toronto: University of Toronto Press.

Anctil, P. 2019. "Vers une sociologie des communautés hassidiques de Montréal." Pp. 13–34 in Anctil, P. and Robinson, I. (eds.) *Les Juifs Hassidiques de Montréal.* Montréal: PUM.

Berger, M. 2009. "Quand pourrons-nous parler des choses? Quelques contraintes à la référentialité des voix profanes dans un dispositif d'urbanisme participatif." Pp. 253–280 in Cantelli, F., Pattaroni, L., Roca, M. and Stavo-Debauge, J. (eds.) *Sensibilités pragmatiques. Enquêter sur l'action publique.* Bruxelles: Peter Lang.

Blondiaux, L. 2003. "Publics imaginés et publics réels. La sollicitation des habitants dans une expérience de participation locale." Pp. 313–326 in Cefaï, D. and Pasquier, D. (eds.) *Les sens du public: publics politiques, publics médiatiques.* Paris: Presses Universitaires de France.

Cardon, D., Heurtin, J.-P. and Lemieux, C. 1995. "Parler en Public." *Politix* 8 (3rd trimester 31): 5–19.

Cefaï, D. and Gardella, E. 2012. "Comment analyser une situation selon le dernier Goffman ? *De Frame Analysis à Forms of Talk.*" Pp. 231–263 in Cefaï, D. and Perreau, L. (eds.) *Erving Goffman et l'ordre de l'interaction.* Paris: CURAPP-ESS/CEMS-IMM.

Cefaï, D. 2007. *Pourquoi se mobilise-t-on ? Les théories de l'action collective.* Paris: La Découverte.

Eliasoph, N. 1998. *Avoiding Politics. How Americans Produce Apathy in Everyday Life.* Cambridge: Cambridge University Press.

Fader, A. 2009. *Mitzvah Girls: Bringing Up the Next Generation of Hasidic Jews in Brooklyn.* Princeton: Princeton University Press.

Gaddi, V. 2016. *La grammaire d'Outremont. Ethnographie de trois controverses autour des hassidim.* Master's thesis. Montreal: Département de Sociologie, Université de Montréal.

Gagnon, J.E., Dansereau, F. and Germain, A. 2004. "Ethnic Dilemmas? Religion, Diversity and Multicultural Planning in Montreal." *Canadian Ethnic Studies Journal* 36 (2): 51–75.

Goffman, E. 1963. *Behavior in Public Places. Notes on the Social Organization of Gatherings*. New York: Simon and Schuster.

Goffman, E. 1974. *Frame Analysis: An Essay on the Organization of Experience*. Harvard: Harvard University Press.

King, J. 2003. *From the Ghetto to the Main: The Story of the Jews of Montreal*. Montreal: Montreal Jewish Publication Society.

Lemieux, C. 2007. "À quoi sert l'analyse des controverses?" *Mil neuf cent. Revue d'histoire intellectuelle* 1 (25): 191–212.

Lightman, E. and Shor, R. 2002. "Askanim: Informal Helpers and Cultural Brokers as a Bridge to Secular Helpers for the Ultra-Orthodox Jewish Communities of Israel and Canada." *Families in Society: The Journal of Contemporary Social Services* 83 (3): 315–324.

Mitnick, Y. 1999. "An Unorthodox Approach for the Orthodox Teen." *The Jewish Observer* 32 (9): 69–73.

Sandercock, L. 1998. *Towards Cosmopolis: Planning for Multicultural Cities*. London: John Wiley.

Scott, R.L. 1991. "Can Controversy Be Analyzed to Yield Useful Insights for Arguments." Pp. 20–21 in Parson, D.W. (ed.) *Argument in Controversy: Proceedings of the Seventh AFA/SCA Conference on Argumentation*. Annandale, VA: Speech Communication Association.

Shahar, C., Weinfeld, M. and Schnoor, R.F. 1997. *Survey of the Hasidic and Ultra-Orthodox Communities in Outremont and Surrounding Areas*. Outremont: COHO, Coalition d'Organisations Hassidiques.

Simon, S. 2016. "Traduire la différence dans une société démocratique: le Québec après la Charte des valeurs." Pp. 67–87 in Gagnon, Alain-G. and St-Louis, Jean-Charles (eds.) *Les conditions du dialogue au Québec: laïcité, réciprocité, pluralisme*. Montréal: Québec Amérique.

Snow, D.A. and Benford, R.D. 1992. "Master Frames and Cycles of Protest." Pp. 133–155 in Morris, A.D. and McClurg Mueller, C. (eds.) *Frontiers in Social Movement Theory*. New Haven: Yale University Press.

Spielman, Y. and Goldberg, A. 1998. *Fostering Cooperation between Social Workers and Religious Leaders*. Jerusalem: Department of Social Services.

Stocker, V. 2003. "Drawing the Line: Hasidic Jews, Eruvim, and the Public Space of Outremont, Quebec." *History of Religions* 43(1): 18–49.

Valverde, M. 2012. *Everyday Law on the Street: City Governance in an Age of Diversity*. Chicago: University of Chicago Press.

Van Praagh, S. 2008. "View from the Succah: Religion and Neighbourly Relations." Pp. 21–40 in Moon, Richard (ed.) *Law and Religious Pluralism in Canada*. Vancouver: UBC Press.

Warner, M. 2005. *Publics and Counterpublics*. New York: Zone Books.

Part III

The rhetoric of contestation

8 Secular and religious reasons for conscientious objection

The case of medical assistance in dying

Isabelle Dumont and Jocelyn Maclure

In this chapter, we wish to participate in the discussion on the rights and duties of physicians with regard to requests for medical assistance in dying (MAID) made by patients. In particular, we want to contribute to the debate on the meaning and status of the right to conscientious objection invoked by some doctors. Our normative argumentation will rely, inter alia, on a qualitative study conducted with 20 physicians who are opposed to MAID, or deeply ambivalent about it (Dumont and Maclure, 2019).

The debate in bioethics and medical ethics on conscientious objection by health professionals suffers from at least two major shortcomings. On the one hand, conscientious objection is generally seen as a freestanding and *sui generis* theme that can be discussed within the typical normative frameworks used in bioethics and medical ethics. We partly disagree. We believe that it cannot be dissociated from the broader philosophical and legal reflections on freedom of conscience and exemption requests (see, for instance, Greenawalt, 2017; Vallier and Weber, 2018). On the other hand, the work in medical ethics for or against conscientious objection by health professionals rarely relies on an analysis of the actual discourse and moral experience of health professionals. We have tried to fill the first gap in a previous paper (Maclure and Dumont, 2016). We now want to contribute to filling the second gap.

In the first section, we will sketch out our interpretation of the principle of freedom of conscience. In the second section, we will present the main elements of the Quebec and Canadian legislative framework allowing MAID. The third section is devoted to some of the arguments put forward to challenge physicians' right to conscientious objection. In the fourth section, we highlight some of the relevant results of our qualitative study with 20 Quebec physicians. In the context of this volume, we focus on the secular and religious reasons which explain why some physicians refrain from including MAID in their practice. In the Discussion section, we argue that legislators were right to recognise a right to conscientious objection for health professionals and plead for a liberal understanding of such a right. We argue that a right to conscientious objection, when coupled with an obligation to refer patients to a competent administrative body, best conciliates the basic rights of the parties involved.

Freedom of conscience and moral identity

Freedom of conscience allows each of us to hold the beliefs we deem true or right with regard to what gives meaning to human life and to the moral obligations we think we have to abide by, as long as we do not infringe upon the basic rights of others. Freedom of conscience targets "conscientious convictions" or "meaning-giving beliefs and commitments", i.e. the beliefs or commitments that are at the core of our moral identity. Such beliefs and commitments, or "strong evaluations", determine the direction we want our life to take or ground our deliberations when we have to resolve ethical dilemmas (Maclure and Taylor, 2011; Taylor 1989: 14). Not respecting a basic value, conviction or commitment gives us the impression that we have betrayed ourselves, that we have lacked integrity or that we have strayed from the kind of person we want to be (Bou-Habib, 2006; Maclure and Taylor, 2011; Laborde, 2017). In that spirit, Ronald Dworkin (1994) distinguishes between our "critical interests" and our "experiential interests". The latter refers to our interest in living positive experiences and emotions in our daily lives, whereas the former refers to our more ethically salient interest in the shape and character of our life as a whole. As moral agents, most of us have at least a rough sense of the kind of person we aim to be, and of values that provide meaning to our life. Critical interests, for Dworkin, should have more weight than experiential ones in our practical deliberations about important life decisions.

Meaning-giving beliefs and commitments can be religious or secular. If they are spontaneously associated with religious beliefs, given the importance that believers generally attach to respecting the precepts of their faith, the source of core values and commitments may also be non-religious. For example, one can be a pacifist or vegetarian on the basis of purely secular philosophical convictions (Maclure and Taylor, 2011; Nussbaum, 2008; Greenawalt, 2017). One can claim the status of conscientious objector in time of war or request an accommodation measure to obtain vegetarian meals without adhering to a religion.

Perhaps closer to the moral experience of many of us today, it is also possible for us to find ourselves in a situation where we discover our attachment to a particular value or commitment without it being part of a complete and structured philosophical or religious doctrine, that is, what John Rawls called a "comprehensive doctrine" (Rawls, 1993). For instance, it can be when a loved one has a serious illness that we become aware of the crucial importance, for us, of the role of being a caregiver – a role that we will wish to take on with dedication and compassion. Reasonable accommodation measures by our employer may be required for us to live up to our commitment to our loved one. It is easy to imagine that a physician can discover, following the legalisation of medically assisted death, that it is inconceivable for her to perform a medical act whose function it is to intentionally cause the death of a patient. Such a procedure may be incompatible with her deepest moral convictions or with her conception of the basic deontological obligations or ends of the medical profession.

Freedom of conscience and religion therefore aims to let people live their life in accordance with their most fundamental commitments, while respecting the rights of others to do the same. While it is rooted in the recognition of human agents' capacity for rational autonomy and right to moral self-determination, it can also be justified on a more pragmatic and prudential basis. From the tragic fate of the main protagonists in Sophocles' Antigone to the present-day conscientious objection and exemption requests, through the Wars of Religion of the early modern era, experience amply demonstrates that the reasonable accommodation of conscience promotes social peace and stability (Greenawalt, 2017).

Medical assistance in dying

Quebec legalised MAID with the adoption of the *Act Respecting End-of-Life Care*[1] in 2014. Unable to amend the Criminal Code, which is a federal jurisdiction, Quebec has chosen to include MAID in the continuum of care provided to people at the end of their life. To be eligible for MAID, persons must be adult, be capable of giving informed consent, have received the diagnosis of a grievous and incurable illness, be approaching the end of their life, and be in a state of suffering that cannot be alleviated under conditions they deem acceptable.

Following the Supreme Court of Canada's *Carter* decision in 2015, access to MAID became a constitutional right across Canada.[2] Reversing the 1993 *Rodriguez*[3] decision, the Supreme Court ruled that patients with serious and incurable diseases causing them persistent and intolerable suffering must now be able to obtain assistance to end their life, an assistance administered or supervised by health professionals. The right to autonomy regarding end-of-life decisions derives from the right to life, liberty and security of the person guaranteed by Section 7 of the Canadian Charter of Rights and Freedoms.[4] According to the Supreme Court, the prohibition of MAID forces some people to commit suicide while they are still able to do so, thus taking their life earlier than desired and unduly restricts their autonomy with regard to decisions regarding their physical integrity and end of life. As has been affirmed by many philosophers and palliative care theorists, the dying process is part of life (Kübler-Ross, 1997). For most of us, a personal reflection on what constitutes a good and meaningful life includes a reflection on the end of life that best coheres with our values or conception of a dignified life (Dworkin, 1994). Late modern societies are characterised by the plurality of the conceptions of the "good life", and by extension, of the "good death" upheld by citizens. Accordingly, the Government of Canada passed the *Act to Amend the Criminal Code and Make Related Amendments to Other Acts* (*Medical Assistance in Dying*)[5] in 2016 to comply with the Supreme Court's decision. The law creates an exemption in the Criminal Code to exclude MAID from the category of "culpable homicide offences".

Physicians caring for people in the end-of-life trajectory or who are suffering from incurable diseases must now respond to patients who wish to avail themselves of MAID. Since death is an issue that raises both metaphysical and ethical questions about the character and value of human life – questions to which several reasonable answers are possible – it was to be expected that many people, including health professionals, would continue to believe that no human intervention intentionally causing death is morally justifiable.

The controversy over conscientious objection

The current legislative framework explicitly provides health care professionals with a right to conscientious objection. No physician should be required to administer a lethal injection or assess a patient's eligibility if they have a conscience-based reason not to do so. While there is a commitment to "respect the personal beliefs of health care providers" in the preamble to the federal law, the Quebec law states that "a physician may refuse to administer medical assistance in dying because of personal beliefs and [that] a health professional may refuse to participate in its administration for the same reason" (An Act respecting end-of-life care, 2014).

However, this right is contested. Both in the medical ethics literature and in the public sphere, some question the legitimacy of statutory exemptions for physicians (Stahl and Emanuel, 2017; Savulescu and Schuklenk, 2017). Countries such as Sweden and Iceland do not recognise a general right to conscientious objection for doctors, although a case-by-case assessment of exemption requests is possible (Fiala et al., 2016; Fiala and Arthur, 2017; Munthe, 2017). According to Stahl and Emanuel (2017), physicians' role morality is incompatible with conscientious objection: "the proliferation of conscientious objection legislation in health care violates the central tenet of professional role morality in the field of medicine: the patient comes first" (Stahl and Emanuel, 2017: 1384). For Savulescu and Schuklenk (2017), respectively editors of *Bioethics* and the *Journal of Medical Ethics*, the respect for patients' right to have access to the full range of care available in a timely fashion requires the repeal of the right to conscientious objection and the exclusion of candidates applying to medical schools who may wish to be exempted from the obligation to perform specific care on the basis of their conscientious convictions:

> We argue that eligible patients could be guaranteed access to medical services that are subject to conscientious objections by: (1) removing a right to conscientious objection; (2) selecting candidates into relevant medical specialities or general practice who do not have objections
>
> (Savulescu and Schuklenk, 2017: 162).

Others argue that the right to conscientious objection is currently being used to justify the decision of physicians who do not wish to participate in the MAID process for reasons that are not philosophical, moral or religious. Some doctors consider that, in a context where they have to increase the number of patients they follow, the management of MAID requests is too cumbersome and time-consuming. Regretting that only a small group of physicians have been offering MAID since it came into effect in Quebec, Dr. Pierre Viens suggests that "[t]he real objection of conscience, based on religious or philosophical grounds, is very rare in my experience. What we are experiencing in Quebec are objections of inconvenience rather than conscience" (Viens, 2018; Naud, 2018).

In a similar vein, researchers who conducted interviews with physicians maintain that "the term conscientious objection was used for various reasons that go beyond the traditional meaning of the term" (Opatrny and Bouthillier, 2017: 38). An analysis of the 22 qualitative interviews they conducted "reveals that only a minority of physicians oppose MAID on genuine moral or religious grounds" (Id: 39). They conclude that conscientious objection is often used as a subterfuge (Id: 40). The main reasons for opting out from MAID they extracted from their interviews were "the heaviness of the emotional load, the perception of their incompetence to proceed and time constraints" (Id: 40).

A qualitative study with conscientious objectors

The overall objective of the qualitative study that we conducted was to advance ethical reflection on physician requests for exemption from MAID (Dumont and Maclure, 2019). Normative arguments pro and con conscientious objection for physicians, including our previous work (Maclure and Dumont, 2016), overwhelmingly lack empirical grounding. One of the goals of our study was to better understand and describe, on the basis of the participants' discourse, the reasons (religious and secular) justifying their opposition or reservations with regard to MAID.

Our participants were physicians who, in their practice, receive or could receive requests for MAID and who are opposed to, or have serious reservations about, MAID. Twenty physicians were recruited from November 2017 to May 2018. A network sampling method (snowball) was chosen. The information about the study was first sent to a few physicians who matched the desired profile and who, in turn, forwarded the information to other physicians with a similar profile. The criteria for selecting participants were as follows:

- Be a member of the Quebec Collège des Médecins.
- Be called upon, in their practice, to receive MAID requests.
- Have exercised or plan to exercise the right to conscientious objection.

The qualitative study we conducted does not claim to be statistically representative and does not allow large-scale generalisations with regard to the reasons and motivations of physicians who do not wish to include MAID in their medical practice. However, it shows at the very least that a subset of physicians among those who do not wish to be involved in the MAID process reached their decision on the basis of religious and moral reasons that correspond to the type of beliefs protected by freedom of conscience. Our participants' positions on MAID ensued from genuine moral deliberations about the relationship between their (professional and personal) values and the act of intentionally causing a patient's death. The legalisation of MAID has forced many physicians to reflect on the meaning and telos of medicine, on the relationship between their personal beliefs and their professional ethics and on the ethical and social consequences of creating a right to MAID. It is clear to us that many of the reasons given by our participants fell within the ambit of freedom of conscience. Although not statistically representative of the category made up of those Quebec physicians who do not want to include MAID in their practice, the value of the study lies mainly in the richness of the points of view obtained.

A quarter of our participants (5/20) stated that their religious beliefs and affiliation are an integral part of their personal identity and influence their understanding of their moral duties. It should be noted that these five participants also all have "public" reasons to oppose MAID and claim the right to conscientious objection. As one participant stated: "it's interesting, because any good secular argument that I may give I would say comes from my religious beliefs". For John Rawls, reasons are "public" when they are not derived from a particular (secular or religious) comprehensive conception of the good and are potentially endorsable by all citizens notwithstanding their worldview (1993). For Rawls, given the "fact of reasonable pluralism" with regard to the conceptions of the good, the justifications for legislations and other public norms should be based on political principles that can figure in an "overlapping consensus".

> Five other participants said that their religious education or culture may unconsciously influence their position on MAID, but were keen to point out that their explicit and conclusive reasons for not wanting to perform MAID were not religious: "Yes, the religious dimension is present in me, but let's say it would be the last one invoked", declared a participant. Answering a question about whether his religious beliefs influenced his views on MAID, another participant hesitated and responded: "yes and no … probably so. … I'm not fully an atheist. … I'd say I'm deistic agnostic. … So perhaps it influences me a little".

The other ten participants said they were atheists or that religion had nothing to do with their decision. One of the participants stressed that she was a staunch atheist:

> I know conscientious objectors who are very Catholic, and then I know people who are atheistic conscientious objectors. I'm in the atheistic category. I am … very very very atheistic (laughs).

These results call for caution with regard to the perception that conscientious objectors to MAID are mainly motivated by their religious faith.

We clustered the public reasons given by the participants to justify their opposition or ambivalence towards MAID into four categories: (1) professional identity and the ends of medicine; (2) philosophy of palliative medicine and resource allocation in palliative care; (3) benevolent paternalism, the good death and the interests of future self; (4) the slippery slope argument and the protection of vulnerable persons. We discussed these four clusters in a previous paper (Dumont and Maclure, 2019).

Discussion

The moral cost of repealing the right to conscientious objection

The responses of many of the participants clearly show the importance of meaning-giving beliefs and commitments or strong evaluations in one's conception of oneself and of what a meaningful life is. It also suggests that removing the right to conscientious objection would put many of them in a potentially harrowing situation in virtue of which they would have to choose between respecting their conscience and the opportunity to practice medicine. As two different participants stated:

> Because, at the end of the day, what I'm being told is that in order to be able to be a doctor you're going to have to sacrifice one of your fundamental rights, your freedom of conscience. I can't accept that. … I'm talking to you strictly on a human basis. You can't ask someone that in order to practice his profession he must do something that he considers morally wrong.
>
> You can't force me to kill you. Because it goes against everything I've done in my life … OK? I've been following you for 30 years, for 40 years. You're asking me to kill you. I won't do it. If you absolutely want to have it, at any time you can change doctors. … But I say you can't force me, as a human being, to do that.

This kind of testimony leads us to believe that those who challenge the health professional's right to conscientious objection underestimate the moral cost of repealing it. As the excerpts show, the refusal of conscience-based exemptions forces the agent to choose between upholding one of his basic commitments and the possibility of practising medicine. This should not be taken lightly. Any plausible theory of justice includes a right to equal opportunity and non-discrimination in the access to the various roles, positions and offices available. The first subprinciple of John Rawls' second principle of justice states that offices and positions must be "open to all under conditions of fair equality of opportunity" (1971: 266).

This highlights one of the weaknesses of one of the most widely used arguments in the critique of conscientious objection, namely that there is no right to become a physician (or any other professional) and that physicians are not "conscripts". Unlike healthy adults in times of military conscription, people voluntarily choose to become health care professionals: "[u]nlike conscripted soldiers, health care professionals voluntarily choose their roles and thus become obligated to provide, perform, and refer patients for interventions according to the standards of the profession" (Stahl and Emanuel, 2017: 1380).

No one denies that there is no such thing as a right to become a physician or any other health professional. The debate is about the meaning and implications of the fair opportunity principle in conjunction with the basic right to freedom of conscience. As alluded to, those who think that a conditional right to conscientious objection should be recognised argue that people should not be placed in a situation where they have to renounce one of their fundamental rights in order to avail themselves of another right (Quong, 2006; Maclure, 2018). It should be added that, unlike abortions which are performed, with few exceptions, in specialised clinics, physicians practising in a wide range of settings may receive MAID requests or be called upon to assess a patient's eligibility. While the majority of our participants practise in family medicine and palliative care, physicians from other specialties (internal medicine, thoracic surgery, public and community health, anaesthesiology, intensive care, endocrinology, psychiatry and geriatrics) also participated in our study. While it seems reasonable and justified to hire doctors who do not oppose abortion in specialised clinics or in settings where abortions are frequent, MAID potentially concerns all physicians. Excluding people who do not wish to administer the MAID for moral reasons would practically amount to closing the doors of medicine to them. As one participant said: "If ever I am told: "Well, you have no right to conscientious objection. You must execute your patient's request. I'm withdrawing from palliative care".

The normative conclusion we draw from this observation is not that the right to conscientious objection is unconditional, but rather that its outright abrogation is blunt and unjustified. Limiting the right to freedom of conscience by refusing requests for exemption or accommodation is sometimes justified, but it needs to be established contextually (Greenawalt, 2017). From a normative perspective, the objective is to conciliate as well as possible the legitimate interests of the parties involved, which is not possible with the a priori refusal of all conscience-based exemption requests. A conditional right to exemption prevents agents from having to choose between honouring a deep moral commitment and their right to aspire to a career in medicine.

A narrow conception of the right to conscientious objection

We believe that the critics' interpretation of the right to freedom of conscience and conscientious objection by health professionals is often too narrow. If the right to conscientious objection first aimed at protecting religious, and later, secular and moral convictions that were derived from structured metaphysical or moral doctrines, this can no longer be the case today (Maclure and Taylor, 2011; Laborde, 2017). An agent may have a conviction or commitment that is central to their conception of herself and the type of person she wishes to be without it ensuing from a deep philosophical reflection or comprehensive worldview. In secularised societies characterised by the diversity of the conceptions of the good life, a more flexible conception of freedom of conscience and of conscientious objection is required.

It is possibly on the basis of a narrow conception of conscientious objection that Opatrny and Bouthillier (2017) conclude that reasons such as an "excessive emotional burden", given by one of the participants in their study on conscientious objection and MAID, should not be seen as protected by freedom of conscience. A participant who was quoted in their article said:

> The conscientious objection I declared is not really a conscientious objection. It's more at an emotional level. I couldn't live with the fact of doing that at this time. If a patient I've known for 30 years asked me, I'd be there for him. I could assist him, but it would affect me deeply.
>
> (Opatrny and Bouthillier, 2017: 39)

The participant probably believes that conscientious objection requires having explicit and structured religious or philosophical convictions nested in a comprehensive doctrine or worldview. But how should the feeling of not being able to "live with" performing MAID be interpreted? Is the emotion felt devoid of any cognitive and moral dimension?[6] Is the feeling connected to beliefs regarding voluntary euthanasia and the values of medicine? Does the exclusion of emotional burden from the scope of freedom of conscience presuppose a non-cognitivist account of emotions? What about cases where rational thinking and emotions are inextricably linked, such as when a person who considers that their role as a caregiver for a terminally ill spouse confers responsibilities that they strongly want to take on? To take one of the paradigmatic examples of conscientious objection: Is a pacifist who refuses to serve in times of war not likely to say that they could not live with himself after fighting against an enemy combatant? The fear of not being able to live with oneself if one acts in a certain way is generally based on the belief that it would undermine one's moral integrity and be at odds with the kind of person one wants to be. One of the participants in our study said, "killing someone seems absolutely inconceivable to me. I don't think I could live with the idea that I killed someone". Not having interviewed the participant in Opatrny and Bouthillier's study, we are not asserting that she had moral reasons not to participate in the MAID process. Our point is that a more in-depth exploration of her moral experience would have been desirable before concluding that her refusal did not match the requirements of a genuine conscientious objection.

In short, a conception of freedom of conscience that is broader and better adapted to the conditions of morally pluralistic societies leads to caution and nuance regarding the idea that conscientious objection is for the most part instrumentalised by physicians. Among other things, it is increasingly recognised that emotions have a cognitive dimension and cannot be dissociated from rational deliberation. While it is clear that some doctors instrumentalise the right to conscientious objection – which is deplorable and reprehensible – others legitimately invoke it.

A richer Interpretation of the reasons for conscientious objection

The relatively small number of Quebec physicians willing to provide MAID in the years following the implementation of the End-of-Life Care Act in 2014 made the access to MAID difficult in certain regions. This shortage also had the effect of overtaxing physicians who were the first to add MAID to their medical practice. The number of physicians who have administered MAID is increasing each year, but access to MAID varies according to geographical location and some physicians remain over-solicited.

This shortage led some to question the motives of the physicians who decided to opt out from MAID. As mentioned above, one physician opined that the physicians who invoked their conscience found MAID more inconvenient than unconscionable (Viens, 2018). Other critics argue that moral conservatism and religious dogmatism are the main, albeit sometimes veiled, source of conscientious refusal.

According to Dr. Alain Naud, who was one of the first to accept MAID requests from patients and to talk publicly about his experience, some of the opposition to MAID is "ideological and religious". This "hidden and efficacious opposition" would deprive hundreds of patients of their right to MAID (Breton, 2019).

Again, our study invites a more nuanced and charitable interpretation of the reasons motivating at the very least a subset of the physicians who want to be exempted from the MAID process. On the one hand, 15 out of 20 participants are opposed to MAID, or ambivalent about it, because of secular reasons that cannot be dismissed out of hand. The five participants who have strong religious reasons also have serious secular reasons for their exemption requests. The expression of such public reasons is a necessary condition for an informed public debate on the implications of the legalisation of medically assisted dying. As pointed out above, the most salient and frequent reasons given by our participants were derived from concerns related to: (1) professional identity and the ends of medicine, (2) the philosophy of palliative medicine and resource allocation in palliative care, (3) benevolent paternalism, the good death and the interests of future self, and (4) the slippery slope argument and the protection of vulnerable persons. One of our participants insisted on pointing out that "politically", she was on the "far left", including on morally laden issues such as abortion and gay marriages.

On the other hand, as Dr. Naud (2018) made clear in an earlier intervention, his point is not to deny the right to conscientious objection to those whose religious beliefs are incompatible with performing MAID, but rather to stress the importance of being transparent when justifying one's conscientious refusal. He also rightly argues that conscientious objectors have a duty to refer their patients to a colleague or to the appropriate administrative unit (Naud, 2018; Grant, 2019). It should be noted that 16 out of our 20 participants did not object to referring their patients to either a colleague or, more frequently, to a designated administrative unit such as a Professional Services Directorate (Dumont and Maclure, 2019).

Even if it was true, as it surely is, that some physicians falsely invoke moral scruples, this doesn't justify depriving those who request exemptions on the basis of a genuine moral deliberation of their right to conscientious objection. That would be an instance of the "two-wrongs-make-a-right" fallacy.

Conclusion

The legalisation of MAID is a major social reform. The adoption of the Quebec and Canadian laws establishing a conditional constitutional right to MAID has prompted many physicians to question and articulate their understanding of the meaning and purposes of medicine, as well as their views on death and dying. While it is true that health care facilities will have to find ways to increase the number of physicians prepared to add MAID to their practice, it is also important to recognise that some physicians have serious secular and religious moral reasons for not wanting to do so. On the one hand, institutional measures should be implemented to encourage physicians who have no conscientious objection to be part of the MAID process. Clear and effective referral systems need to be established so that patients who are monitored by conscientious objectors can be quickly directed to another physician. On the other hand, acknowledging the importance of respecting freedom of conscience and the seriousness of the moral opposition or ambivalence felt by the objectors could potentially contribute to the appeasement of the relationship between participating and non-participating physicians. Moreover, one does need to endorse the reasons given when claiming exemptions for granting that objectors are also the ones most likely to alert the rest of society to the risks inherent in legalising assisted dying. From a normative standpoint, the goal is to harmonise as best as possible the basic rights of physicians and patients. We believe that recognition of the right to conscientious objection, combined with a duty to refer, best achieve this objective.

Notes

1 *Act respecting end-of-life care* (2014), LRQ., chapter S-32.0001.
2 *Carter v. Canada* (Procureur général) (Attorney General) (2015) CSC 5, 1 R.C.S. 331.
3 *Rodriguez c. Colombie-Britannique* (Procureur général) (1993) 3 R.C.S. 519.
4 *Loi Constitutionnelle de 1982* (1982) LRC., art 7.
5 *Act to Amend the Criminal Code and Make Related Amendments to Other Acts (Medical Assistance in Dying)* (2016), S.C., Chapter 3, First Session, Forty-second Parliament, Canada.
6 For cognitivist accounts of emotions, see Damasio, 2005; Nussbaum, 2003.

Bibliography

Bou-Habib, P. 2006. “A Theory of Religious Accommodation.” *Journal of Applied Philosophy* 23 (1): 109–126.

Breton, B. 2019. “Moins d’idéologie, moins de souffrances.” Le Soleil. Retrieved on September 25th, 2020. https://www.lesoleil.com/chroniques/moins-dideologie-moins-de-souffrances-57c2bc379e6fca898502dac2e606fcb0.

Damasio, A. 2005. *Descartes' Error: Emotion, Reason, and the Human Brain*. New York: Penguin Book.

Deschamps, P. 2017. *Les soins de fin de vie: repères éthiques, juridiques et sociétaux*. Montréal: LexisNexis.

Dumont, I. and Maclure, J. 2019. "Conscientious Objection to Medical Assistance in Dying: A Qualitative Study with Quebec Physicians/Objection de conscience et aide médicale à mourir: une étude qualitative auprès de médecins québécois". *Canadian Journal of Bioethics/Revue canadienne de bioéthique* 2 (2): 110–134.

Dworkin, R. 1994. “Dying and Living.” Pp. 209–216 in Dworkin, R. *Life's Dominion: An Argument about Abortion, Euthanasia, and Individual Freedom*. New York: Vintage Books.

Fiala, C. et al. 2016. “Yes We Can! Successful Examples of Disallowing ‘Conscientious Objection’ in Reproductive Health Care.” *European Journal of Contraception and Reproductive Health Care* 21 (3): 201–206.

Fiala, C. and Arthur, J.H. 2017. “There Is No Defence for ‘Conscientious Objection’ in Reproductive Health Care.” *European Journal of Obstetrics and Gynecology and Reproductive Biology* 216: 254–258.

Granda-Cameron, C. and Houldin, A. 2012. "Concept Analysis of Good Death in Terminally Ill Patients." *American Journal of Hospice and Palliative Care* 29 (8): 632–339.

Grant, K. 2019. "Ontario's Top Court Rules Religious Doctors Must Offer Patients an 'Effective Referral' for Assisted Dying, Abortion." The Globe and Mail. Retrieved on May 15th, 2019. https://www.theglobeandmail.com/canada/article-religious-doctors-must-make-referrals-for-assisted-dying-abortion.

Greenawalt, K. 2017. *Exemptions, Necessary, Justified, or Misguided?* Cambridge: Harvard University Press.

Kübler-Ross, E. 1997. *Living with Death and Dying*. New York: Touchstone.

Laborde, C. 2017. *Liberalism' Religion*. Cambridge: Harvard University Press.

Maclure, J. and Dumont, I. 2016. "Selling Conscience Short: A Response to Schuklenk and Smalling on Conscientious Objections by Medical Professionals." *Journal of Medical Ethics* 43: 241–244.

Maclure, J. and Dumont, I. 2018. "Conscience, Religion, and Exemptions: An Egalitarian View." Pp. 9–20 in Vallier, K. and Weber, M. (eds.) *Religious Exemptions*. Oxford: Oxford University Press.

Maclure, J. and Taylor, C. 2011. *Secularism and Freedom of Conscience*. Cambridge: Harvard University Press.

Munthe, C. 2017. "Conscientious Refusal in Healthcare: The Swedish Solution." *Journal of Medical Ethics* 43 (4): 257–259.

Naud, A. 2018. "Médecine, religion et péché." Le Devoir. Retrieved on Februrary 8th, 2020. https://www.ledevoir.com/opinion/idees/519592/medecine-religion-et-peche.

Nussbaum, M. 2003. *Upheavals of Thought: The Intelligence of Emotions*. Cambridge: Cambridge University Press.

Nussbaum, M. 2008. *Liberty of Conscience: In Defense of America's Tradition of Religious Equality*. New York: Basic Books.

Opatrny, L. and Bouthillier, M.-È. 2017. "Décoder l'objection de conscience dans le cas de l'aide médicale à mourir: Premiers résultats d'une étude unique." *Le spécialiste* 19 (4): 36–40.

Quong, J. 2006. "Cultural Exemptions, Expensive Tastes, and Equal Opportunities." *Journal of Applied Philosophy* 23 (1): 53–71.

Rawls, J. 1971. *A Theory of Justice*. Cambridge: Harvard University Press.

Rawls, J. 1993. *Political Liberalism*. New York: Columbia University Press.

Robichaud, V. 2018. *L'accompagnement en fin de vie – Nouveau regard sur les soins palliatifs*. Montréal: Éditions du CRAM.

Savulescu, J. and Schuklenk, U. 2017. "Doctors Have No Right to Refuse Medical Assistance in Dying, Abortion or Contraception." *Bioethics* 31 (3): 162–170.

Stahl, R.Y. and Emanuel, E.J. 2017. "Not Conscripts — Conscientious Objection in Health Care." *New England Journal of Medicine* 376 (14): 1380–1385.

Taylor, C. 1989. *Sources of the Self: The Making of the Modern Identity*. Cambridge: Harvard University Press.

Vallier, K. and Weber, M. (eds.). 2018. *Religious Exemptions*. New York: Oxford University Press.

Viens, P. 2018. "L'objection de conscience, vraiment?" La Presse +. Retrieved on Februrary 18th, 2020. http://plus.lapresse.ca/screens/54739b58-d9d1-44ed-8a4f-b0a3925c6b70__7C___0.html.

9 The impossibility of contesting in the name of religion? A comparative perspective on assistance in dying in Quebec (Canada) and the canton of Vaud (Switzerland)

Samuel Blouin

Introduction

I conducted a comparative ethnography of the administration of death requests through euthanasia in the province of Quebec (Canada) and assisted suicide in the canton of Vaud (Switzerland). The relevance of my research to reflections on contestation in the name of religion was initially not clear to me for two reasons. First, I observed and interviewed mainly people who participate in assistance in dying,[1] not people who contest this practice. Second, I witnessed little contestation *in the name of* religion while compiling my ethnography, either in public debates or practice. What caught my attention was the contrast between what I had read about the things I should have observed and what I in fact documented.

Studies on the relationships between assistance in dying and religion indicate that strong religious belief increases the odds of opposing assistance in dying. Based on the European Values Study and the World Values Survey, religious people and people living in religious contexts are more likely to oppose this practice (Verbakel and Jaspers, 2010). In Canada, a study shows that religious/spiritual beliefs and teachings contribute to medical students being less willing to provide assistance in dying (Bator et al., 2017). In Switzerland, "[h]aving no religious affiliation and being Protestant were associated with higher rates of assisted suicide than being Catholic" (Steck et al., 2018). Nonetheless, some physicians and nurses who participate in assistance in dying have religious beliefs (Georges et al., 2007). After reading those studies and on the basis of assumptions based on common knowledge, the expectation is that religion plays a significant role in the contestation of assistance in dying.

However, Verbakel and Jaspers (2010: 133) found that "[t]he difference in opinions toward euthanasia of religious and nonreligious individuals is more strongly expressed in devout societies than in secular societies". The researchers have no explanation for this effect of secularised contexts. My ethnographic research provides some insights into this relationship. Instead of contributing to reflections on contestation in the name of religion, my research helps us to reflect on its impossibility, or at least on the difficulty of contesting in the name of religion in secularised contexts.

The legalisation of assistance in dying is part of the process of dissociating religion from culture (Roy, 2010). In the contexts that authorise assistance in dying, religious arguments, such as the sanctity of life, are no longer publicly accepted as sufficient reasons for prohibiting assistance in dying. These public policies thus indirectly contribute to the secularisation of a society by giving expression to a new moral order. As such, they are open to contestation on religious grounds. Assistance in dying laws either allow for individual exemptions for providers or simply allow this practice without requiring that it be provided. In fact, such legislation makes the decision to participate in assistance in dying a fundamentally individual one that nonetheless relies on shared cultural and moral frames of reference, including human rights (Blouin, 2020). Far from blowing society apart or opening the door to strategies adopted by religious actors to render laws inoperative, individual exemptions in Quebec and the canton of Vaud seem to be recognised as legitimate and as allowing various moral convictions to coexist, even though their coexistence might sometimes prove to be challenging.

This chapter draws on a four-year ethnography conducted in Quebec and Vaud, which involved observation of the assistance in dying process, interviews with active players in public debates, professionals, applicants, and with their loved ones, and also secondary sources, such as a press review, public reports and court decisions.[2] In the first section, I outline the system for regulating assistance in dying and religious pluralism in Quebec and Vaud. In the second and third sections, I explore evidence of contestation in the name of religion in both contexts. I end with reflections on constraints that weigh on the possibility of contesting in the name of religion in contexts that tend to relegate religion to the sphere of private choice.

Two contexts, two forms of regulation

The province of Quebec and the canton of Vaud are interesting situations to compare because of their contrasting systems for regulating assistance in dying and their religious pluralism. They shed a different light on how contestation of assistance in dying in the name of religion is constrained. In Quebec, medical aid in dying (MAID) has been part of health care services offered by the state since 2015. Following years of public consultations and ethical reflections by the medical profession, the National Assembly passed the *Act respecting end-of-life care* (hereafter the Act) that notably creates a right to access end-of-life care, including palliative care and MAID if the legal conditions are met.[3] In Quebec, MAID is also regulated by the Federal Criminal Code that was modified by Parliament in 2016 in response to a Supreme Court decision which ruled that the prohibition of assistance in dying violates rights guaranteed by the Constitution.[4] In matters of religious pluralism, the freedom of conscience and religion of individuals is protected by the provincial and federal charters of rights. This traditionally predominantly Catholic province experienced a rapid secularisation process in the last century. Health care institutions that were run by religious organisations are now controlled and financed by the provincial government.

In Switzerland, assisted suicide is a civil act that has been tolerated since 1942. According to the Federal Criminal Code, assisted suicide is not punishable if a provider without a selfish motive assists a person with decision-making capacity.[5] Since the 1990s, not-for-profit "right-to-die societies" have mostly provided organised assisted suicide to their members, who pay an annual membership fee. Volunteers, who are not necessarily health professionals, assist members and connect them with physicians agreeing to prescribe the lethal substance when certain conditions are met. In Vaud, the *Law on public health*, adopted following a referendum, has also regulated assisted suicide in publicly funded health care institutions since 2013.[6] However, it does not make it a service offered by institutions and it explicitly prevents employees from participating in the assistance *per se* in a professional capacity. As in Quebec, freedom of conscience and religion is protected by both federal and cantonal constitutions. Vaud also recognises three institutional religions – the *Église évangélique réformée du canton de Vaud* (Reformed Protestant Church of Vaud) (EERV), the *Église catholique dans le canton de Vaud* (Catholic Church of Vaud) (ECVD), and the *Communauté israélite à Lausanne et dans le canton de Vaud* (Jewish Community in Lausanne and the canton of Vaud) (CILV), which are predominantly split between two faiths: the Catholic and Reformed Churches (Becci and Bovay, 2007). This recognition by the canton comes with public funding but also with the obligation to provide some services to the general population, such as chaplaincy in hospitals. This historically Protestant region now has a diverse population made up of similar proportions of people identified as Protestants, Catholics and those without religious affiliation.[7] Unlike the institutional religions, *EXIT A.D.M.D. Suisse romande*, the most active right-to-die society in the region, has no formal recognition, even though it informally and formally collaborates with the state to facilitate the oversight of assistance in suicide.

Legally, Quebec and Vaud present two different ways of treating religious and secular convictions. I now turn to how those convictions are handled in public debates and practice to see what this means for the possibility of contestation in the name of religion.

Looking for evidence of religious contestation in Quebec

In public debates

When I began researching assistance in dying in Quebec, I first looked at what was publicly available. I did the same to find evidence of contestation in the name of religion. I read briefs submitted by explicitly religious organisations[8] to the *Select Committee on Dying with Dignity* that was mandated in 2009 by the National Assembly to consult the public, organisations and experts. I also read the interventions of these organisations in the parliamentary proceedings relating to the adoption of the Act. In addition, I consulted statements by religious institutions, public reports and my press review to find traces of contestation.

What stands out is that very few religious actors use religious frames of reference as their only arguments against assistance in dying. For example, my analysis of briefs submitted to the *Select Committee* shows that out of 273 interventions, 19 involved explicitly religious groups, all Christian (Select Committee, 2012: 13). Some organisations, such as the *Association d'Églises Baptistes Évangéliques au Québec* (Association of Protestant Baptist Churches in Quebec), suggest that life is a gift from God and that individuals cannot decide on its beginning and end (AÉBÉQ, 2010: 4–5). Most religious organisations, however, use arguments similar to those put forward by secular groups who oppose the legalisation of euthanasia.[9] They defend the right to life. They argue that a euthanasia request is a sign of distress or a cry for help, and not a genuine wish to die. Those organisations also consider that legalising euthanasia would counteract efforts to prevent suicide and put vulnerable people at risk. They favour the improvement of palliative care and an "ethics of solidarity".

When organisations do resort to religious frames of reference, they often stress that their arguments are not different from those used by secular actors. For instance, the *Assemblée des Évêques catholiques du Québec* (Assembly of Catholic Bishops of Quebec) mentions at the end of its brief that it must "add more meaning"[10] to its contribution by referring to its convictions of faith after having stated arguments that it considers acceptable to all (Assemblée des Évêques catholiques, 2010: 11). After the implementation of the Act in 2015, the *Assemblée* did not condemn a priest who refused to bless the urn of a man who had received assistance in dying "because he [the priest] must have had his reasons", but nor did it encourage other priests to imitate him (Radio-Canada, 2016a). The man's wife, a believer, felt hurt by the priest's attitude. Moreover, the Quebec clergy did not follow the same path as some Canadian bishops who deny religious funerals for those who die by assistance in dying (Radio-Canada, 2016b). Within the Catholic Church, some forms of contestation and objection, or at least disagreement, can be found.

A scandal in the news media illustrates the public treatment of religious and secular convictions in Quebec with regard to assistance in dying. Physicians complained to the media about the "over-representation" of Opus Dei members in the parliamentary consultation on the draft Act (Buzzetti, 2013). Six physicians who are Opus Dei members were reported to have participated in the consultation to oppose assistance in dying. The physicians who contacted the media were concerned that these individuals lacked "neutrality" and that they were speaking from the viewpoint of medical expertise without making their religious beliefs explicit. This is surprising in a context where suspicion towards the expression of religion in public is very strong (Rousseau, 2016), to the point where bills are regularly tabled in parliament to prohibit the wearing of religious symbols by government employees. One might have expected the religious discretion exercised by these physicians to be acceptable. Furthermore, the physicians risked losing all legitimacy to express themselves publicly if they revealed their religious affiliation.

This injunction for religious transparency (Amiraux, 2018) does not constrain those with secular convictions and values, yet religious actors have to disclose their convictions so that they can better be discredited.

This episode made me realise the contrast between the positions expressed by two groups of actors in public debates. According to my interview with a former president of the *Association québécoise pour le droit de mourir dans la dignité* (Quebec Association for the Right to Die with Dignity), the Association received offers of support from the secularist movement, which it declined, and an award from the *Fondation humaniste du Québec* (Humanist Foundation of Quebec) in 2013 for its work in favour of the adoption of a bill on assistance in dying (Fondation humaniste du Québec, 2013). However, the Association chose to stay away from debates on secularism to avoid confounding the two issues. Doing so could have harmed the popularity of the legalisation of assisted dying that it was defending.

On the one hand, the Association defends free choice in matters of end of life and is supported by a movement that considers religion to be an ideology that imposes its views and that is incompatible with rational thought. The press articles reporting arguments adopted by people in favour of assistance in dying also tend to convey a discourse that is common in right-to-die circles (Gandsman, 2018: 330). On the other hand, some religious groups are in favour of respecting religious convictions in debates on state secularism. However, they consider that free choice at the end of life is the expression of a mortiferous ideology, a loss of meaning of suffering, a culture of death, and that it consequently does not reflect a real and sincere wish for hastened death. Between these two extremes, there is a range of intermediate positions. The two extremes nonetheless pinpoint a fundamental mutual misunderstanding of the relationship between individuals and the collective, between what is considered to be a matter of choice and what is imposed on people.

Table 9.1 Two polarised extremes in public debates on assistance in dying and wearing of religious symbols in Quebec

	Some organisations in the right-to-die movement	*Some organised religions*
Wish for hastened death	Choice, free will	Distress, call for help
Religion	Irrationality, imposition	Choice, conviction

How has the State of Quebec positioned itself in the face of this plurality of perspectives? With regard to assistance in dying, the report of the *Select Committee* (2012: 63) affirms “that in a secular State such as ours, the beliefs of some cannot serve as a basis for the development of legislation applicable to all”. Parliamentarians also state,

> The medical aid in dying option is compatible with changes in social values, medicine and the law. Fuelled by diverse ideas, our social values have shifted

> from religious or ideological beliefs to notions of personal liberty, respect for autonomy, inviolability and integrity of the individual, all consistent with the concept of medical aid in dying.
>
> (Select Committee, 2012: 76)

Parliamentarians are more nuanced in other places in the report where they recognise that Quebec is a plural society, that the meaning of death and suffering has changed, and that each person can live their life according to their values and beliefs. Overall, the report describes a set of values that would be characteristic of a secular relationship with the world as distinct from "religious or ideological beliefs".

Regarding religious pluralism, in 2019 the National Assembly adopted the *Loi sur la laïcité de l'État* (State Secularism Act),[11] which prohibits the wearing of religious symbols for certain categories of state employees, thereby endorsing the position that religious beliefs should not be apparent at the risk that they might influence the provision of services or the perception of their delivery. The state endorses a policy that denies certain persons the right to exercise their religion in a manner consistent with their convictions without its having demonstrated any impact on their work performance. Public debates on secularism in Quebec construct religion as a problem that requires the regulation of the expression of individual religious convictions (Dalpé and Koussens, 2016).

On the subject of assistance in dying, the state adopts a policy that promotes the moral autonomy of individuals on the basis that such decisions that affect values are a matter of individual freedom. This public policy treats beliefs as a matter of individual choice about how to live one's life, although it limits the expression thereof to medical contexts (suffering must be related to a medical condition). In this sense, this policy does not discriminate between people with religious or secular beliefs about the end of life, since each person can decide how they wish to end their life as per the conditions set out in the law. Moreover, health professionals' right to freedom of conscience is reaffirmed in the legislation. In the end, contestation in the name of religion appears to be quite marginal and marginalised in public debates on assistance in dying as the state promotes a secularist worldview. The divide between the ways that religious and secular convictions are treated – however powerful it may be in public debates – is not completely borne out in the practice of assistance in dying.

And in practice?

During my observations of the assistance in dying process in a hospital of the Montreal area, I was made aware of numerous cases of conscientious objection by physicians and nurses for a variety of secular and religious reasons. According to Bouthillier and Opatrny (2019), who carried out a study on physicians' conscientious objections in Quebec, religious reasons do not particularly stand out: 4 physicians out of 22 interviewed refused to participate, mainly for religious reasons. In fact, the majority of physicians who refuse to participate do not oppose

MAID and support patients' right to request this intervention. They refuse on other grounds, such as "emotional reasons" and concerns "related to capacity and competence". Dumont and Maclure (2019), who conducted a similar study with a different interpretative framework, show that secular reasons for refusing to participate were largely predominant among objecting physicians, including among those who have religious convictions.[12] My own observations, which focus on conditions of interaction rather than on reasons for objecting, point in the same direction.

I observed several health care team meetings where the issue of conscientious objections was discussed. Two of the themes that came up most often in the discourse of nurses and caregivers were respect for the patient's decision but also respect for their own convictions. For example, it was stressed repeatedly that one should not judge the person who requests an assisted death. The phrase "don't judge" was not used to mean that a request should not be evaluated but that a sphere of intimacy should be preserved from the judgement of others. The extent of this sphere depends on the interveners. It can include the state of the person's relationships with others, financial concerns and other reasons for requesting MAID. However, in some cases, reasons are taken into account by the clinicians tasked with assessing a request. Along with the respect for the person's "choice", "not judging" emerged as one of the moral maxims fundamental to the practice of assistance in dying.

Clinicians also insist on respecting their own convictions. For instance, the nurse in charge of MAID at the hospital keeps repeating to her colleagues in different care units that they have to be "consistent with [their] values and beliefs". Imposing consequences on nurses who refuse to provide ordinary care to people requesting assistance in dying was considered by head nurses, but so far this possibility has been ruled out. Instead, an educational process is being undertaken to accompany nurses and train them in the hope of convincing more of them to help with certain steps of the process (inserting the catheter, handling drugs, meeting the family). When meeting teams, the ethics counsellor also insists on the fact that "[i]t is not because a person participates [in MAID] that they are in favour". Also, health professionals set their own limits, such as only assessing requests without administering MAID, for physicians or accompanying the person without touching the medication, for nurses. A nurse consulted her pastor before agreeing to accompany a patient until the last moment. Actors involved in the administration of MAID have developed a common language and ways of interaction that allow them to manage diverging views about this practice, whatever the reasons behind principled opposition or ambivalence.

However, some people told me that they had experienced stigmatisation, either because they participate in assistance in dying or because they do not. Mixed feelings towards people who do not participate have more to do with organisational issues (lack of staff, concerns for access, etc.) than with the reasons why they refuse to participate. People who participate in MAID also sometimes feel disparaged by colleagues who give them a judgemental look or whisper when they pass by. The number of conscientious objections is perceived as a challenge by the institution and there is a certain frustration among the people on whose shoulders the task of assisting with MAID regularly falls, to the point where a nurse said, "It's not racist, but I wonder if it's only ethnic Quebecers [*Québécois de souche*] who will agree to participate". There is a potential for discourse in practice to end up embracing the anti-religious public discourse that also crosses racial lines.

Opposition to MAID sometimes comes from applicants' families. In one case, a Catholic family vocally challenged the decision of one of its members to get MAID. The physician and the team respected the applicant's decision as they have no legal obligation to follow the family's wishes. Contestation in the name of religion was quickly defused, but the situation made it harder for health professionals to provide the requested intervention and left difficult memories for the people involved.

Disagreements regarding MAID can be felt in daily work interactions without amounting to anything close to contestation in the name of religion. I have found no evidence of religious contestation in the sense of preventing the practice or blocking the administration of a request, which does not mean that it does not exist. Overall, the regime of non-discriminatory state intervention to offer MAID and protect freedom of conscience seems to be working.

Is contestation in the name of religion impossible in Quebec?

In short, the Quebec context leaves little room for contestation in the name of religion. The possibility of contesting in the name of religion does exist, but it is severely constrained by the context, which instead favours individual objections that do not question its secular nature. Several aspects of the Quebec context bear witness to the constraints that weigh on contestation in the name of religion. In public debates, religious actors mostly use secular arguments against assistance in dying, and public speech in the name of religion is deemed suspicious and discredited. In practice, the health care system is familiar with the personalisation of care (Audy, 2017), and conscientious objections are respected. In short, in the Quebec context, the conditions for the relationship between the state and its citizens are not only secular but also "secularist" in the sense that religion is publicly treated as an individual belief, as against secular convictions (Asad, 2003) and is reduced to a private preference (Amiraux, 2016).

Looking for evidence of religious contestation in Vaud

In public debates

As in Quebec, in Vaud I also looked for evidence of religious contestation in the name of religion in publicly available documents. Over the years, institutional religions in Vaud have voiced their concerns regarding assisted suicide. From 2009 to 2012, the controversy around EXIT's popular initiative on the regulation of assisted suicide in nursing homes forced the state and institutional religions recognised by the state to adopt a position. EXIT's initiative was aimed at compelling those nursing homes recognised as being "of public interest" and therefore benefiting from public subsidies, to allow assisted suicide within their walls. In 2012, about 10% of nursing homes were opposed to assisted suicide being conducted on their premises (Bedeau, 2012). The spirit of EXIT's proposal was to guarantee equal rights for persons living at home and residents of nursing homes. The state replied with a counter-plan, which featured a different proposal that was also submitted to the population to vote on at the same time. This proposal would regulate assisted suicide in public health care institutions, both nursing homes and hospitals, provided that certain legal conditions were met. The counter-plan had the support of all political parties and the three recognised institutional religions. It was accepted by 62% of the population in 2012 (Roulet, 2012).

Before the referendum, Catholic, Reformed and Jewish institutions, the three religious communities recognised as being "of public interest" in Vaud, jointly decided not to give voting instructions, as their positions did not completely overlap. Instead, they published a joint statement reminding voters that Swiss law provides for freedom of choice, which implies the "right not to be prevented" from ending one's life and not an "absolute right to a service" (EERV, CILV and ECVD, 2012, my trans.). According to the episcopal vicar of the canton of Vaud, they issued this joint statement because of their "close collaboration in health settings" (Corradini, 2012, my trans.). In their statement, these institutions stress the specific nature of making an end-of-life decision in nursing homes as it necessarily involves other people, while noting that "institutional constraints cannot, as a matter of principle, seriously restrict the individual's choices" (EERV, CILV and ECVD, 2012, my trans.). They also defend the idea that no authority can claim a monopoly on the conception of dignity. They add that "God alone is Lord of life, and that he entrusts responsibility for it to us". From this, they draw the consequence that everyone can "express his or her choices regarding his or her care, way of dying and last wishes". The wish to die defies "in the last instance our moral or legal judgments". As in Quebec, the arguments used by religious actors are similar to those used by secular actors, with the distinction that their justification rests in part on theological grounds. In the joint statement, the three institutions propose a discourse similar to the consensus that is emerging in Vaud: individuals are free to make decisions for themselves, without interference from the state or religious institutions, provided they have the necessary decision-making capacity, except if assisted suicide is to take place in a health institution where additional checks are required. This exception is based on the fact that these are collective places. The EERV and the ECVD are also critical of the fact that public subsidies to nursing homes are made conditional on their acceptance of assisted suicide (Corradini, 2012), a fear shared by *Living with Dignity* in Quebec regarding palliative care hospices as its general director told me in an interview in 2016.

The positions of individual religious institutions differ. Over the years, the EERV has repeatedly taken a stand on assisted suicide. It encourages the use of palliative care without opposing assisted suicide (Troilo, 2015; Réformés, 2019). It leaves pastors free to decide whether or not they wish to accompany those making this decision: "Each minister is called upon to forge his or her own convictions. There is no right or wrong way to think. Our Church accepts this tension within her" (EERV, 2016: 2; my trans.). On the institution's website, it says that existential decisions at the end of life cannot be evaluated according to moral or ethical principles, provided that "all those involved are willing to take responsibility for putting (themselves) in the place of the other, to invest themselves and even, when things become serious, to accept guilt, consciously and deliberately" (Troilo, 2015; my trans.). This position is similar to those adopted by the Swiss federal state and the State of Vaud, which refuse to take decisions based on legislated criteria as to which lives should be protected or not, if they go beyond aspects such as decision-making capacity and the presence of a medical condition when health care professionals are involved. The responsibility must be borne by the persons concerned. In this, the state reflects a historical Protestant sensitivity, which is implicitly recognised by the spokesman of the EERV: "It is part of our culture to finally leave total freedom of choice to citizens and parishioners" (Corradini, 2012; my trans.).

Following the adoption of the counter-project, the ECVD affirms that its mission continues "to accompany people at the end of life and towards the mystery of death" (ECVD, 2012, my trans.). Chaplains remain available for discussions with people considering assisted suicide. In several publications on the Swiss Catholic Portal cath.ch, the Swiss Church relays the positions expressed by Canadian bishops that funerals and the anointing of the sick are incompatible with euthanasia, or the Pope's statements on euthanasia and assisted suicide, which he likens to "the most alarming symptoms of the culture of death" (Zbinden, 2019, my trans.). In 2008, the Swiss Bishops' Conference called for a ban on organised and commercial assisted suicide and refused that it be enshrined in law. Moreover, according to a press article, it maintains that "the desire for death is rarely a freely taken decision" (Ehrbar, 2008, my trans.). The ECVD seems to admit this possibility more clearly than the Swiss Church. During the debates on the vote, the ECVD put forward an attitude of compassion and non-judgement, according to the episcopal vicar: "Since the Canon Law of 1983, the Catholic Church, in the name of mercy, has welcomed for funerals those who have chosen to leave by suicide. This is an attitude of non-judgment" (Corradini, 2012, my trans.). It thus joins the Swiss consensus that assisted suicide can be freely chosen without being facilitated or condemned by institutions. Like the Church in Quebec, the Church in Vaud seems to have adopted a position that falls in line with the views of the population. The Swiss assisted dying regime ultimately accommodates the religious sensitivities of the two main Churches by considering assisted suicide as an exercise of individual freedom and by refusing to authorise euthanasia,[13] which is explicitly condemned by the Roman Catholic doctrine.

Some ten nursing homes publicly declared themselves to be "conscientious objectors", accompanied by the *Fédération Romande d'Églises évangéliques* (FREE) (Federation of Evangelical Churches of the French-speaking region of Switzerland), the ECVD, and the Salvation Army. This circumstantial alliance favours the status quo but considers that the counter-plan is preferable to EXIT's initiative (Bourgeois, 2012). Once the new article of the law on public health came into force, some nursing homes associated with religious institutions persisted in their opposition. In 2015, State Councillor Pierre-Yves Maillard reminded institutions dependent on the Salvation Army that they could not continue to assert their intention not to apply the law (24 heures, 2015). They risked seeing their public funding suspended if they were to persist.

Public funding of major religious organisations helps defuse the possibility of contestation in the name of religion. Traditionally, state-funded religious institutions must abide by the law and chaplains, who are employees of state-funded religious organisations, play a dual role that is difficult to fulfil, as some told me, because they must provide chaplaincy services for everyone, not just for people who share their beliefs. As "the State takes into account the spiritual dimension of the human person" (my trans.) according to the cantonal Constitution,[14] religious communities must, in the exercise of their common missions, provide services to users regardless of their spiritual convictions.

And in practice?

In Vaud, religion is scarcely an obstacle to the practice of assisted suicide. Assisted suicide takes place mostly outside of health care institutions according to EXIT numbers. In 2018, 99 assistances were provided at the requester's home, while 16 were administered in nursing homes and 4 in hospitals (Exit, 2019: 13). Outside health care institutions, conscientious objections on religious grounds are not an issue. The EXIT volunteers who provide assisted suicide ask the requester's treating physician if they would agree to prescribe the lethal substance. If the physician refuses for personal reasons not related to legal requirements, the volunteer will contact a physician who is on the panel of those who regularly work with EXIT.

Some EXIT volunteers have religious or spiritual convictions, but this does not prevent them from providing assisted suicide. For instance, a volunteer told me in an interview that she had doubts in relation to her Catholic faith when she started practising assisted suicide. She decided to meet a priest to find out if what she was doing was "right". He responded, "You are a person of faith, don't change anything". Another volunteer told me a similar story. A priest reassured her that she was right to do it if she has "peace of mind". Loved ones to whom applicants disclose their intention to access assisted suicide also tend to help them with the administrative process regardless of their personal position on assisted suicide (Gamondi et al., 2018). A devout practising Catholic woman told me how she had not hesitated to accompany a friend who requested assisted suicide because of her refractory depression. In the situations I have been told about where relatives disagreed or even attempted to prevent the applicant from having access to assisted suicide, religious convictions were never an issue, which does not mean that this is never the case, however. When there are disagreements among a family, relatives can complicate the process. As they have no definitive role, they cannot, however, completely hamper the process. Respect for the person's decision and autonomy usually prevails among the informed relatives (Pott et al., 2015).

While the religious convictions of care providers and relatives cannot prevent someone from getting access to assisted suicide at home, the situation can be more complicated in health care institutions. In Vaud, medical directors of public health care institutions have a legal obligation to assess assisted suicide requests to determine if the person can proceed within the institution. As previously mentioned, this step may be an issue in religiously affiliated nursing homes, but pressure from the state seems to have eased those situations. The bylaw allows applicants to appeal to the regional health authority if they feel that their requests have not been assessed in conformity with the law. EXIT officials told me in interviews that they observe that collaboration from institutions has considerably improved in recent years. Individual conscientious objections are possible for health care professionals, but this possibility is not likely to be used since employees of public institutions are not authorised to participate in assisted suicide in a professional capacity.

In hospitals, access to assisted suicide can be a real challenge. However, again, religion does not appear to be a major issue. The daughter of a woman who wanted to leave the hospital to get assisted suicide at home told me her mother's story. Hospitalised following a fall and feeling unwell, her 90-something mother told the staff that she wanted to have an assisted suicide because of the multiple conditions that caused her pain and made her lose autonomy. The hospital staff initiated a process of assessment that lasted more than ten days. Several physicians visited her during the process to constantly re-assess her decision-making capacity, which was felt as infantilising by the mother and the daughter. The daughter could not explain why the staff would do all this as her mother was perfectly coherent and did not even want to get assisted suicide in the hospital. In this case, secular hospital protocols and culture seemed to be the issue, and not religious convictions, even though the daughter was tempted to attribute this attitude to religion. She could not tell why she thought that religious convictions could be involved. Her reflex seems to be in line with public debates that tend to associate religions with opposition to assistance in dying, even though there seemed to be no evidence of religious involvement in this situation.

As in Quebec, the portrait of the interactions between religion and assistance in dying is more nuanced than what can be expected based on public debates. The government's non-intervention regime works to accommodate a variety of moral convictions but comes at the price of placing a heavy burden on an association of volunteers that has no formal recognition or funding from the state.[15] This regime leaves virtually no room for the contestation of assistance in dying in the name of religion, as long as the state and medicine remain marginal actors.

The impossibility of contesting in the name of religion in Vaud?

In Vaud as in Quebec, the possibilities for contesting assistance in dying in the name of religion are quite limited. At the institutional and public debate level, the main organised religions do not oppose the cantonal state's limited intervention regime in the area of assisted suicide. Because they receive public funding and have a mandate to provide services to the general population, organised religions need to maintain a position of openness. The political justification for state support of institutional religions is no longer based on their historical role or the values they promote but on their role as service providers (Pahud de Mortanges, 2018: 130). Institutional religions must deal with the fact of being the partners of a state that is both secularist and pluralistic (Becci, 2020). The partnership between the state and the established religions has no equivalent concerning the end of life. EXIT does not enjoy the same "social integration" recognition as some churches (Pahud de Mortanges, 2018: 123). Rather, the association is seen as an acceptable, tolerable source of disturbance of the social order. Its legitimacy comes not from the provision of services deemed useful by the state, but from the principle of self-determination and the recognition that it responds to a demand, or even a need, in the population.

Unlike Quebec, where the state intervenes heavily to regulate religious convictions in public service and end-of-life choices, Vaud adopts different approaches regarding the end of life and religious matters. For assisted suicide, the state respects the convictions of individuals by intervening in a very limited manner, whereas for religious freedom, Vaud funds certain religious institutions and prohibits its agents from wearing religious symbols.

Although contestation of the current regime in the name of religion is very limited, organised religions strongly oppose the legalisation of euthanasia as a medical act offered by health care institutions. The state already defends such a view, not believing that helping people to die is part of the state's mission. It is easy for the state to maintain this position when assisted suicide is already available through private associations.

Conclusion

In conclusion, I suggest that the "ethics of the secular" (Lavi, 2014) weighs heavily on the possibility of contesting assistance in dying in the name of religion. Building on Talal Asad's work, Shai Lavi concludes that "a new secular ethics and cosmology … has made the pangs of death 'unnecessary'" (Lavi, 2014: 300). As a matter of fact, the assistance in dying regimes of Quebec and Vaud are united around the concept of "intolerable suffering", despite the many differences between them. Experiencing intolerable suffering is one of the eligibility criteria for MAID in Quebec and is also one of the criteria used by right-to-die societies in Switzerland. In 2018, the Swiss Academy of Medical Sciences, an organisation that issues guidelines for the medical profession, modified its guidelines for the practice of assisted suicide. It replaced the criterion that stipulates that a person must be at the end of life to get an assisted suicide with the requirement that the requester is experiencing intolerable suffering (SAMS, 2018). This tendency to distinguish deaths that can be facilitated based on the concept of "intolerable suffering" is symptomatic of the ethics of the secular. This ethics has dissociated suffering from dying and aims not simply at reducing suffering but at eliminating it and is concerned about making death appear to be without suffering (Lavi, 2014). This is in line with the view of the Dutch physician and philosopher Henri Wijsbek (2012) who argues that intolerable suffering is a public norm by which physicians assess requests for euthanasia, which is also demonstrated by ethnographic studies (see, for example, Norwood, 2009).

Based on my observations of the two contexts, contesting assistance in dying in the name of religion appears very difficult because it implies contesting not only this practice but also contesting the ethics of the secular, which makes religion an individual conviction and which has made suffering lose its meaning in the face of death. The only form of contestation or rather accommodation that remains is individual conscientious objection. I also form the hypothesis that it is hard for religions to contest assistance in dying because it can potentially concern everyone directly, as opposed to issues such as abortion or same-sex marriage.

Finally, I had been told so often that I was going to encounter contestation in the name of religion that I am surprised that I have not found more. Indeed, secularism limits the capacity to read and interpret religious actions and constrains the behaviour of religious actors (Amiraux, 2018: 176). I had underestimated the strength of secularised contexts that have the potential to make every moral question an issue of individual conviction, which does not mean that it is an egotistic conviction, as Émile Durkheim so aptly perceived it. Durkheim (1898) describes the "religion of the individual", which, according to him, is not a threat if it is the foundation of a culture of human rights. What seems to differentiate people's positions on assistance in dying, whether secular or religious or both, is the way they articulate personal convictions and public values, giving more or less weight to the collective or to the individual. This comes back to Durkheim's classic question about the dynamics of regulation and integration that explain the suicide rate, or, it could be argued, other forms of voluntary deaths (Durkheim, 2007 [1897]). Without being able to contest in the name of religion, the only thing religions can do is to propose other ways of articulating individual and public values. In Quebec and Vaud, freedom of conscience is thus not a means mostly used to contest assistance in dying in the name of religion. It is rather a tool that makes room for conciliating responses to suffering in individual cases and preoccupations of justice, social care, and freedom that transcend individual cases.

Notes

1 I use the phrase "assistance in dying" to designate both euthanasia and assisted suicide.

2 In total, my ethnography includes 60 hours of observation (50 in Quebec and 10 in Vaud) and 85 interviews (56 in Quebec and 29 in Vaud). The press review was compiled from three daily newspapers in each context and covers the period 1988–2018 (depending on the availability of the electronic database).

3 S-32.0001 – Act Respecting End-of-Life Care (10 December 2015). Quebec. Retrieved on 16 September 2020. http://legisquebec.gouv.qc.ca/fr/showdoc/cs/s-32.0001?langCont=en

4 Act to amend the Criminal Code and to make related amendments to other Acts (medical assistance in dying, C 14). (17 June 2016). (S.C. 2016, c. 3). Canada. Retrieved on 16 September 2020. https://laws-lois.justice.gc.ca/eng/annualstatutes/2016_3/ See also Supreme Court of Canada (2015, February). *Carter v. Canada* [2015], 1 SCR 331. Retrieved on 16 September 2020. https://scc-csc.lexum.com/scc-csc/scc-csc/fr/item/14637/index.do

5 CC 311.0 Swiss Criminal Code of 21 December 1937, art. 115. See also the decision of the Federal Tribunal of 2006, ATF 133 I 58. Retrieved on 16 September 2020. https://www.admin.ch/opc/en/classified-compilation/19370083/index.html
6 800.01 Loi sur la santé publique du 29 mai 1985, art. 27d (800.01: law on public health care of 29 May 1985, art. 27d). Retrieved on 16 September 2020. https://prestations.vd.ch/pub/blv-publication/actes/consolide/800.01?key=1577921418951&id=258cb2db-b772-411c-b0c5-6ed80967c762
7 Office fédéral de la statistique (2019) (Swiss Federal Office of Statistics), "Population résidante permanente âgée de 15 ans ou plus selon l'appartenance religieuse par canton et ville". Retrieved on 16 September 2020. https://www.bfs.admin.ch/bfs/fr/home/statistiques/population/langues-religions/religions.assetdetail.7226716.html
8 Based on their name and/or website.
9 All briefs can be found on the website of the National Assembly of Quebec (2010–2011).
10 "*confèrent un supplément de sens*" in the French original.
11 L-0.3 – Loi sur la laïcité de l'État (law on the secularism of the state [16 June 2019]). Quebec. Retrieved on 16 September 2020. http://legisquebec.gouv.qc.ca/fr/ShowDoc/cs/L-0.3
12 In this book, see also Chapter 8 by Dumont and Maclure and Chapter 3 by Weinstock on conscientious objections in Quebec in relation to medical aid in dying.
13 On several occasions, the federal government has refused to authorise euthanasia, among other things because it would go against the State's duty to protect life and the set of values on which the Swiss Constitution is founded. To characterise this set of values, the Federal Council mentions the intangibility of human life from a human rights perspective and the Christian heritage, which the State must take into account given its importance in Switzerland, even though the State, which claims to be secular, cannot give an absolute character to the vision of the churches. The Federal Council says that it cannot base its decision on this heritage, but that it attaches significant value to it in view of the imprint that the Judeo-Christian tradition has made on Swiss society (report of the Swiss Federal Council, 2000).
14 Constitution vaudoise de 2003, art.169, al. 1. (Constitution of the State of Vaud, art. 169, paragraph 1). Retrieved on 16 September 2020. https://www.admin.ch/opc/fr/classified-compilation/20030172/index.html
15 Nonetheless, the association's finances are in very good shape, thanks to annual membership fees and donations.

Bibliography

24 heures. 2015. "Quand les Églises ont de la peine à se plier à la loi." *24 heures* May 9: 11.

Agence de presse internationale catholique. 2012. "Vaud: Prise de position du vicaire épiscopal sur l'assistance au suicide." *Cath.ch*. Retrieved on September 16th, 2020. https://www.cath.ch/newsf/la-mission-de-l-eglise-demeure-la-meme/.

Amiraux, V. 2016. "Visibility, Transparency and Gossip: How Did the Religion of Some (Muslims) Become the Public Concern of Others?" *Critical Research on Religion* 4 (1): 37–56.

Amiraux, V. 2018. "Citoyens, piété et démocratie. Réflexions sur l'occultation des corps croyants, l'intimité et le droit au secret." *Social Compass* 65 (2): 168–186.

Asad, T. 2003. *Formations of the Secular*. Stanford: Stanford University Press.

Assemblée des Évêques catholiques du Québec. 2010. *Mémoire*. In Commission on Dying with Dignity, Assemblée nationale du Québec, 39e législature, 1ère session. Retrieved on September 16th 2020. http://www.assnat.qc.ca/Media/Process.aspx?MediaId=ANQ.

Vigie.Bll.DocumentGenerique_36095&process=Default&token=ZyMoxNwUn8ikQ+TRKYwPCjWrKwg+vIv9rjij7p3xLGTZDmLVSmJLoqe/vG7/YWzz.

Association d'Églises Baptistes Évangéliques au Québec. 2010. *Mémoire présenté par Michel Michel-Habib et Éric Lanthier*. Commission on Dying with Dignity, Assemblée nationale du Quebec, 39e législature, 1ère session. Retrieved on September 16th, 2020. http://www.assnat.qc.ca/Media/Process.aspx?MediaId=ANQ.Vigie.Bll.DocumentGenerique_37581&process=Default&token=ZyMoxNwUn8ikQ+TRKYwPCjWrKwg+vIv9rjij7p3xLGTZDmLVSmJLoqe/vG7/YWzz.

Audy, E. 2017. *L'infirmière, la pratique de soin et la négociation: Ethnographie des suivis postnatals à domicile en milieu multiethnique à Montréal*. Doctoral thesis. Montréal: Université de Montréal. Retrieved on September 16th 2020. https://papyrus.bib.umontreal.ca/xmlui/handle/1866/18524.

Bator, E.X., Philpott, B. and Costa, A.P. 2017. "This Moral Coil : A Cross-Sectional Survey of Canadian Medical Student Attitudes Toward Medical Assistance in Dying." *BMC Medical Ethics* 18 (1): 58–66.

Becci, I. 2020. "*Gouverner en reconnaissant ou en séparant ? Deux cantons romands face à la nouvelle diversité religieuse »*. Pp. 263–281 in Pahud de Mortanges, R. (ed.) Jubiläumsband zum 40-jährigen Bestehen des Instituts für Religionsrech. Freiburg : Schulthess-Verlag.

Becci, I. and Bovay, C. 2007. "Les représentations sociales concernant la pluralisation religieuse en Suisse." *Social Compass* 54 (2): 145–159.

Bedeau. 2012. "La plupart des EMS Vaudois Acceptent Exit." *Le Matin* March 11: 9.

Blouin, S. 2020. *Administrer les demandes de mort: comparaison de l'aide médicale à mourir (Québec) et de l'assistance au suicide (canton de Vaud)*. Doctoral dissertation. Montréal: Université de Montréal and Université de Lausanne.

Bourgeois, L. 2012. "Une dizaine d'EMS prêts à l'objection de conscience." *24 heures* May 31: 24.

Bouthillier, M.-E. and Opatrny, L. 2019. "A Qualitative Study of Physicians' Conscientious Objections to Medical Aid in Dying." *Palliative Medicine* 33 (9): 1212–1220.

Buzzetti, H. 2013. "Mourir dans la dignité – L'influence discrète de l'Opus Dei." *Le Devoir*. October 29. Retrieved on September 16th, 2020. https://www.ledevoir.com/politique/quebec/391209/l-influence-discrete-de-l-opus-dei.

Corradini. 2012. "Les Églises vaudoises butent sur Exit." *Le Matin* April 1: 10.

Dalpé, S. and Koussens, D. 2016. "Les discours sur la laïcité pendant le débat sur la 'Charte des valeurs de la laïcité'. Une analyse lexicométrique de la presse francophone québécoise." *Recherches sociographiques* 57 (23): 455–474.

Dumont, I. and Maclure, J. 2019. "Objection de conscience et aide médicale à mourir: Une étude qualitative auprès de médecins québécois." *Canadian Journal of Bioethics/Revue canadienne de bioéthique* 2 (2): 110–134.

Durkheim, É. 1897. *Le suicide: Étude de sociologie* (Nouv. éd.). Paris: Presses universitaires de France. 2002.

Durkheim, É. [1898] 2002. "L'individualisme et les intellectuels". *Revue bleue, 4e série* X: 7–13.

Église Évangélique Réformée du canton de Vaud (EERV). 2016. *Assistance au suicide et accompagnement pastoral*. Conseil synodal. Retrieved on September 16th 2020. https://eerv.ch/download/6203/.

Église Évangélique Réformée du canton de Vaud (EERV), Communauté israélite de Lausanne et du canton de Vaud (CILV) and Église catholique dans le canton de Vaud (ECVD). 2012. *Quelques réflexions des Eglises réformée et catholique du canton de*

Vaud et de la Communauté israélite de Lausanne et du canton de Vaud en vue de la votation de juin 2012 sur l'initiative "assistance au suicide en EMS" et sur le contre-projet du Grand Conseil. March 30.

Ehrbar. 2008. "Aide au suicide: non des évêques." *Le Matin* July 9: 6.

Exit. 2019. *Bulletin no 70*. April. Retrieved on September 16th, 2020. https://exit-romandie.ch/pdf/bul70.pdf.

Fondation humaniste du Québec. 2013. "Prix Humaniste 2013." March 21. Retrieved on September 16th, 2020. http://fondhum.org/nouvelles/prix_humaniste_2013.

Gamondi, C., Pott, M., Preston, N. and Payne, S. 2018. "Family Caregivers' Reflections on Experiences of Assisted Suicide in Switzerland : A Qualitative Interview Study." *Journal of Pain and Symptom Management* 55 (4): 1085–1094.

Gandsman, A. 2018. "Paradox of Choice and the Illusion of Autonomy: The Construction of Ethical Subjects in Right-To-Die Activism." *Death Studies* 42 (5): 329–335.

Georges, J.-J. et al. 2007. "Dealing with Requests for Euthanasia : A Qualitative Study Investigating the Experience of General Practitioners." *Journal of Medical Ethics* 34 (3): 150–155.

Lavi, S. 2014. "Humane Killing and the Ethics of the Secular: Regulating the Death Penalty, Euthanasia, and Animal Slaughter." *UC Irvine Law Review* 4 (1): 297–324.

National Assembly of Quebec. 2010–2011. *Briefs Tabled Under the Order to the Committee Consultation générale sur la question de mourir dans la dignité*. 39e legislature. Retrieved on September 16th, 2020. http://www.assnat.qc.ca/en/travaux-parlementaires/commissions/CSMD/mandats/Mandat-12989/memoires-deposes.html

Norwood, F. 2009. *The Maintenance of Life : Preventing Social Death Through Euthanasia Talk and End-of-Life Care—Lessons from the Netherlands*. Durham: Carolina Academic Press.

Pahud de Mortanges, R. 2018. "Entre pluralisation religieuse et sécularisation : L'évolution récente de la reconnaissance étatique des communautés religieuses en Suisse." Pp. 121–131 in Becci, I., Monnot, C. and Voirol, O. (eds.) *Pluralisme et reconnaissance : Face à la diversité religieuse*. Rennes: Presses universitaires de Rennes.

Pott, M., Stauffer, L. and Gamondi, C. 2015. "Quand accompagnement de fin de vie rime avec assistance au suicide: L'expérience des proches en Suisse latine." *Anthropologie & Santé* 10: 1704–1723.

Radio-Canada. 2016a. "Refus de bénir l'urne après l'aide médicale à mourir : les évêques ne cautionnent pas, mais ne condamnent pas". *Radio-Canada*. December 8. Retrieved on September 16th, 2020. https://ici.radio-canada.ca/nouvelle/1004748/aide-mourir-euthanasie-eveques-catholiques-pretre-diocese-trois-rivieres.

Radio-Canada. 2016b. "Aide à mourir et funérailles religieuses : la position d'évêques canadiens soulève l'indignation." *Radio-Canada*. September 29. Retrieved on September 16th, 2020. https://ici.radio-canada.ca/nouvelle/806013/aide-medicale-mourir-eglise-funerailles-debat.

Réformés.ch. 2019. "Libérer la parole sur le suicide assisté." *Réformés.ch*. January 22. Retrieved on September 16th, 2020. https://www.reformes.ch/ethique/2019/01/liberer-la-parole-sur-le-suicide-assiste-suicide-assiste-eerv-formation-reformes.

Roulet, Y. 2012. "Suicide assisté dans le canton de Vaud: la version de l'État triomphe." *Le Temps*. June 17. Retrieved on September 16th, 2020. https://www.letemps.ch/suisse/suicide-assiste-canton-vaud-version-letat-triomphe.

Rousseau, L. 2016. "Le travail obscur de la mémoire identitaire dans les débats nés d'une nouvelle diversité religieuse au Québec." *Recherches sociographiques* 57 (23): 289–310.

Roy, O. 2010. *Holy Ignorance. When Religion and Culture Part Ways*. New York: Columbia University Press.

Select Committee on Dying With Dignity. 2012. *Report. Assemblée nationale du Québec*. Retrieved on September 16th, 2020. http://www.assnat.qc.ca/Media/Process.aspx?MediaId=ANQ.Vigie.Bll.DocumentGenerique_54787en&process=Default&token=ZyMoxNwUn8ikQ+TRKYwPCjWrKwg+vIv9rjij7p3xLGTZDmLVSmJLoqe/vG7/YWzz.

Steck, N., Junker, C. and Zwahlen, M. 2018. "Increase in Assisted Suicide in Switzerland : Did the Socioeconomic Predictors Change? Results from the Swiss National Cohort." *BMJ Open* 8 (4): 1–11.

Swiss Academy of Medical Sciences (SAMS). 2018. *Management of Dying and Death*. Retrieved on September 16th, 2020. https://www.samw.ch/en/Ethics/Ethics-in-end-of-life-care/Guidelines-management-dying-death.html.

Swiss Federal Council. 2000. *Rapport du Conseil fédéral donnant suite au postulat Ruffy. Assistance au décès. Adjonction au Code pénal Suisse*. Retrieved on September 16th, 2020. https://www.bj.admin.ch/dam/data/bj/gesellschaft/gesetzgebung/archiv/sterbehilfe/ber-ruffy-f.pdf.

Troilo, D. 2015. "EXIT: Éléments d'orientation et d'appréciation théologico-éthiques protestants". *Église évangélique réformée dans le canton de Vaud*. April 16. Retrieved on September 16th, 2020. https://aumonerieems.eerv.ch/2015/04/16/elements-dorientation-et-dappreciation-theologico-ethiques-protestants/.

Verbakel, E. and Jaspers, E. 2010. "A Comparative Study on Permissiveness Toward Euthanasia Religiosity, Slippery Slope, Autonomy, and Death with Dignity". *Public Opinion Quarterly* 74 (1): 109–139.

Wijsbek, H. 2012. "The Subjectivity of Suffering and the Normativity of Unbearableness". Pp. 319–332 in Kimsma, G.K. and Youngner, S.J. (eds.) *Physician-Assisted Death in Perspective : Assessing the Dutch Experience*. Cambridge: Cambridge University Press.

Zbinden, R. 2019. "Le pape François s'élève à nouveau contre l'euthanasie". *Cath.ch portail catholique suisse*. June 5. Retrieved on September 16th, 2020. https://www.cath.ch/newsf/le-pape-francois-seleve-a-nouveau-contre-leuthanasie/.

10 The politicisation of French Catholics on intimate issues through the promotion of lay expertise

A case study based on the Emmanuel Community's magazine *Il est vivant!* (1975–2018)

Samuel Dolbeau[1]

French society is one of the most secularised in Europe (Béraud, 2017). Its public institutions are among those most impermeable to religious arguments. However, contemporary Catholic campaigns centred around issues related to policies regarding intimate issues[2] have acquired greater visibility in the public space, particularly in the past ten years (Balas and Tricou, 2019; Béraud, 2011, 2014; Béraud and Portier, 2015; Bréjon de Lavergnée and Della Sudda, 2015; Massei, 2017). The opposition to same-sex marriage in 2012–2013 or the debates surrounding the amendment of bioethics laws[3] in 2017–2019 have highlighted the politicisation of some French Catholics, whom the political scientist Yann Raison du Cleuziou calls "observants" (Raison du Cleuziou, 2014). For him, these observant Catholics:

> retain from the Gospels elements that legitimise a certain opposition to the dominant social values. Often critical of a society that they consider to be decadent and relativistic, they expect the Church to be a beacon that illuminates their path of truth both in season and out of season. … Even if these Catholics can be labelled as conservatives, this is therefore not related to the defence of the established order since they contest it.[4]
>
> (Raison du Cleuziou, 2019: 19)

In a social context in which religious arguments are neutralised in the public space, these Catholics must use various strategies to make their voices heard. As the sociologists Michael Stambolis-Ruhstorfer and Josselin Tricou have demonstrated for the movement that opposes the "gender ideology",[5] which began in France in 2011, this visibility in the public space is the result of a rhetorical framework based on republican values and of the exploitation of a propitious political context "both on the national political scene and within the French Church" (Stambolis-Ruhstorfer and Tricou, 2017: 80). These two authors identify various types of contextualising techniques used by these observant

Catholics, such as positioning themselves as "whistle-blowers", defenders of children's rights, using the English word "gender" (not the French word *genre*) in order "to portray 'gender' as a dangerous ideology imported from abroad" (Stambolis-Ruhstorfer and Tricou, 2017: 86), drawing "explicitly on the images and rhetoric of progressive political campaigning" (ibid.), especially Gay Pride Parades, trying to hide their religious and social background (upper class), and using their professional expertise and scientific arguments. In short, these Catholics have strategically adopted a secular positioning in a secularised public space.

Here, as with the other two chapters in this final part of book, I shall be analysing how the rhetoric of contestation adopted by these religious actors has evolved. From a historical perspective, I shall seek to understand "from within" how these observant Catholics have constructed their secular rhetorical framing. The purpose of this chapter is to contribute to the analysis of this contestation by viewing this phenomenon in the light of an internal dynamic of contemporary Catholicism, that of laypeople taking responsibility in the running of the Catholic Church. According to the sociologist Céline Béraud, this "silent revolution" (Béraud, 2007), which largely evolved from the 1970s onwards, has its roots in three phenomena: the shortage of priests, "the ecclesiological renewal initiated by the Second Vatican Council" (1962–1965), and "the extension of democratic culture to all spheres of social activity" (Béraud, 2007: 41). Céline Béraud showed, on a diocesan scale, how the Catholic Church adapted to the shortage of priests by developing new types of permanent lay workers (Béraud, 2008), mostly women, to fulfil different tasks in day-to-day religious life (parish administration, catechism classes, baptisms, funerals and so on). My theory is that this approach can provide a fruitful analytical framework for understanding the politicisation of these observant Catholics around issues related to policies regarding intimate issues. While the use of professional expertise and scientific arguments was part of a strategy of creating a framework based on republican values in the French public space, it has also contributed to the legitimisation of "lay expertise" in the religious field. In this case, the term "lay" does not refer to a lack of specialised knowledge on a subject, that is, to a lack of expertise, but only to the laity. To study this phenomenon, I will focus on one of the most dynamic French ecclesial movements: the Emmanuel Community.

The Emmanuel Community was initially a prayer group founded in Paris in 1972 by two laypeople: Pierre Goursat (1914–1994) and Martine Laffitte-Catta. It can now be found in about 60 countries and has around 11,500 and 12,000 members, including priests and laypeople (some married, some celibate). Half of these members live in France. They belong mostly to the upper class, even though the group's activities have a wider reach. The members of the Emmanuel Community go more or less through the same type of religious socialisation, that is, a background in a practising Catholic family, with baptism, first communion, confirmation, scouting,[6] serving as an altar boy and so on. According to the typology drawn up by Yann Raison du Cleuziou, they can be labelled as "observant" Catholics (Raison du Cleuziou, 2019).

The Emmanuel Community is also part of a larger movement in contemporary Catholicism, known as Charismatic Renewal. It appeared in Europe in the early 1970s and imported a number of theological and ecclesiological elements from American Pentecostalism (Maurer, 2010). In Europe, France is the country where Charismatic Renewal has spread the most rapidly and extensively (Landron, 2004). In a social context of intense community experiments, dozens of prayer groups flourished, experiencing religious sentiments focused on explicit evangelism, a culture of praise and the expression of charisms[7] and Baptism in the Spirit.[8] Many of these groups disappeared after the death of their founder.

However, the growth and formation of some of these communities and of the Emmanuel Community in particular was encouraged by some bishops[9] at the turn of the 1980s. It was part of a desire to break with the left-wing and far left-wing politicisation of the previous generation of Catholics (Horn, 2015; Pelletier and Schlegel, 2013). This politicisation centred around the events of May 1968 in France, during which several Catholic organisations were involved in the protests (Hervieu-Léger, 1973; Pelletier, 2002; Raison du Cleuziou, 2016). Today, the contrast between these factions is widely disseminated in the French historiography of Catholicism, that is, left-wing Catholics versus "Catholics of identity" to use a concept created by French political scientist Philippe Portier (Baudouin and Portier, 2002). Therefore, it was a little surprising when in 2012–2013, several commentators stressed the important role played by the Emmanuel Community during the campaigns against same-sex marriage in France (Brustier, 2014).

To understand the politicisation of these Catholics around issues related to policies regarding intimate issues, I studied a magazine that has been published by the Emmanuel Community since 1975: *Il est vivant!* (He is alive). The publication was initially a 35-page bimonthly magazine, intended to be a bulletin for prayer groups and communities involved in French Catholic Charismatic Renewal. In the first few issues, a great deal of space was devoted to reports on charismatic gatherings, articles about prayer groups or communities, and personal testimonies. The Emmanuel Community published French translations of a number of extracts from American books popular in charismatic circles (Ranaghan and Ranaghan, 1969; Wilkerson, 1963). There were also some in-depth theological articles on specific charismatic issues: charisms, baptism in the Holy Spirit and so on. From the mid-1980s on, and in particular in 1987 with the magazine's change of editorship, the audience expanded considerably beyond the boundaries of Charismatic Renewal. In September 1994, the magazine became a monthly publication. During the 1990s, the number of pages increased to around 50. At this time, *Il est vivant!* had about 20,000 subscribers, and was distributed beyond ecclesial circles on newsstands. Ever since, the number of subscribers has declined significantly, and the magazine has changed its focus and has become an internal training tool. All French-speaking members of the Emmanuel Community receive it automatically. Since December 2010, *Il est vivant!* has been published in an 80-page A5 format. The decline in the number of subscribers is partly due to the fact that the Emmanuel Community launched a new magazine called *L'1visible* (The Invisible) in 2010. It is a 24-page monthly, distributed free to a wide Catholic audience mainly through the parish network. For this study, I examined all of the issues of *Il est vivant!* between 1975 and 2001 and the years 2004, 2007, 2011 and 2012, plus a special 2018 issue on bioethics.[10] I focused on the contents page, the various advertisements that appear (i.e. for conferences, training sessions, and retreats), the readers' letters section, and the articles related to policies regarding intimate issues.[11] This research material was supplemented with observations made during the 2017 and 2018 *Journées Bioéthique* (Bioethics days[12]) in Paris, and study of the archives of the French Episcopal Commission for Pastoral Care of the Family.[13]

This chapter is structured in three sections, on a chronological basis. First, I will describe how the attention to the "Development of Peoples" shifts towards issues related to policies regarding intimate issues. The study of *Il est vivant!* shows that this shift is not a generational shift (from left-wing Catholics concerned about world development issues to observant Catholics concerned about birth control issues). Second, I will focus on the promotion of women's medical expertise in *Il est vivant!* This phenomenon emerges in the early 1980s and grows throughout the 1990s. For these women, this scientific expertise is an instrument of legitimisation within the religious field. Finally, I will highlight the gradual dissociation of concerns about policies regarding intimate issues from concerns about the pastoral care of the family. This dissociation is the result of this lay expertise becoming institutionalised.

The link between the "Development of Peoples" and policies regarding intimate issues at the turn of the 1980s

It is not surprising, coming from a charismatic community, that the first issues of the magazine are quite strongly characterised by a countercultural positioning (Cohen, 1998: 335; Pina, 2001). Many articles promote "true" fraternal bonds uniting Catholics against a liberal society. For example, in an article from April 1977, a certain Thomas Mornay writes:

> In our capitalist society, the measure of everything is money. … the values that are increasingly prevalent are decadent pagan values. … Only one solution seems possible to us: the community path. … Our objective is not a global political revolution … but a transformation of society based on personal conversion.
>
> (*Il est vivant!*, April 1977, no. 12, pp. 14–15)

As the end of the quotation suggests, the criticism of liberalism is not limited to the establishment of a closed Utopian community. With each issue of the magazine, there is a real desire for the transformation of society. This desire is reflected in the special attention paid to the working class. From 1976 on, the Emmanuel Community has organised "specialised" weekends with the theme "union involvement, politics and renewal" (*Il est vivant!*, October 1976, no. 9, p. 36). This method of placing apostolates or outreach workers "according to social milieu" was clearly influenced by an apostolate model promoted by Specialised Catholic Action. From February 1977 on, a "political and social" chronicle was published in *Il est vivant!*, and in February 1978 the first meetings run by Specialised Catholic Action and entitled "Renewal and the working world" were held in Paris.[14] This concern for the working class was mainly the result of the will of one man: Francis Kohn. A former delegate of the General Confederation of Labour,[15] which was closely allied to the *Communion de Boquen* (Lebel, 2015), he was one of the first members of the Emmanuel Community. He entered the seminary in 1979 and was ordained a priest in 1985. In addition to hosting these "Renewal and the working world" meetings, he conducted several interviews for *Il est vivant!*, including one with Father Yvan Daniel (1909–1986) in December 1977 (*Il est vivant!*, December 1977, no.16, pp. 17–21). This priest was co-author, with Father Henri Godin (1906-1944), of *La France Pays de mission?* in 1943 (Daniel and Godin, 1943). This bestseller had a profound impact on French Catholicism, partly influencing the experience of priest-workers (Poulat, 1965; Cavalin and Viet-Depaule, 2009).

The other issue prevalent in the late 1970s was the issue of Christian "third-worldism". The magazine published several articles on the development of populations from non-industrialised countries. There were reports on Latin American countries, especially Mexico, describing Catholic charismatic initiatives to combat situations of extreme poverty. The reports were always presented from the charismatic perspective of personal conversion, conveying the message that it is the action of the Holy Spirit in the life of the born-again Christian that subverts the established order and reverses injustices. For example, an article from July 1975 tells the story of a group of Marxist social workers in a northern Mexican city. They try to improve the conditions of exploited workers in a waste-reprocessing plant (the article states that they are paid $8 a week). Through the conversion of these Marxists, the situation is resolved, and the mayor of the city ends up giving 45% of the company's shares to the workers. A subtitle for the article refers to "an oppressive structure transformed by the Lord" (*Il est vivant!*, July 1975, no. 4, p. 11). This type of article remains in a minority in the pages of the magazine, but it illustrates a widespread line of thinking among the first generation of members of the Emmanuel Community. Indeed, the issue of Third Worldism led them in 1981 to set up *FIDESCO*.[16] *FIDESCO* is an international non-governmental organisation, which sends volunteers to countries in the southern hemisphere to carry out humanitarian missions lasting one to two years. *FIDESCO* is now one of the largest volunteer-based NGOs in France, with an annual budget of between three and four million euros.[17]

From the end of 1980, we see the gradual emergence of a new theme that went on to become a main focus of the magazine, namely the theme of the family. This change was clearly linked to the Fifth Ordinary General Assembly of the Synod of Bishops, the theme of which was "the Christian family". This was the first synod held by the new Pope John Paul II (1920–2005), who was elected in 1978. It was held in the Vatican from 26 September to 25 October 1980 and resulted a year later in the publication of the apostolic exhortation *Familiaris Consortio* on the role of the family in the world (John Paul II, 1981). This change in focus can be traced from one issue to another. In July–August 1980, issue 29 of the magazine was entitled "Changing the World: A Task for the Church" and included the transcript of a lecture given by the Dominican theologian Vincent Cosmao (1923–2006), which described his work to promote the development of non-industrialised countries. In September–October 1980, the 30th issue of the magazine was published with the title "Synod on the Family". The issue contained a rather long article by Gotfried Daneels (1933–2019), the new Archbishop of Mechelen-Brussels, appointed in December 1979. It stated: "The presentation of conjugal morality cannot be cut off from its doctrinal and spiritual root" (*Il est vivant!*, September 1980, no. 30, p. 36). It should be pointed out that these concerns about the couple and the family were not new to the Emmanuel Community. In the first few years of the movement, its members, specially Martine Laffitte-Catta, were very close to Father Henri Caffarel (1903–1996), the founder in 1939 of the *Équipes Notre-Dame*, a French conjugal spirituality movement (Walch, 2002, 2011). In the subsequent issues, we observe the creation of a "family life" section in the catalogue of books and audio cassettes available by mail order. This section gradually expands until it starts to overshadow other sections such as that devoted to ecumenism. It illustrates the formation of a pro-family[18] community network, committed to fight against abortion and so-called chemical contraception, which had been condemned since the publication of the encyclical *Humanae Vitae* (Paul VI, 1968). For example, the mail order catalogue in the June–July 1983 issue includes audio cassettes produced by the *C.L.E.R.*[19] Created in 1961, the *C.L.E.R.* is an association with a special interest in conjugal and sexual morality, which in particular promotes natural methods of birth control (Fradois, 2017; Sevegrand, 1995). It is still active today in the current debates around policies regarding intimate issues in France, especially with regard to sex education in private schools (Gauglin, 2019).

In the same catalogue, among recommended authors, there are two books by Father Jean Toulat (1915–1994): *Droit de naître*[20] (Toulat, 1979) and *Contraception sans violence*[21] (Toulat, 1980) (*Il est vivant!*, June–July 1983, no. 42, p. 18). Jean Toulat was a priest who was born in 1915 and died in 1994. He was involved in the French Resistance during World War II, and was an ardent pacifist, supporting the Fight for the Larzac[22] (Toulat, 1972). He was also concerned about the issue of development in South America (Toulat, 1965). His brother, Father Pierre Toulat (1922–2018), was the secretary of the French Episcopal Commission "Justice and Peace" between 1967 and 1989 (Toulat, 2014). In 1973, Jean Toulat published *L'avortement, crime ou libération?*[23] (Toulat, 1973), in which he made a strong case for the use of natural birth control methods rather than abortion. The sudden change in this author's concerns is indicative of an interesting process. Indeed, the concerns of these observant Catholics around issues such as abortion and contraception tended to be understood as a generational shift. The rise of the "intimate" (Pérez-Agote and Dobbelaere, 2015) and pro-family issues, embodied in the election of Pope John Paul II, would seem to have "laid to rest" the social themes promoted by left-wing Catholics (Pelletier and Schlegel, 2013). However, among authors like Father Jean Toulat, there was a clear link between a social development-based line of thinking, which was critical of liberalism, and opposition to contraception and abortion. From the 1990s onwards, the major figure who embodied this link, and was widely read in the Emmanuel Community was Father Michel Schooyans. This Belgian priest, born in 1930, is Professor Emeritus at the Faculty of Theology at the *Université catholique de Louvain* in Belgium, and was Professor at the *Pontifícia Universidade Católica de São Paulo* in Brazil for ten years. He was very active in developmental issues in Latin America (Sappia, 2010) and was a consultant to the Pontifical Council for Justice and Peace between 1977 and 1994. Today, according to Sarah Bracke, Wannes Dupont and David Paternotte, Michel Schooyans is considered to be one of "the main architects of the discourse against the 'gender ideology'" (Kuhar and Paternotte, 2017: 79). In 1990, in the 75th issue of *Il est vivant!* magazine, Michel Schooyans gave an interview that clearly illustrated the link between the social and political aspects of issues regarding intimate issues.

> It should not be said that people are poor because there are too many of them, but on the contrary that there are too many of them because they are poor. When environmentalists vote for the liberalisation of abortion, I wonder what other values they can still credibly defend.
>
> (*Il est vivant!*, July–August 1990, no. 75, pp. 13–14)

As this excerpt shows, the theme of birth control is of paramount importance. For these Catholics, it allows them to articulate a rhetoric on the "Development of Peoples" and issues related to policies regarding intimate issues. Of course, this link was already visible in the encyclical *Populorum Progressio* (Paul VI, 1967), considered to be the first authoritative document to outline the theory underlying the concept of "integral human development" (Bertina, 2013). But it is interesting to study this link from a more micro-social perspective in order to identify the nuances in the dichotomy that was running through French Catholicism at the turn of the 1980s (left-wing Catholics *vs.* observant Catholics). Otherwise, this phenomenon could be reduced "to an ideological split that combined theological options (open to or closed to change) and political options (right-wing/left-wing)" (Hervieu-Léger, 2017: 605).

The promotion of women's medical expertise in the 1980s and 1990s

The Emmanuel Community, like many groups that emerged after the Second Vatican Council (1962–1965), demanded a greater participation of the laity in ecclesial life. This participation was promoted through a common theme found in the movements of Specialised Catholic Action, that is, the "ongoing training" of its members. Within this context, the Emmanuel Community founded the *Centre International Jean-Paul II* in 1979. This centre, which was housed in the Convent of the Annunciation of the Dominicans in Paris (*Il est vivant!*, June 1979, no. 24, p. 16), was to survive until 1986. From the very beginning, the courses on offer covered both ecclesiastical and secular disciplines, such as psychology, economics, ecology and so on. The theological courses were mostly provided by Dominican brothers, in particular by Marie-Dominique Philippe[24] (1912–2006), whereas the secular courses were mostly provided by laypeople, who contributed professional expertise. These evening classes were recorded, marketed in the form of audio cassettes, and sold by mail order through the magazine's catalogue. This method allowed the Emmanuel Community to spread its message to a wider Catholic audience in the 1980s.

Among the regular speakers at the *Centre International Jean-Paul II* was the co-founder of the Emmanuel Community: Martine Laffitte-Catta. At that time she was a doctor practising at the Cochin Hospital in Paris, married to Hervé-Marie Catta, a former lawyer responsible for public relations in the Emmanuel Community. It is interesting to note that her lectures did not strictly cover her professional expertise, but always adopted a combined religious and a secular approach. In the first course at the *Centre International Jean-Paul II*, she gave lectures entitled "medicine and healing", about the expression of gifts of healing in charismatic prayer groups. In the second course, she also gave lectures on the "psychology of love" and the "psychology of the Christian couple". These two examples show how her symbolic professional capital (as a doctor) and her social capital (as a wife) could be converted into a symbolic religious capital (of expertise on the theology of charisms and the pastoral care of the family). At the end of 1981, with the help of her husband and another doctor who was a member of the Emmanuel Community, Charles-Éric Hauguel, Martine Laffitte-Catta started to organise the first weekends for couples at the Convent of the Annunciation (*Il est vivant!,* October–November 1981, no. 34, p. 2). These weekend retreats, soon to bear the name *Amour et Vérité* (Love and Truth), were to become a vehicle for the promotion of natural methods of birth control and of the sexual morality promoted by Pope John Paul II. From 1985 on, Professor Jérôme Lejeune (1926–1994), who discovered the chromosomal abnormality responsible for Down's syndrome together with Marthe Gautier and Raymond Turpin (1895–1988) and who was a member of Opus Dei and a pro-life activist, was invited to speak at the meetings held by the Emmanuel Community at Paray-le-Monial (Saône-et-Loire). During this time, advertisements began to appear in *Il est vivant!* featuring the *Office chrétien des personnes handicapées* (Christian Office for People with Disabilities) or the *Associations Familiales Catholiques* (Catholic Family Associations). These associations also organised pro-life conferences. In short, this pro-family community network that had been formed a few years earlier was gradually gaining ground.

Moving into the 1990s, a discourse constructed specifically around bioethical issues began to emerge. This discourse was no longer confined to the theme of natural birth control. In 1992, the first special issue entitled "50 questions on life and love" was published (*Il est vivant!*, May–June 1992, no. 90–91). It discussed abortion, contraception, medically assisted reproduction techniques, and euthanasia. What is striking is that the language used is extremely techno-scientific rather than being at all theological. The experts who write these articles are laypeople, mostly women, who have mastered this techno-scientific mode of discourse. For example, the June–July 1995 issue, entitled "Give Life", was devoted specifically to reproductive and sexual issues (*Il est vivant!*, June–July 1995, no. 115). It contained 12 in-depth articles, plus various testimonies. To illustrate the typical content of this issue, an insert set out in precise detail all the various possible *in vitro* fertilisation procedures, such as embryo transfer, intracytoplasmic sperm injection and so on (ibid., p. 24). Six of the articles were written by women, and only one by a man (a priest). This was the only theological reflection in the issue, the main theme of which was the dignity of the embryo. The other five articles were written by couples, in which the woman is not only introduced as the "wife of" but also has real expertise in the scientific field. These women writers are biologists, doctors and such like. Again, this phenomenon illustrates how a symbolic professional and social capital has been transposed into the religious field. These laypeople do not only translate an authoritative discourse on bioethics into techno-scientific language, but in the 1980s and the 1990s they also gradually became the main vehicles, the "experts", disseminating such a discourse.

The ubiquitous nature of this scientific language also appears to inflate the importance of problems concerning reproduction and embryo research at the expense of issues more closely related to sexuality or the family. Of course, the first French bioethics laws in 1994 dealt specifically with embryo research and reproduction. Therefore, it is not surprising for a Catholic magazine to mention these issues. However, very little is said, for example, about homosexuality, except in articles about AIDS. In a special issue in February 1993 entitled "Family Today", it is quite striking to see that the main concern of the authors is the question of hyper-consumption of both material (toys, etc.) and immaterial goods (i.e. the threat that television represents for the family) (*Il est vivant!*, March 1993, pp. 8–23). There is no mention of new family structures (such as single-parent families or homoparental families). The first articles defending a "traditional" family model appear at the end of the 1990s, in the context of the debates on the *Pacs* bill in France. This law relating to the Civil Solidarity Pact, which was passed in October 1999, offered legal recognition to same-sex couples.

The overrepresentation of women's medical expertise, which was mentioned above, still persists today. During the observations that I made at the 2017 and 2018 *Journées Bioéthique* (Bioethics days) in Paris, most of the speakers were women. In the question and answer sessions after each lecture, most of the questions were asked by women, often nurses or doctors, who talked about their own professional experiences.

Of course, we must not think that the readers of *Il est vivant!* fully agree with the rhetoric that features in the magazine. In this respect, the readers' letters column offers a different perspective. Around the time of the *Pacs* bill, in 1999, there were letters criticising *Il est vivant!*, the circulation of which was then at its peak, for not addressing this issue and for failing to incite readers to campaign against the bill (*Il est vivant!*, February 1999, no. 150, p. 32). The editorial staff responded by calling for participation in the demonstration in Paris on 31 January 1999. This demonstration was later considered to be the biggest anti-*Pacs* rally, with 100,000 people marching. In many ways, this demonstration foreshadowed the various forms of public action adopted by *La Manif' pour Tous* 14 years later to protest against the same-sex marriage bill. As Céline Béraud and Philippe Portier state, "the look of the event has changed (floats were used with variety music, copying Gay Pride parades), as is the look of the demonstrators (casual clothing is recommended)" (Béraud and Portier, 2015: 33). Yet, some readers were unhappy with the call to protest and wrote back to complain about the politicisation of the magazine. During the same period, in readers' letters, several women also strongly contested natural birth control methods. In the March 1997 issue, entitled "Living compassion", a reader wrote about medically assisted reproductive techniques:

> Apart from the processes used, where is the difference? Should an infertile couple be denied the opportunity to give birth? Please do not make young people feel guilty if they cannot have children by natural means and resort to *in vitro* fertilisation.
>
> (*Il est vivant!*, March 1997, no. 132, p. 33)

In a social environment where the expertise is traditionally mastered by priests, that is, by men, these bioethical issues offer Catholic laywomen a space that gives them authority in the religious field. We can now focus on how this expertise has become institutionalised.

The gradual dissociation of bioethical issues from the pastoral care of the family in the 2000s

From the late 1990s, and especially from the early 2000s onwards, bioethical issues, which were becoming a central theme in *Il est vivant!*, were progressively handled separately from marriage and family issues. We find evidence of the structuring of specific arguments, specific training facilities, and specific movements and associations. As indicated above, in the 1980s and 1990s, the *C.L.E.R.* was the main association supported by the magazine *Il est vivant!*, through conference advertisements or audio tapes. This association initially emerged from the *Centre de Préparation au Mariage* (Marriage Preparation Centre) (Sevegrand, 1995: 192–193), which was a movement founded in 1956 by Father Henri Caffarel and directly linked to the French Episcopal Commission for Family Pastoral Care.

From the 2000s onwards, a new leading association emerges, namely *l'Alliance pour les droits de la vie* (Alliance for the Rights to Life), which was renamed *Alliance Vita* in 2011. This lay association was founded in 1993 by Christine Boutin, a former French Minister of Housing and Member of Parliament, in the context of the first French bioethics laws. Throughout the 2000s, this association was extremely active on bioethical issues, and specialised in providing a secular framework for pro-life arguments in the public space, as described by Michael Stambolis-Ruhstorfer and Josselin Tricou (Strambolis-Ruhstorfer and Tricou,

2017), in particular through the use of scientific expertise. Since the *Manif' pour Tous* protests in 2012–2013, *Alliance Vita* has been considered to be one of the most important pro-life lobbies in France. Since 2004, its leaders have had very regular platforms for their views in *Il est vivant!* and the events they organise are widely publicised.

This shift from the *C.L.E.R.* to *Alliance Vita* illustrates the dissociation of bioethical issues from family pastoral care, as well as demonstrating the legitimacy gained by Catholic lay movements in the religious field. This phenomenon can be observed in the history of the Emmanuel Community itself. The archives of the Bishops' Conference of France show that since the early stages of its development, the Emmanuel Community has been accused of operating on its own, outside the traditional structures of the French Catholic Church. Its subsidiary associations such as *FIDESCO* in the humanitarian sector, for example, have been accused of replicating existing associations like the *Comité catholique contre la faim et pour le développement*,[25] which is controlled by the ecclesiastical hierarchy.

Another significant phenomenon is the fact that, from 2001 onwards, the Emmanuel Community has organised the *Journées Bioéthique* (Bioethics days) mentioned above. Bioethical issues were previously discussed in a parochial context, or in the context of *Amour et Vérité* weekends, and were therefore clearly part of a family pastoral care approach. Initially, these *Journées Bioéthique* were conceived as an extension of the *Amour et Vérité* weekends. The first adverts in the magazine for this event showed the *Amour et Vérité* logo, but these *Journées Bioéthique* now clearly function autonomously. The organiser of the 2018 session, a lay doctor, introduces them in an issue of *Il est vivant!*:

> 50% of the people we reach are carers or work in the health sector. … We encourage health professionals to group themselves by region … meet up two or three times a year to … help each other … and welcome young people who want to get involved.
>
> (*Il est vivant!*, April–May–June 2018, no. 339, pp. 37–38)

As this interview suggests, the *Journées Bioéthique* are not primarily targeted at Catholic couples who want to learn about bioethical issues. They are mainly a platform for religious, professional and political networking aimed at health care professionals. This type of event has specifically existed for doctors since the end of the 2000s. The declared objective is networking. Health care professionals are encouraged to interact and talk to one another, wearing name badges. For example, during the 2017 session, Sophie Lutz, the mother of a little girl with multiple disabilities and a pro-life writer, said: "resistance is not easy these days. We must connect and network. [We must] shine as Christians. … Some people are called upon to lobby, others to get involved in community networks, or to promote interpersonal dialogue". This autonomy of bioethical issues is accompanied by an urgent call for involvement in public debate. From the 2000s onwards, the magazine has widely promoted conscientious objection for doctors and pharmacists. In a 2011 issue, Doctor Henri Couraye writes:

> The issue of conscientious objection is a more burning one than ever. First, because the "culture of death" … has invaded our society. Second, because … our society is conveying a reductive vision of man that is characterised by relativism.
>
> (*Il est vivant!*, May 2011, no. 282, pp. 34–35)

But it is with *La Manif' pour Tous*, in 2012–2013, that the magazine started to provide its readers with practical tools for intervening in the public space. This phenomenon continued with the amendment of the bioethics laws, in 2017–2019. In an issue published in the summer of 2018, an article entitled "Bioethics: human where are you?" offered a seven bullet-point presentation on how its readers could intervene in the public debate. The fifth point suggested:

> Commit to memory two or three important ethical arguments. … Do not go to the debate alone but in pairs. Respond at the appropriate time with calm and non-aggressive action. Rely on each other's interventions, speak on your own behalf, make your argument clear, … base it on your personal experience.
>
> (*Il est vivant!*, April–May–June 2018, no. 339, p. 40)

This dissociation from family pastoral care should not be considered as being some kind of internal secularisation of Catholic discourse on policies regarding intimate issues. The 2018–2019 debates about assisted reproductive technology and surrogacy are very much linked, in the minds of these observant Catholics, to a specific view of the family that is built on a religious background. For them, opposing these bills means defending what they consider to be the core unit of the universal Church. Moreover, especially in the Emmanuel Community, many of these Catholics receive a good theological training (through the *Collège des Bernardins* in Paris for example). What I am suggesting here is that this dissociation from family pastoral care illustrates how lay expertise, rooted in the world of work, is being legitimised in the religious field.

Conclusion

Compared with the academic and media interest that Catholic campaigns around policies regarding intimate issues have generated, the political success of such campaigns is almost non-existent. In their conclusion, Michael Stambolis-Ruhstorfer and Josselin Tricou note with regard to *La Manif' pour Tous*:

> Despite its failure to prevent same-sex marriage and adoption by same-sex couples in 2012, the movement has successfully derailed a number of

> planned reforms, such as those intended to address lesbian couples' access to reproductive technologies, and forces lawmakers to gingerly avoid discussing the needs of women, LGBT people and gender and sexual equality more generally.
>
> (Stambolis-Ruhstorfer, Tricou, 2017: 94).

However, on 15 October 2019, the French National Assembly voted in favour of giving lesbian couples access to reproductive technology. The defeat of the proudly Catholic candidate François-Xavier Bellamy in the May 2019 European elections, who received only 8.48% of the votes cast, is also symptomatic of Catholics' poor performance on the political front.

However, in the religious field, these campaigns have undoubtedly been a success. They have enhanced the public profile of a new ecclesiastical "elite" of laypeople, including many women, which first emerged in the early 1980s. In this respect, it was a natural step for someone like Professor Jérôme Lejeune to become the first president of the Pontifical Academy for Life, which was founded in 1994 by Pope John Paul II. This study of the legitimacy gained by lay movements within the Catholic Church could be transposed to other areas, such as evangelisation, management of the Church and so on.

During these Catholic campaigns around policies regarding intimate issues, the Emmanuel Community has really acted as a catalyst for various associations and movements even though it did not directly organise demonstrations in the public space. This is perhaps why its role was only featured at a late stage in research produced at the time of the *Manif pour Tous* in 2012–2013. However, the Emmanuel Community has had the ability to bring together several key personalities in one place to create links and networks, and to politicise Catholics.

Notes

1 I would like to thank Petre Maican and Anaïs Vignoles for their help.

2 That is, dealing with the body, sexuality, family, and the beginning and end-of-life (Berrebi-Hoffmann, 2009).

3 These debates focused mostly on medically assisted reproduction for single mothers and lesbian couples.

4 The translation of this extract and also of those that follow was produced by the author.

5 The debates on the "gender ideology" started with the introduction of the concept of "gender" in biology textbooks.

6 Rather the *Scouts unitaires de France* (Unitary Scouts of France) and the *Scouts* d'Europe (Scouts of Europe), which are considered to be more conservative than the *Scouts et Guides de France* (Scouts and Guides of France).

7 Charisms are spiritual gifts given by the Holy Spirit.

8 Baptism in the Spirit is an experience of personal conversion.

9 The first three bishops to officially recognise the Emmanuel Community in France were the Bishop of Nanterre Jacques Delarue (1914–1982), Archbishop Roger Etchegaray (1922–2019) in Marseille, and most importantly Archbishop Jean-Marie Lustiger (1926–2007) in Paris.

10 I focused on 2004 and 2011 because they were years when the bioethics laws in France were revised. The 2011–2012 sequence is interesting because of the debates around

"gender ideology", and of course the same-sex marriage bill. I chose 2007 because it was a French presidential election year in which bioethical issues were discussed (Raison du Cleuziou, 2019).

11 This work was conducted at the *Bibliothèque Nationale de France* in Paris.

12 Bioethics days, which have been in existence since 2001, are training days for professionals or retired staff in the medical sector.

13 This work was conducted at the *Centre national des Archives de l'Église de France* in Issy-les-Moulineaux.

14 Those meetings were to continue until 1987.

15 The General Confederation of Labour (known in France as the CGT) is one of the biggest French trade unions. Founded in 1895, it was close to the French Communist Party for a long time (and still was in the 1970s).

16 *FIDESCO* stands in French for International Foundation for the Economic, Social and Spiritual Development of Cooperation. Its purpose is to support "the development and evangelism work of dioceses among the poorest in the Third World. In the power of the Spirit, every Christian is called to a renewal of the North-South dialogue, at home and abroad, so that justice may grow, and the inevitability of poverty may be overcome" (*Il est vivant!*, March–April 1984, no. 46, p. 17).

17 http://www.sharesolidaire.com/?product=fidesco, accessed 1 October 2019.

18 This term refers to the defence of a "traditional" view of family.

19 *C.L.E.R.* stands in French for Research Team Liaison Centre.

20 The right to be born.

21 Contraception without violence.

22 Fight for the Larzac was a protest movement against the plan to expand a military base in the south of France. This movement lasted from 1971 to 1981.

23 Abortion, crime or liberation?

24 Even though the founder of the Saint John Family had only a tenuous relationship with the Order of Preachers at that time, he never officially left it.

25 The Catholic Committee against Hunger and for Development was a non-governmental organisation created by French Bishops in 1961.

Bibliography

Balas, M. and Tricou, J. 2019. "'Nous, maintenant, on veut poursuivre cette occupation de la rue': les catholiques attestataires entre contre-culture, mission et défense patrimoniale." *Social Compass* 66 (1): 62–74.

Baudouin, J. and Portier, P. (eds.). 2002. *Le mouvement catholique français à l'épreuve de la pluralité: enquêtes autour d'une militance éclatée*. Rennes: Presses universitaires de Rennes.

Béraud, C. 2007. *Prêtres, diacres, laïcs: Révolution silencieuse dans le catholicisme français*. Paris: Presses universitaires de France (Le lien social).

Béraud, C. 2008. "The Church's Lay Workforce: Employment in the French Catholic Church." *Sociologie du Travail* 50: 66–82.

Béraud, C. 2011. "Quand les questions de genre travaillent le catholicisme." *Etudes* 414 (2): 211–221.

Béraud, C. 2014. "Un front commun des religions contre le mariage pour tous?" *Contemporary French Civilisation* 39 (3): 335–349.

Béraud, C. 2017. "Ce que l'épisode du mariage pour tous nous dit du catholicisme français." *Revue du Maus* 1 (49): 327–337.

Béraud, C. and Portier, P. 2015. *Métamorphoses Catholiques, Acteurs, enjeux et mobilisations depuis le mariage pour tous*. Paris: Éditions de la Maison des sciences de l'homme.

Berrebi-Hoffmann, I. (ed.). 2009. *Politiques de l'intime: des utopies sociales d'hier aux mondes du travail d'aujourd'hui*. Paris: La Découverte (Recherches).

Bertina, L. 2013. "La doctrine catholique du 'développement humain intégral' et son influence sur la communauté internationale du développement." *Revue internationale de politique de développement* 4 (1): 141–154.

Brejon de Lavergnée, M. and Della Sudda, M. (eds.). 2015. *Genre et christianisme: plaidoyers pour une histoire croisée*. Paris: Beauchesne.

Brustier, G. 2014. *Le mai 68 conservateur: que restera-t-il de la Manif pour tous?* Paris: Les Éditions du Cerf.

Cavalin, T. and Viet-Depaule, N. 2009. "Des prêtres-ouvriers au mouvement missionnaire français. Bilan historiographique et nouvelles perspectives." *Histoire et missions chrétiennes* 1 (9): 9–41.

Cohen, M. 1998. "Le renouveau charismatique français: mouvement de sainteté et protestation socioreligieuse". In Kerrou, M. (ed.) *L'autorité des saints: perspectives historiques et socio-anthropologiques en Méditerranée occidentale*. Paris: Ministère des Affaires Étrangères (Éditions recherche sur les civilisations).

Daniel, Y. and Godin, H. 1943. *La France, pays de mission?* Lyon: Éditions de l'Abeille (Rencontres).

Dolbeau, S. 2019a. "Le rapport de la Communauté de l'Emmanuel avec ses paroisses parisiennes. S'accommoder sans se diluer, se spécifier sans s'isoler." *Émulations*. Retrieved on September 25th, 2020. https://ojs.uclouvain.be/index.php/emulations/article/view/dolbeau.

Dolbeau, S. 2019b. "L'engagement des laïcs porté par la Communauté de l'Emmanuel." Pp. 223–238 in Coutel, C. and Rota, O. (eds.) *Se faire apôtre du XIXe siècle à nos jours: l'Eglise catholique et les différents régimes d'apostolat dans le monde modern*. Les-Plans-sur-Bex: Parole et Silence.

Fradois, G. 2017. "De la cure des âmes à l'évangélisation des corps. Le CLER Amour et Famille: classes dominantes et morale sexuelle." *Genre, sexualité & société* 18. Retrieved on March 15th, 2020. http://journals.openedition.org/gss/4062 ; DOI : 10.4000/gss.4062

Garbagnoli, S. and Prearo, M. 2017. *La croisade anti-genre: du Vatican aux manifs pour tous*. Paris: Textuel (Petite encyclopédie critique).

Gauglin, M. 2019. "Traduction et appropriation des prescriptions du Saint Siège et du Conseil Pontifical de la Famille dans les associations d'éducation sexuelle et affective". *Journée d'étude 'Religions et associations'*. Nanterre: Université Paris Nanterre. June 4.

Hervieu-Léger, D. 1973. *De la mission à la protestation. L'évolution des étudiants chrétiens en France (1965–1970)*. Paris: Cerf.

Hervieu-Léger, D. 2017. *Le temps des moines: clôture et hospitalité* (1st ed.). Paris: Presses universitaires de France.

Horn, G.-R. 2015. *The Spirit of Vatican II: Western European Progressive Catholicism in the Long Sixties*. Oxford: Oxford University Press.

John-Paul II. 1981. Apostolic Exhortation *Familiaris consortio*. Retrieved on September 25th, 2020. http://www.vatican.va/content/john-paul-ii/en/apost_exhortations/documents/hf_jp-ii_exh_19811122_familiaris-consortio.html.

Kuhar, R. and Paternotte, D. (eds.). 2017. *Anti-Gender Campaigns in Europe: Mobilizing Against Equality*. Londres: Rowman & Littlefield International.

Landron, O. 2004. *Les communautés nouvelles: nouveaux visages du catholicisme français*. Paris: Les Éditions du Cerf, (Histoire).

Lebel, B. 2015. *Boquen: entre utopie et révolution*, 1965–1976. Rennes: Presses universitaires de Rennes, (Histoire).

Massei, S. 2017. "S'engager contre l'enseignement de la 'théorie du genre'. Trajectoires sociales et carrières militantes dans les mouvements anti- 'ABCD de l'égalité'." *Genre, sexualité et société* 18. Retrieved on March 15th, 2020. http://journals.openedition.org/gss/4095 ; DOI : 10.4000/gss.4095

Maurer, S.A. 2010. *The Spirit of Enthusiasm: A History of the Catholic Charismatic Renewal, 1967–2000*. Lanham, MD: University Press of America.

Paul VI. 1967. Encyclical Letter *Populorum Progressio*. Retrieved on September 25th, 2020. http://w2.vatican.va/content/paul-vi/fr/encyclicals/documents/hf_p-vi_enc_26031967_populorum.html.

Paul VI. 1968. Encyclical Letter *Humanae Vitae*. Retrieved on September 25th, 2020. https://w2.vatican.va/content/paul-vi/fr/encyclicals/documents/hf_p-vi_enc_25071968_humanae-vitae.html.

Pelletier, D. 2002. *La crise catholique: religion, société, politique en France, (1965–1978)*. Paris: Payot.

Pelletier, D. and Schlegel, J.-L. (eds.). 2013. *À la gauche du Christ: les chrétiens de gauche en France de 1945 à nos jours*. Paris: Seuil.

Pérez-Agote, A. and Dobbelaere, K. (eds.). 2015. *The Intimate: Polity and the Catholic Church: Laws about Life, Death and the Family in So-Called Catholic Countries*. Leuven: Leuven University Press (KADOC Studies on Religion, Culture and Society).

Pina, C. 2001. *Voyage chez les charismatiques français*. Paris: Éditions de l'Atelier.

Poulat, E. 1965. *Naissance des prêtres-ouvriers*. Paris-Tournai: Casterman.

Raison du Cleuziou, Y. 2014. *Qui sont les cathos aujourd'hui?: sociologie d'un monde divisé*. Paris: Desclée de Brouwer (Confrontations).

Raison du Cleuziou, Y. 2016. *De la contemplation à la contestation: la politisation des Dominicains de la province de France (années 1940–1970)*. Paris: Socio-histoires.

Raison du Cleuziou, Y. 2019. Une contre-révolution catholique: aux origines de La Manif pour tous" Paris: Seuil.

Ranaghan, K. and Ranaghan, D. 1969. *Catholic Pentecostals*. New York: Paulist Press.

Sappia, C. 2010. "Un Institut des hautes études doctrinales pour l'Amérique latine à Louvain? Reflet des conflits idéologiques latino-américains à l'Université catholique de Louvain (1964–1970)." *Histoire et missions chrétiennes* 14 (2): 125–144.

Schooyans, M. 1969. *Chrétienté en contestation: l'Amérique latine. Essai de prospective pastorale*. Paris: Éditions du Cerf.

Schooyans, M. 1974. "L'avortement, problème politique." *Nouvelle Revue Théologique* 96 (10): 1031–1053.

Sevegrand, M. 1995. *Les enfants du bon Dieu: les catholiques français et la procréation au XXe siècle*. Paris: Albin Michel.

Stambolis-Ruhstorfer, M. and Tricou, J. 2017. "Resisting 'Gender Theory' in France: A Fulcrum for Religious Action in a Secular Society." Pp. 79–98 in Kuhar, R. and Paternotte, D. (eds.) *Anti-Gender Campaigns in Europe: Mobilizing Against Equality*. Londres: Rowman & Littlefield International.

Toulat, J. 1965. *Espérance en Amérique du Sud*. Paris: Perrin.

Toulat, J. 1972. *Le Larzac et la paix*. Poitiers: Jean Toulat.

Toulat, J. 1973. *L'avortement, crime ou libération?* Paris: Fayard.

Toulat, J. 1979, *Le droit de naître*, Paris: Pygmalion.

Toulat, J. 1980, *Contraception sans violence.*, Paris: Pygmalion.
Toulat, P. 2014. Un chemin d'humanité. Paris: Karthala.
Verloo, M. (ed.). 2018. *Varieties of Opposition to Gender Equality*. Londres: Routledge.
Walch, A. 2002. *La spiritualité conjugale dans le catholicisme français: XVIe - XXe siècle*. Paris: Les Éditions du Cerf (Histoire religieuse de la France, 19).
Walch, A. (ed.). 2011. *Le père Caffarel: des Équipes Notre-Dame à la Maison de prière, 1903–1996*. Paris: Lethielleux.
Wilkerson, D. 1963. *The Cross and the Switchblade*. New York: Random House.

Index

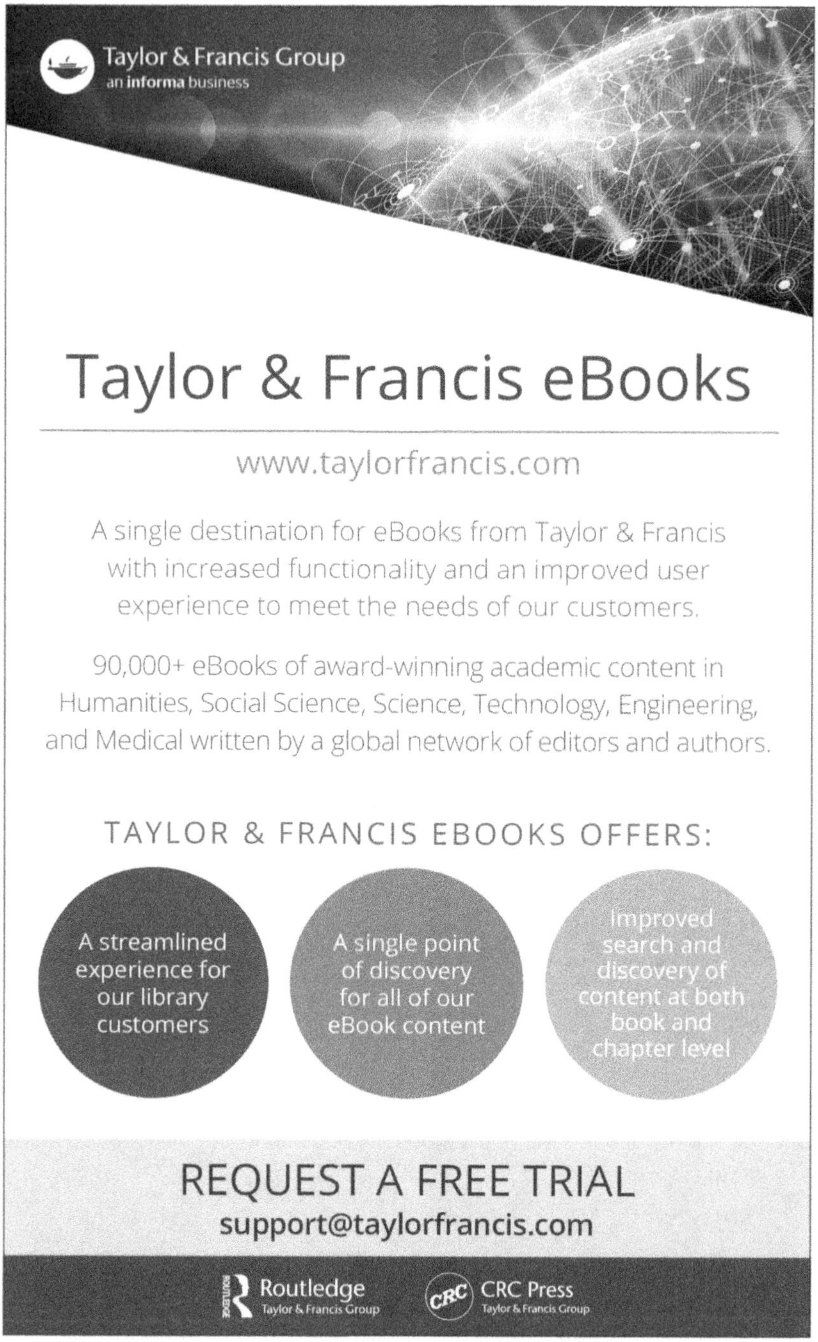

Taylor & Francis Group
an informa business
Taylor & Francis eBooks
www.taylorfrancis.com
A single destination for eBooks from Taylor & Francis with increased functionality and an improved user experience to meet the needs of our customers.
90,000+ eBooks of award-winning academic content in Humanities, Social Science, Science, Technology, Engineering, and Medical written by a global network of editors and authors.
TAYLOR & FRANCIS EBOOKS OFFERS:
A streamlined experience for our library customers
A single point of discovery for all of our eBook content
Improved search and discovery of content at both book and chapter level
REQUEST A FREE TRIAL
support@taylorfrancis.com
Routledge
Taylor & Francis Group
CRC Press
Taylor & Francis Group

For Product Safety Concerns and Information please contact our EU representative GPSR@taylorandfrancis.com
Taylor & Francis Verlag GmbH, Kaufingerstraße 24, 80331 München, Germany

www.ingramcontent.com/pod-product-compliance
Lightning Source LLC
LaVergne TN
LVHW021127300926
849160LV00010B/903

9780367673796